Challenging Corruption in Asia

in Asia

*Case Studies and a
Framework for Action*

DIRECTIONS IN DEVELOPMENT

Challenging Corruption in Asia
Case Studies and a Framework for Action

Vinay Bhargava and Emil Bolongaita

THE WORLD BANK
Washington, D.C.

© 2004 The International Bank for Reconstruction and Development / The World Bank
1818 H Street, NW
Washington, DC 20433
Telephone 202-473-1000
Internet www.worldbank.org
E-mail feedback@worldbank.org

1 2 3 4 06 05 04 03

The findings, interpretations, and conclusions expressed herein are those of the author(s) and do not necessarily reflect the views of the Board of Executive Directors of the World Bank or the governments they represent.

The World Bank does not guarantee the accuracy of the data included in this work. The boundaries, colors, denominations, and other information shown on any map in this work do not imply any judgment on the part of the World Bank concerning the legal status of any territory or the endorsement or acceptance of such boundaries.

Rights and Permissions

ISBN 0-8213-5683-6

Library of Congress Cataloging-in-Publication Data has been applied for.

Contents

Foreword

In East Asia, the challenge of controlling corruption in both public and private sectors remains formidable, and governments in the region frequently call upon the World Bank for advice on designing, implementing, and strengthening anticorruption programs in their countries. The Bank is happy to respond to such requests, as we know that corruption is one of the single biggest obstacles to growth and poverty reduction. Corruption hurts the poor and raises the cost of doing business in a myriad of different ways. Interference in public procurement and deliberate distortions to laws and policies in order to favor personal or private interests weaken competitiveness and can undermine the functioning of the whole economy. Many countries in this region suffer from weak and corrupt judicial systems, sabotaging the enforcement of contracts and property rights, not to mention access to justice for the whole society. The costs of corruption stretch further, raising public expenditure and lowering the tax take, with consequent damage in terms of fiscal deficits and macroeconomic instability. Corruption in building standards and inspections results in unsafe buildings and loss of life.

And corruption hurts the poor most of all. While the rich bribe for speed, the poor have to bribe for access, even to basic services. The poor pay a higher proportion of their income in bribes than any other income group, they find it harder to get jobs or start businesses, their property rights are more insecure, and they suffer from poor services or no services at all—such as lack of access to clean water. They pay with low life expectancy as well as with money.

We also know that fighting corruption takes time and can be risky. Powerful groups whose interests are threatened can be dangerous. But leaving corruption to fester can be even more dangerous. We have seen how prolonged systemic corruption undermines institutions, alienates investors, and ultimately erodes the legitimacy of the state. The region cannot afford that.

Earlier this year we published *Fighting Corruption in East Asia: Solutions from the Private Sector*. This volume focuses on the public sector agenda. Both these offerings are based upon the Bank's own research and cross-country experience as a global development finance institution and are published for the benefit and use of development practitioners and researchers around the world. In this regard, I am delighted by the publication of this book, which responds to the needs and demands of policymakers for a practical framework to assess and improve anticorruption policies and programs.

Across the board in Asia, the champions of corruption control are seeking to improve the effectiveness of tools, instruments, and approaches to this complex and dangerous problem. Many have adopted policies and programs that worked in other countries only to find them wanting at home. In some instances, what worked well elsewhere actually worsened the problem when transplanted to a different country. This book uses case studies of four Asian countries, written by local specialists, to tackle that critical dilemma: how to design and deliver policies and programs so that they are appropriate, relevant, and effective in specific country governance environments.

The case studies and the analytical framework proposed by the authors were subjected to a reality check during discussions, facilitated by the Bank's Global Development Learning Network, with a wide variety of individuals from the countries concerned. They confirmed that measures that do not fit the country context are unlikely to work, or may even aggravate the problem. Corruption does not come in standard sizes and types. It is essential to assess the strength or weakness of the country's institutions, and understand the particular patterns, mechanisms and incidence of corruption, in order to design effective strategies.

It is therefore critical, the book contends, to assess a country's governance conditions accurately and to choose those anticorruption measures that are appropriate to a country's governance environment. The authors emphasize that building a broad coalition with ethical leadership can be the deciding factor in shifting the balance of forces in favor of anticorruption. They also argue that execution is only as good as its evaluation, and they therefore emphasize monitoring and feedback mechanisms to help fine-tune the program and give citizens the information they need to hold the state to account.

In sum, this book aims to provide policymakers with a functional framework to help them design and implement anticorruption agendas that are relevant to the national context. It seeks to encourage policymakers to learn and draw from a global menu of anticorruption instruments. The method is appealing for its simplicity and straightforwardness: its six-step approach to anticorruption should help guide the deliberations and decisions of policymakers and stakeholders. It does not purport to provide clear-cut answers, but it does offer an informed way to ask better questions and identify ways and means to improve the effectiveness of anticorruption programs.

I commend the editors and contributors for this important volume, and I recommend the book to anyone seeking to sharpen their thinking and tools to combat corruption. It is in all our interests to help good governance prevail.

Jemal-ud-din Kassum
Vice President, East Asia and Pacific Region
The World Bank

Preface and Acknowledgments

Our interest and involvement in anticorruption converged from different paths. Vinay Bhargava's work at the World Bank, advising policymakers and implementing development projects, exposed him to many countries with different qualities of governance, and to their interplay with development. The final spark for writing this book came in 1998 when the president of the Philippines asked Bhargava to organize World Bank advice on improving the effectiveness of anticorruption programs in the Philippines. That led to a two-year effort covering not only the Philippines but also neighboring countries facing similar challenges. Emil Bolongaita learned about the complexity of governance environments and corrupt practices in Asia while teaching and consulting in different countries in the region. Our paths crossed a few times and our discussions would often turn to the region's problems of corruption and governance. We realized that there cannot be a one-size-fits-all solution to the problems in the face of such country diversity. The solutions to a country's problems must surface from and be suited to its conditions.

After a series of discussions we were fortunate to be able to convert our conversations into a collaboration in the World Bank's Global Development Learning Program (GDLN) series in Making National Anti-Corruption Policies and Programs More Effective. In that venture we sought to develop an analytical framework that would address a common need among progressive policymakers in the region—a tool to help them make anticorruption measures more appropriate to and effective in their particular country governance and operating environments. We were not alone or ahead in thinking about this issue—some of our World Bank and academic colleagues were in one way or another already involved in research and action. We are grateful to colleagues at the Bank whose work in this regard has been seminal and influential, particularly Anwar Shah and Daniel Kaufmann and his colleagues at the World Bank Institute.

To illustrate the heuristic and practical value of the analytical framework we selected four countries for case studies. We chose countries that reflect varying degrees of corruption and different levels of governance quality. We were fortunate to find and work with outstanding local scholars who contributed ably in this regard, namely Jhungsoo Park

(University of Seoul) for the Republic of Korea, Nualnoi Treerat (Chulalongkorn University) for Thailand, Eduardo Gonzalez and Magdalena Mendoza (Development Academy of the Philippines) for the Philippines, and Hamid Awaluddin (Partnership for Governance Reform) for Indonesia. The country case studies drafted by these scholars and practitioners served as discussion papers in the various GDLN sessions around the region. Vedi R. Hadiz later joined the project to contribute the case study of Indonesia included in this volume. We thank each of them for their contributions in their write-ups and in the videoconference sessions.

The GDLN seminars in different cities in the region were designed to discuss the analytical framework and country case studies with policymakers and stakeholders onsite. Through the aid of World Bank videoconference facilities, the reach of each seminar extended to other countries. We are grateful to the government officials, private sector leaders, heads of nongovernmental organizations, and other concerned people who participated in the seminars in Bangkok, Jakarta, Manila, and Singapore, and who provided highly valuable reality checks on the practical applicability for the framework and approach we have proposed. On a couple of occasions we had videoconference participation from Dili, East Timor. Bolongaita thanks his former students in the Public Policy Program at the National University of Singapore who avidly shared their views about their respective countries. We thank May Olalia and the World Bank staff in Manila for their effective coordination of the various GDLN sessions.

In the course of the GDLN videoconference seminar series we realized that we could only cover a particular segment of the anticorruption population of policymakers and stakeholders. To further meet the growing demand for anticorruption tools we decided to propose bringing together the analytical papers and case studies into an edited volume. We gratefully acknowledge the support for the GDLN program extended by the World Bank's East Asia and Pacific Region as well as the production and publication of this book. In that regard we are grateful for the support of Homi Kharas and Barbara Nunberg. We are also grateful for support from other colleagues at the World Bank. The perceptive comments from Daniel Kaufmann and Ed Campos helped us revisit and revise the text. We also received helpful feedback from Sarwar Lateef, Helen Sutch, and Joel Hellman. Ana M. Cardona-Geis provided us with efficient secretarial support.

At present, Bhargava is director of international affairs at the World Bank and continues to work on governance and anticorruption matters. Bolongaita currently heads the Public Sector Governance Group of the Economic Governance Technical Assistance Program of the U.S. Agency for International Development in the Philippines. Our responsibilities continue to give us learning opportunities to improve the framework proposed in this volume. We are pleased and privileged to be able to work with capable colleagues and staff. Together, fighting corruption is less the lonely and dangerous activity that it can be.

Finally, we would like to thank our spouses, Nimmi and Kerrie-Anne, for the unstinting support that gave us the time and energy to complete this volume.

1
Introduction:
Challenging Corruption in Asia

We are all deeply concerned about the spread of corruption, which is a virus capable of crippling governments, discrediting public institutions and private corporations and having a devastating impact on the human rights of populations, and thus undermining society and its development, affecting in particular the poor.
— Final Declaration, Global Forum II

Corruption in Asia: who cares? The citizens in every country where corruption is prevalent care. Corruption is now recognized as perhaps the most challenging governance problem afflicting many countries. The growing condemnation of corrupt activities is a seismic shift in national mood. Many practices once part of business- and politics-as-usual are now regarded as corrupt. Two events in the last decade—the East Asian financial crisis and the corruption scandals involving the highest government officials—helped catalyze the change in perception of corrupt practices. As a result, public awareness about the corrosive effects of corruption is at an all-time high and corruption is invariably among the top problems cited in citizen surveys.

At the economic level, corruption is seen as a contributing factor to the East Asian financial crisis. The crisis focused people's attention on the staggering impact of corruption, particularly in Indonesia, the Republic of Korea, and Thailand. The interlocking relationship of business and government were previously viewed as part of the way of doing business and practicing politics—a useful partnership crucial to strategic policy-making. As one scholar noted, "Not too many years ago, the economic successes of the countries of East Asia were attributed by some observers to a presumably positive impact of corruption in facilitating decision-making" (Tanzi 1999, p. 2). Many actors justified questionable practices by explaining them to be necessary conditions for rapid economic development. Today those specific practices constitute the problematic areas of corruption.

At the political level, corruption has risen in recent years in national agendas because of its role in political developments. At one point the heads of government themselves of Indonesia, the Philippines, and Thailand were in the dock on corruption-related charges. Peaceful populist protest forced the Philippine president, Joseph Estrada, to step down in January 2001. In July 2001 Indonesia's parliament removed President Abdurrahman Wahid from office partly because of corruption allegations. Thaksin Shinawatra, prime minister of Thailand, was indicted by the National Counter-Corruption Commission but was eventually acquitted in a controversial decision by the country's Constitutional Court. In 2002 the convictions of two sons of President Kim Dae-Jung of the Republic of Korea on corruption charges tarnished the president's achievements. Other high-level political leaders have also been convicted recently on corruption-related charges in China, Indonesia, the Philippines, and Thailand.

Although many countries now face corruption as a major national issue, its causes, patterns, and consequences are highly country specific. Differences—in terms of political and legal institutions, level of economic development, and social values—mean variable effects in dealing with corruption. For instance, all things being equal, a country that has an independent judiciary is more likely to be able to succeed in combating corruption than a country weak in the rule of law. (For an empirical analysis, see Ades and di Tella 1997.) Thus the heterogeneity of Asia's political and electoral processes (Hsieh and Newman 2001; Taylor 1996), economic patterns (Rodan, Hewison, and Robison 1997), and social and cultural conditions (for example, see Steinberg 1987) mean different country capabilities for controlling corruption.

In this introductory chapter we give an overview of the costs and consequences of corruption. We then present a survey of recent efforts to address the problem at the international and national levels, and we highlight the role of government, the private sector, and civil society in dealing with the problem. We continue by presenting some recent data on dimensions of the corruption problem in Asia and the progress in challenging it. The data will show that Asia is lagging behind some of the other regions in this fight and has a huge challenge ahead.

In chapter 2 we discuss a strategic framework for combating corruption, emphasizing that an effective anticorruption program must be crafted on the basis of an extensive review of a country's governance and operating environment and the nature of its corruption problems. The anticorruption strategy must be grounded on actual governance conditions, not grafted simply from a one-size-fits-all approach. We then provide an overview of a global menu of anticorruption instruments and explain the importance of selecting and prioritizing from that menu, based on a country's particular circumstances. We explain the importance of building a broad anticorruption coalition and the need for ethical leadership and management. Critically, we underscore the need for a monitoring and evaluation process that ensures feedback to benchmark and improve implementation.

Chapters 3 through 6 are case studies of the Philippines, Korea, Thailand, and Indonesia, respectively. Each case study discusses the problems of corruption in the country in the context of the country's governance and operating environment. It likewise assesses the relevance of recent approaches to combating corruption in those countries and suggests how such anticorruption measures may be improved. It is not our intention to make a comprehensive presentation of the full range of each country's anticorruption programs. Rather, we focus on a subset of anticorruption measures in each country, distill some lessons, and show how application of the framework can improve the effectiveness of anticorruption programs.

Corruption Increasingly Damages Economic Development

Corruption is plainly deleterious to enterprises even if it is more calculable than variable.[1] To be sure, many firms see bribery as a cost of doing business. Others believe bribery to be acceptable because it increases business and sales. For these firms, playing by the rules in a game in which rules are being bent would be disastrous. Recent research, however, has shown that firms that practice bribery end up paying more for their money—they actually become inefficient as well. In reality these firms spend significant amounts of effort negotiating with bureaucrats and they are burdened with higher cost of capital (Kaufmann and Ji-Wei 1999).

Corruption is corrosive to economies. Because many Asian countries were rapidly growing for years, the tradeoff between economic growth and good governance was tolerated, if not extolled. But the events in June 1997 and onward made it clear that the tradeoff was a false bargain. Corruption was hollowing out Asia's economies. Indonesia, Korea, and Thailand came close to economic collapse (Arndt and Hill 1999). In Indonesia's case, the economic drop was accompanied by a political upheaval that brought down the Suharto government. In Thailand, the government of Prime Minister Chuan Leekpai subsequently faced defeat at the polls. The magnitude of the Asian crisis was huge because the problems were glossed and rolled over for a long time—a situation made possible by the lack of transparency in those countries, particularly in their banking systems, which were not adequately prepared for the effects of financial liberalization (Mehrez and Kaufmann 1999; McLeod and Garnaut 1988). The financial crisis was an expensive lesson about the costs and effects of corruption.

There is growing international realization that corruption cripples development in many ways (Gray and Kaufmann 1988; Hutchcroft 1997). It worsens income inequality and poverty (Gupta, Davoodi, and Alonso-Terme 1998), reduces investment rates (Mauro 1997), lowers economic growth (Tanzi and Davoodi 1998), diminishes democratization, and weakens representation (Ocampo 2001). It enervates economy and society in insidious ways. It is, as World Bank president James Wolfensohn put it, a "cancer."

Given corruption's negative multiple effects, it stands to reason that controlling it can yield multiple benefits. Indeed, in countries where corruption is contained, critical socioeconomic indicators are performing well: there are greater foreign investments, higher per capita income growth, lower infant mortality, higher literacy, stronger property rights, increased business growth, and so on (see Kaufmann, Kraay, and Zoido-Lobatón 2000). Controlling corruption is, therefore, nothing less than promoting economic development, increasing country competitiveness, improving social conditions, and reducing poverty.

Globalization of the Fight against Corruption

International efforts to combat corruption have played a pivotal role in setting the agenda of many governments. Two global gatherings of anticorruption practitioners from country governments, international organizations, donor countries, international nongovernmental organizations, and national political leaders have gained in stature and reach. These are the International Anti-Corruption Conference (IACC) series (www.11iacc.org) and the Global Forum series (www.globalforum3.org). The IACC series has included a wide range of anticorruption stakeholders (governments, civil society organizations, international institutions, media, and so forth) whereas the Global Forum series has been primarily a gathering of government ministers with participation from invited experts, multilateral institutions, and leading civil society organizations. The IACC series started in 1983 whereas the Global Forum is of more recent origin and had its first meeting in 1999.

The 11th IACC and Global Forum III were scheduled back to back in May 2003 in Seoul, Korea. This conjunction underscored efforts at international coalition-building to foster advocacy and implementation of the anticorruption agenda. The participants included ministers, senior officials, and representatives of various state bodies representing 123 countries and various intergovernmental and nongovernmental organizations. The final declaration at the end of the forum sought to ensure that corruption will continue to be a high priority on international and national agendas.

In the 11th IACC and Global Forum III, an anticipated event discussed among the participants was the proposed U.N. convention against corruption. As of this writing, negotiations are ongoing with a view to completing the document for signing by the end of 2003. This initiative builds on other important international initiatives, among them the following:

- Convention on Combating Bribery of Foreign Public Officials in International Business Transactions (www.oecd.org)
- Financial Action Task Force—established to fight money laundering (www.oecd.org/fatf/)
- Transparency International—the pioneering global civil society–driven coalition against corruption (www.transparency.org)
- Multilateral Development Banks' Working Group on Anticorruption, Governance and Capacity Building (www.worldbank.org/publicsector)
- United Nations Development Programme—a thematic program for promoting accountability, transparency, and anticorruption (www.undp.org/governance/account.htm).

Recent Initiatives in Combating Corruption in Asia

In Asia, the Asian Development Bank (ADB) and the Organisation for Economic Co-operation and Development (OECD) have pledged to support the Anti-Corruption Action Plan for Asia and the Pacific that has now been endorsed by 20 ADB member states since November 2001.[2] The ADB-OECD action plan aims to support regional activities related to the plan's "three pillars": (1) developing effective and transparent systems of public service, (2) strengthening antibribery actions and promoting integrity in business operations, and (3) supporting active public involvement.[3] Both organizations have taken the lead in mobilizing resources for countries that seek support under the action plan. By pledging support to help countries secure resources for their anticorruption initiatives, the ADB and OECD aim to provide action incentives to governments. Nevertheless, it is a testimony to the difficult problem of corruption that originally only 18 of the 33 member governments in attendance in Tokyo in November 2001 signed the action plan.[4] Designed to be as broadly appealing as possible, the plan is actually nonbinding in nature.

A similar situation applies in the efforts of the World Trade Organization (WTO) to promote its Agreement on Government Procurement in which signatories adopt nondiscriminatory and transparent procurement processes. To date, in Asia only Hong Kong (China), Japan, Korea, and Singapore have signed. For various reasons and with the exception of Taiwan (China), the rest of the economies in the region have not even started to negotiate accession or adopted observer status.[5] The closest that economies in the region have come to moving toward WTO standards is Asia Pacific Economic Cooperation's (APEC's) creation of a Government Procurement Experts Group that in 1999 adopted "Non-Binding Principles on Government Procurement."[6]

Several international organizations have also sought to shape the anti-corruption agenda more directly. The World Bank, for example, has established a number of country initiatives in governance and anticorruption. Among its supported projects in the region are the Economic and Public Sector Capacity Building Project in Cambodia (2002), the Transitional Support Program for East Timor (2002), and the Partnership for Governance Reform (2002) in Indonesia.

Some international organizations have been particularly energetic in certain anticorruption issues, notably those involving money laundering. Recently, the Financial Action Task Force (FATF) placed Indonesia and the Philippines on its "blacklist" of noncooperative countries. After periods of postponement by the Philippine congress on a money-laundering bill, the FATF blacklisting finally prodded the passage of the measure by the congress. (However, the FATF decided to keep the Philippines on the list because, in its view, the law "contains a number of important deficiencies."[7]) Indonesia, added to the FATF blacklist in June 2001, has yet to pass a similar anti-money-laundering law. An offshoot of the FATF's work is the Asia/Pacific Group on Money Laundering (www.apgml.org) that was formed in 1997 to facilitate the adoption, implementation, and enforcement of the FATF's 40 recommendations.

There are continuing efforts by other international organizations to weigh in on the corruption agenda of governments through the establishment of various covenants. Among the efforts are the Basel Capital Accord of the Bank for International Settlements,[8] the OECD's various initiatives,[9] and international private sector associations like the Pacific Basin Economic Council (PBEC). PBEC is an association of senior business leaders in the Asia-Pacific region and it has adopted a charter on standards for transactions between business and government and it promotes the involvement of business in curbing corruption in the region.[10]

Finally, a few donor countries themselves have been involved directly in corruption agenda setting in the region, notably the Australian Agency for International Development (AusAID), the Canadian International Development Agency (CIDA) and the U.S. Agency for International Development (USAID). Those agencies have been active in pursuing programs in democracy and governance in several countries in the region that have anticorruption dimensions.[11]

In summary, partly because of rising public pressure in Asia fueled somewhat by the East Asian financial crisis, the sundry corruption scandals, and the advocacy work of multilateral institutions, government reformers, and civil society, challenging corruption has become a high priority for many governments. Because of their economic resources and diplomatic reach, external actors have continued to influence those evolving agendas. At times their leverage is relatively unilateral; at other times it is combinatorial, as when international organizations join forces with domestic groups to multiply and magnify pressure points. In many ways the universalization of anticorruption efforts testifies to the powerful nexus that can develop among international and domestic processes and players. This nexus augurs well in tilting the balance of forces between those who benefit from the status quo, and therefore naturally have interests to protect and are often equipped to do so, and the more disparate and less-organized forces for reform.

Challenge of Combating Corruption in Asia

Growing numbers of citizens in several Asian countries, like other countries increasingly influenced by external forces of globalization and internal pressures for democratization, are becoming increasingly aware of the effects of corruption. With newfound voices they are demanding better behavior from their leaders even as they wish for better lives themselves. The clamor of citizens resonates with the concerns of an international community that is itself increasingly aware of the costs and consequences of corruption. Because of their networks and resources, international actors have uncommon leverage in demanding better governance in exchange for the support they provide. In seeking change and reform in governance, there is a burgeoning demand among national and international anticorruption players and stakeholders for more knowledge, greater information, and increased insight about corruption.

To meet that demand, a number of institutions have worked to overcome the inherent difficulties of generating and analyzing information on the naturally secretive world of corruption. To be sure, data concerning the extent of corruption across countries are hard to collect. Despite these methodological constraints, a number of institutions are regularly assessing corruption comparatively.

Transparency International's (TI's) Corruption Perceptions Index (CPI), for instance, is among the more prominently used measures of corruption. Drawing on various international and country surveys, TI's CPI scores provide a useful partial measure of the challenge of combating corruption in Asia. CPI scores relate to perceptions of the degree of corruption based on surveys of businesspeople, academics, and risk analysts, and range between 10 (highly clean) and 0 (highly corrupt). Using this measure we see, as listed in table 1.1, that most of the developing countries in Asia have CPI scores at or below 4 and thus have a long way to go to reach a corruption-controlled state.

Table 1.1. Corruption Perceptions Index Scores, Selected
          Economies in Asia, 2000–03

Economy	2000	2001	2002	2003
Singapore	9.1	9.2	9.3	9.4
Australia	8.3	8.5	8.6	8.8
Hong Kong, China	7.7	7.9	8.2	8.0
Japan	6.4	7.1	7.1	7.0
Taiwan, China	5.5	5.9	5.6	5.7
Malaysia	4.8	5.0	4.9	5.2
Republic of Korea	4.0	4.2	4.5	4.3
China	3.1	3.5	3.5	3.4
Thailand	3.2	3.2	3.2	3.3
India	2.8	2.7	2.7	2.8
Philippines	2.8	2.9	2.6	2.5
Pakistan	n.a.	2.3	2.6	2.5
Vietnam	2.5	2.6	2.4	2.4
Indonesia	1.7	1.9	1.9	1.9
Bangladesh	n.a.	0.4	1.2	1.3
Regional average	4.4	4.3	4.6	4.5

n.a. Not available.
Source: Transparency International, at www.transparency.org.

The World Bank is contributing to efforts to measure corruption as part of a broader attempt to understand and improve governance. Corruption is viewed as one of six indicators of governance, namely (1) voice and accountability, (2) political stability, (3) government effectiveness, (4) regulatory quality, (5) rule of law, and (6) control of corruption. In developing its corruption-control indicators the World Bank uses original survey sources, such as DRI/McGraw-Hill, the Economist Intelligence Unit, the Political Risk Services Group, and the World Bank's business surveys. (It does not use the TI index directly because the CPI actually is also a survey of surveys.)

In our view it is important to situate the problem of corruption as part of the comprehensive challenge of good governance. In the analytical framework we discuss in the following chapter, we will emphasize the importance of understanding a country's full governance environment as a critical foundation to crafting appropriate anticorruption policies and programs. In this regard the World Bank's work in developing six aggregate indicators of governance helps us better understand the magnitude and dimensions of the problem of corruption among countries. At the same time, it also helps us to understand the strengths and weaknesses in the governance of a country and its shifts over time, which can affect the way we assess and develop anticorruption strategies.

Table 1.2 presents the World Bank's governance indicators for the period 1996–2002 for the four countries covered by the case studies in this volume, Indonesia, Korea, the Philippines, and Thailand. The table gives each country's percentile rank for each indicator in recent years. The number

Table 1.2. Governance Indicators, Selected Years, 1996–2002
(percentile ranking of selected countries)

Governance indicator	Year	Indonesia	Republic of Korea	Philippines	Thailand
Voice and accountability	2002	34.8	67.7	54.0	57.1
	2000	32.5	68.6	60.2	58.1
	1998	12.0	68.6	63.4	55.5
	1996	16.2	68.1	58.6	52.9
Political stability	2002	12.4	60.5	29.7	62.7
	2000	3.0	64.8	40.0	57.0
	1998	9.1	56.4	49.7	59.4
	1996	30.5	54.3	43.3	55.5
Government effectiveness	2002	34.0	79.4	55.7	64.9
	2000	33.2	72.8	60.3	64.1
	1998	26.8	75.4	66.7	62.8
	1996	66.5	78.2	67.6	73.7
Regulatory quality	2002	26.3	76.3	57.7	65.5
	2000	28.1	67.6	62.2	77.3
	1998	47.3	58.7	72.8	56.5
	1996	65.7	78.5	68.5	70.2
Rule of law	2002	23.2	77.8	38.1	62.4
	2000	15.1	74.6	41.6	69.7
	1998	14.1	77.3	60.0	69.2
	1996	39.8	81.9	54.8	71.1
Control of corruption	2002	6.7	66.5	37.6	53.6
	2000	8.7	72.8	37.5	46.2
	1998	6.6	69.9	45.9	61.2
	1996	35.3	76.7	38.0	42.7

Note: The database for these governance indicators is comprehensive, based on 275 governance variables from 20 sources and 18 organizations, including among others Freedom House, Gallup International, Economist Intelligence Unit, DRI/McGraw-Hill, the World Bank, the Heritage Foundation, and the European Bank for Reconstruction and Development. The methodology of aggregation is sensitive to measurement errors; the authors placed greater weight on survey results with smaller measurement errors and lesser weight on those with higher margins of error. By drawing on multiple sources, the governance indicators reduce their margins of error, which would not have been possible if they relied on one or a few sources. For a fuller explanation, see chapter 2 in Radelet (2003).
Source: Kaufmann, Kraay, and Mastruzzi 2003.

for each indicator refers to the percentage of countries worldwide that rate below the selected country (subject to a margin of error). This multidimensional snapshot of governance for each country thus highlights the individual governance contexts in which corruption in each country operates. It suggests that the challenge of combating corruption needs to be clearly differentiated by understanding certain governance strengths and by accounting for particular governance weaknesses.

In part because of the growing information about the costs and effects of corruption, and with corruption prominent in the agendas of international organizations and domestic groups, many governments have been prodded if not pressured to launch or reinvigorate anticorruption policies and programs. In this regard, the number of proposals or ideas on ways and means to combat corruption has grown. An increasing stock of knowledge provides ample information on such efforts. There is hardly any country in which no anticorruption agency exists and few anticorruption instruments are in place. However, the evidence from manifold sources more than suggests that these institutions and instruments are not getting the job done for most countries. In fact, either the counter-corruption policies are not working or the anticorruption institutions themselves are among the most corrupt.

Thus, although vertical and horizontal demands for policies and programs to challenge corruption in Asia are growing, the progress thus far has been less than satisfactory. Metaphorically, in the view of many leading officials and key stakeholders, the goal of anticorruption is clear but the road ahead is uncertain because there are no useful road maps.

At the outset some type of road map is precisely what we seek to provide: the development of an analytical framework to evaluate and increase the effectiveness of existing and proposed anticorruption policies and programs. With varying, if not at times contradictory, recommendations and prescriptions coming from different sources, public officials and anticorruption advocates need a framework to assess and prioritize recommended policies and programs. At the same time they have called for such a framework that would be sensitive to the political, economic, and social realities of their respective environments. These concerns were clearly articulated in the general principles of the Final Declaration of Global Forum III: "anti-corruption measures tailored to the specific circumstances of a particular society should be devised in order to effectively deliver practical solutions." To clarify that this declared need was not a cultural cover to exonerate corruption, the Final Declaration in Global Forum III stated at the outset that there was a "universally held value of integrity" and that the participants' "...call for cultural and historical particularity should not be used as a pretext for justifying corruption...."[12]

The sense of urgency among governments, the private sector, and civil society to control corruption stems in part from the economic damages—and its numerous negative externalities—that continue to be wrought by insidious mutations of transnational and domestic corruption. At the same time there is a growing realization among those sectors that there are enormous benefits to be gained by building a coalition that can control corruption effectively. The World Bank's research, as alluded to earlier, has found that controlling corruption has numerous positive externalities in the political, economic, and social spheres. A less-corrupt Asia would mean its countries are likely to have more growth, improved foreign investments, higher per capita income, lower infant mortality, increased literacy, stronger property rights, increased business growth, and many additional benefits (see, for example, Kaufman, Kraay, and Zoido-Lobatón 2000). The challenge, of course, is how to get from here to there.

Drawing on the growing and compelling body of research about governance and corruption, we discuss and propose an analytical framework—elaborated in the next chapter—that can be used to assess, prioritize, and improve existing and recommended anticorruption policies and programs. A fundamental premise of this framework is that different countries require differentiated policies. Because of the historical, political, economic, and social differences among countries, there is no one-size-fits-all anticorruption agenda. What the analytical framework offers is a practical approach to drawing lessons from the global experience of anticorruption tools and instruments and to crafting and implementing an appropriate reform agenda effectively.

Outline of the Book

In this book we present four case studies: one each from Indonesia, Korea, the Philippines, and Thailand. These cases illustrate the universal nature of the problem of corruption as it afflicts even countries considered to demonstrate relatively good governance (for example, Korea). Two cases—the Philippines and Thailand—highlight the problems of corruption for countries with fair governance, and Indonesia demonstrates the challenges of dealing with corruption under poor governance conditions.

Using these case studies we explain that the choice and design of counter-corruption policies need to be calibrated according to the respective governance and corruption conditions in specific countries. That is no merely academic point. We contend that certain anticorruption policies may not simply be ineffective or inefficient in certain contexts, but may actually worsen the situation. We discuss this tragic irony in our case studies where some anticorruption policies have exacerbated conditions.

In chapter 2 we propose a multidisciplinary analytical framework to help understand the patterns of governance and the nature of corruption in a country and then to use that knowledge to improve the effectiveness of national anticorruption policies and programs. The framework goes beyond improving the technical design of anticorruption programs. It explains the importance of three other elements needed to improve their effectiveness: (1) building coalitions of anticorruption champions, (2) creating effective management and leadership structures, and (3) supporting regular monitoring and reporting on corruption.

The Philippine case is discussed in chapter 3. Written by Eduardo Gonzalez and Magdalena Mendoza of the Development Academy of the Philippines, the case illustrates the challenge of tackling corruption in a fair governance environment characterized by persistent patterns of state capture and petty corruption.

Chapter 4 focuses on the Republic of Korea. The country has joined the ranks of the OECD but continues to encounter serious problems of state capture. The article, written by University of Seoul professor Jhungsoo Park, discusses the challenge of confronting corruption in a relatively well-developed economy.

In chapter 5, the case of Thailand is addressed by Chulalongkorn University professor Nualnoi Treerat. She discusses the dilemma of countering corruption in another fair governance environment where the role of "money politics" continues to perpetuate a significant degree of state capture and administrative corruption.

Chapter 6 deals with Indonesia, and the "untraceable" anticorruption initiatives that have dotted its history (untraceable because they have left no marks against corruption). Written by National University of Singapore professor Vedi R. Hadiz, the article describes the complexity of combating corruption in the poor governance conditions existing in the country—conditions compounded by difficulties in the transition from authoritarianism.

Finally, chapter 7 seeks to draw key lessons from challenging corruption in the four case studies and highlights issues that need to be addressed. We then try to illustrate how to use the analytical framework discussed in chapter 2 to improve the effectiveness of national anticorruption policies and programs.

Notes

1. Some studies suggest that countries with more predictable corruption practices will have higher investment rates than those with unpredictable patterns (see Campos, Lien, and Pradhan 1999).

2. For more information see www1.oecd.org/daf/ASIAcom/index.htm.

3. The ADB itself has developed a number of country programs across the region to improve governance and capacity building. For an overview of these various projects see www.adb.org/Projects/default.asp.

4. The plan was originally endorsed by Bangladesh, Cook Islands, Fiji, India, Indonesia, Japan, Korea, Kyrgyz Republic, Malaysia, Mongolia, Nepal, Pakistan, Papua New Guinea, the Philippines, Samoa, Singapore, and Vanuatu. Subsequently three other economies added their support: Cambodia, Hong Kong (China), and Kazakhstan.

5. See the World Trade Organization's "Overview of the Agreement on Government Procurement," available at www.wto.org/English/tratop_e/gproc_e/over_e.htm.

6. See www.apecsec.org.sg.

7. See the FATF statement, "No FATF Counter-Measures to Apply against the Philippines for Now," available at www1.oecd.org/fatf/pdf/PR-20011218_en.pdf. In its meeting in Hong Kong, China, in February 2002, the FATF reaffirmed its December decision ("Philippines Stays" 2002).

8. In December 2001 the Basel Committee on Banking Supervision of the Bank for International Settlements (BIS) reviewed its progress toward a new Basel Capital Accord, which seeks to improve existing capital requirements, conduct supervisory review of an institution's capital adequacy and internal assessment process, and pursue greater market discipline through effective disclosure to encourage safe and sound banking practices. See BIS, "Progress towards Completion of the New Basel Capital Accord." December 13, 2001, available at www.bis.org/press/p011213.htm.

9. The OECD continues to push for implementation of various measures, notably its Convention on Combating Bribery of Foreign Public Officials in International Business Transactions and the Revised Recommendation, the OECD Council Recommendation on Improving Ethical Conduct in the Public Service, and the OECD Principles on Corporate Governance. For details, see www.oecd.org.

10. See PBEC Web site at www.pbec.org.

11. USAID currently has such programs in Myanmar, Cambodia, Indonesia, and the Philippines. In the Philippines, it seeks to support accountability institutions such as the ombudsman and the other member agencies of the Inter-Agency Anti-Graft Coordinating Council. Working with the Philippine Department of Budget and Management, it is helping conduct Integrity Development Reviews and establish anticorruption plans in high-risk agencies. It is also working with the Philippine Department of Finance to establish an Integrity Protection Service. For a general description of USAID's work, see www.usaid.gov/democracy/ane/ane.html. CIDA has ongoing or planned projects in Cambodia, Indonesia, Laos, Malaysia, the Philippines, Thailand, and Vietnam. See www.acdi-cida.gc.ca/CIDAWEB.webcountry.nsf.asia_e.html. AusAID undertook various activities during 2001/02 with governance as the primary focus, at a cost of A$308.3 million. See www.ausaidegov.au/keyaid/gover.cfm.

12. See the Final Declaration at www.worldbank.org/wbi/governance/ pdf/gf3_finaldec.pdf.

References

Ades, Alberto F., and Rafael di Tella. 1997. "The New Economics of Corruption: A Survey and Some New Results." In Paul Heywood, ed., *Political Corruption*. Malden, Mass.: Blackwell.

Arndt, H. W., and Hal Hill, eds. 1999. *Southeast Asia's Economic Crisis: Origins, Lessons, and the Way Forward*. Singapore: Institute of Southeast Asian Studies.

Campos, Jose Edgardo, D. Lien, and Sanjay Pradhan. 1999. "The Impact of Corruption on Investment: Predictability Matters." *World Development* 27 (6): 1059–67.

Gray, Cheryl W., and Daniel Kaufmann. 1988. "Corruption and Development." *Finance and Development* 35 (1): 7–10

Gupta, Sanjeev, Hamid Davoodi, and Rosa Alonso-Terme. 1998. "Does Corruption Affect Income Inequality and Poverty?" Working Paper WP/98/76, International Monetary Fund, Washington, D.C.

Hsieh, John Fuh-Sheng, and David Newman, eds. 2001. *How Asia Votes*. New York: Seven Bridges Press/Chatham House.

Hutchcroft, Paul. 1997. "The Politics of Privilege: Assessing the Impact of Rents, Corruption, and Clientelism in Third World Development." *Political Studies* 45 (3): 639–58.

Kaufmann, Daniel, and Shang Ji-Wei. 1999. "Does 'Grease Money' Speed Up the Wheels of Commerce?" Working Paper 7093, National Bureau of Economic Research, Cambridge, Mass.

Kaufmann, Daniel, Aart Kraay, and Pablo Zoido-Lobatón. 2000. "Governance Matters: From Measurement to Action." *Finance and Development* 37 (2). Available at www.imf.org/external/pubs/ft/fandd/2000/06/kauf.htm.

Kaufmann, Daniel, Aart Kraay, and Massimo Mastruzzi. 2003. "Governance Matters III: Governance Indicators for 1996–2002." World

Bank Policy Research Working Paper 3106. Washington, D.C. Paper and data available at http://www.worldbank.org/wbi/governance/gov data2002/index.html.

Mauro, P. 1997. "The Effects of Corruption on Growth, Investment, and Government Expenditure: A Cross-Country Analysis." In Kimberly Ann Elliott, ed., *Corruption and the Global Economy.* Washington D.C.: Institute for International Economics.

McLeod, Ross H., and Ross Garnaut, eds. 1988. *East Asia in Crisis: From Being a Miracle to Needing One?* London: Routledge.

Mehrez, Gil, and Daniel Kaufmann. 1999. "Transparency, Liberalization, and Financial Crises." Policy Research Working Paper 2286, World Bank Institute, Washington, D.C.

Ocampo, Luis Moreno. 2001. "State Capture: Who Represents the Poor?" *Development Outreach,* World Bank Institute, Winter. Available at www1.worldbank.org/devoutreach/winter01/article.asp?id=100.

Radelet, Steve. 2003. *Challenging Foreign Aid: A Policymaker's Guide to the Millennium Challenge Account.* Washington, D.C.: Center for Global Development.

Rodan, Garr, Kevin Hewison, and Richard Robison, eds. 1997. *The Political Economy of Southeast Asia: An Introduction.* Melbourne: Oxford University Press Australia.

Steinberg, David Joel, ed. 1987. *In Search of Southeast Asia: A Modern History.* Honolulu: University of Hawaii Press.

Tanzi, Vito. 1999. "Governance, Corruption and Public Finance: An Overview." In Salvatore Schiavo-Campo, ed., *Governance, Corruption and Public Management.* Manila: Asian Development Bank.

Tanzi, Vito, and Hamid Davoodi. 1998. "Roads to Nowhere: How Corruption in Public Investment Hurts Growth." *Economic Issues Series.* Washington, D.C.: International Monetary Fund.

Taylor, R. H., ed. 1996. *The Politics of Elections in Southeast Asia.* Cambridge, U.K.: Woodrow Wilson Center Press and the Press Syndicate of the University of Cambridge.

2

An Analytical Framework for Improving the Effectiveness of Anticorruption Policies and Programs

Anti-corruption measures tailored to the specific circumstances of a particular society should be devised in order effectively to deliver practical solutions.

—Final Declaration, Global Forum III

In several countries around the world, opportunities have emerged for the launching or reinvigorating of national anticorruption programs and policies. In many ways the corrupt forces in these countries now face anticorruption forces that are less discrete and more organized than before. Across countries, previously dispersed and silenced elements from within and outside government appear to be overcoming problems of collective action as they create coalitions against corruption. In some countries progress has been remarkable. Groups have taken advantage of problems and openings to form broad-based coalitions, gathering momentum at such inexorable pace that vested interests have been overcome swiftly.

These opportunities have developed for several reasons. First, from a growing body of research and analysis about the consequences of corruption, citizens have learned that the problem is more costly than was previously imagined. Second, reform-oriented officials in the public sector have also found that the risks of challenging corruption are not as high as before because of the increasing numbers of international donors who are demanding that their development assistance be used honestly—a fact reflected in the international treaties being forged that oblige countries to take measures to combat corruption. Third, public officials are seeing that corruption has become riskier than before as they see changes in the political landscape where corrupt behaviors have led to the ouster of politicians from the highest offices. For that same reason some public officials are now calculating, if not deciding, that anticorruption can reap political rewards.

In this context of rather favorable opportunities and somewhat less-ened risks for combating corruption there is a growing interest and a sense of urgency among public officials and key stakeholders for an ana-lytical framework to evaluate and improve anticorruption policies and programs. The opportunities to initiate or improve anticorruption poli-cies and programs will not be available for long. In fact, the forces of cor-ruption are simultaneously trying to counter them. So it is critical for anticorruption coalitions to develop and execute strategies that can take advantage of opportunities in the face of immediately resistant and resourceful forces.

To address this need, in this chapter we outline an analytical frame-work that may be applied to make the design and implementation of anticorruption policies and programs more effective at national and sub-national levels. Building on the emergent research and findings of global corruption studies, this framework provides a "lens" for the thinking about and crafting of strategies to develop and advance anticorruption agendas. It is partly because the annals of global anticorruption action are recent and partly because there are more questions than answers on the matter that we propose this analytical framework. In this vein the frame-work can help reformers learn from the evolving global experience and thus ask better questions as they develop and execute strategies.

We do not mean to suggest that following this framework ensures vic-tory in combating corruption. As in other fields of human endeavor, the struggle against corruption involves far too many factors and forces to be able to predict with absolute confidence the outcome of battle. We do, however, suggest that the framework can help improve reformers' odds.

The analytical framework we propose comprises the following six action elements:

1. *Analyze a country's governance and operating environment.* The develop-ment and improvement of anticorruption policies and programs at national and subnational levels need to begin with a solid understand-ing of the country's governance and operating environment. In many countries the establishment of anticorruption agencies and measures omitted such analysis and study, and this explains in part the ineffec-tiveness of their anticorruption efforts. A thorough analysis of gover-nance and operating environment entails examining various aspects of a country's political, economic, social, and historical experience. The sociopolitical analysis is particularly important in this regard because it is a decisive determinant of anticorruption outcomes. This analysis should include looking at different existing comparative assessments of a country's governance and its patterns of corruption. There are various diagnostic tools, developed by the World Bank and others, that can pro-

vide an in-depth understanding of a country's governance and operating environment. Such a thorough assessment is critical in choosing anticorruption measures that will have the best chances of working in a given national or subnational governance environment.

2. *Review the global menu of anticorruption instruments.* This global review is fundamental in crafting appropriate policies and programs that are likely to succeed in a particular governance environment. A review of the literature indicates that there is a wealth of information now available on instruments being implemented to combat corruption. A global menu of anticorruption instruments can be compiled. This menu can be comprehensive or limited to a subset, such as increasing transparency through disclosure of information. It is likely that a corruption problem that a country is trying to address (for example, ensuring whistleblower protection) is being addressed in other countries. Reviewing the experiences of other countries can help identify policy and program alternatives and answer the following questions: Where, when, and how did the instruments work? What have been their successes and shortcomings? What are the prerequisites for success, and what needs to be avoided?

3. *Select anticorruption instruments according to a country's governance environment.* Choose from the global menu of anticorruption options the policies and programs that are likely to work in the particular governance environment prevailing in a country, state, or district. To be sure, these measures will need to be analyzed and adapted accordingly. It is crucial that selected measures be analyzed in terms of the likelihood of their being effective in a given set of governance conditions. This analysis can help shape the design and calibrate the implementation of the anticorruption measures. The scope of such measures may be quite comprehensive or more targeted based on available opportunities. For example, the public disgust with corrupt behavior by large corporations has opened an opportunity to put in place measures to improve corporate governance. This analysis of the governance environment should include an assessment of the opportunities for reform, which in turn would shape the comprehensiveness of an anticorruption program. Among other things, analysis should include an assessment of the impact of the proposed measure on the drivers of corruption in the country. Such an appraisal can benefit from the information gathered under the first two action elements described above. Based on this analysis, a technically sound anticorruption program can be crafted that is most likely to succeed given a country's governance circumstances.[1] Although necessary, however, a sound technical design is not a sufficient condition for effectiveness, as the following three action elements underscore.

4. *Build broad coalitions to develop and implement anticorruption policies and programs.* Fighting corruption can be characterized as shifting the balance of forces in state and society toward anticorruption policies and programs. In poor-governance countries, the people and groups who benefit from corruption are likely to be small in size and number, but are more or less organized and, not surprisingly, have sizable resources at their disposal. Thus, the greater the corruption in a country, the more critical it is to build a broad coalition. Only a broad coalition can effect a shift in the balance of forces. The broader the coalition, the better. With a critical mass of state and nonstate actors, anticorruption policies and programs can be placed at the top of a government's agenda. Moreover, the probability that the policies and programs will be decided on and implemented is likely to be increased despite expected resistance and opposition from corrupt forces both inside and outside of government.

5. *Establish accountable leadership and management of anticorruption policies and programs.* Almost all national anticorruption programs feature varying leadership and management structures. These include one or more of the following offices: independent commission against corruption, ombudsman, supreme audit institution, investigative and prosecutorial agency, parliamentary oversight body, multisector advisory group, internal affairs unit, and so forth. In countries with poor governance conditions, many if not most of those institutions themselves are plagued with corruption. In establishing or improving anticorruption institutions it is critical that they have sufficient authority and resources combined with broad accountability mechanisms. Whatever the form of the leadership and management structures, their effectiveness may be appraised according to the following criteria: political support, operational independence, subpoena powers and access to documentation, protection and promotion of whistleblowers, authority to introduce greater transparency and disclosure in public sector operations, reputational legacy, credibility and integrity of top leadership, and adequacy of resources.

6. *Monitor and evaluate feedback about anticorruption policies and programs.* In many poor-governance countries with anticorruption policies and programs there are hardly any regular and systematic processes to generate and assess accountable performance indicators. If anything, the facts and figures monitored and reported are often unrelated to measuring the anticorruption effectiveness of the organizations concerned. The lack of systematic assessments of measurable performance indicators retards and compromises anticorruption policies and programs. Such feedback is critical to establishing benchmarks for improvement. Only what is observed and measured can be more effec-

tively achieved. The World Bank and other organizations have developed various tools, such as diagnostic surveys and report cards, and the information they provide is critical to helping anticorruption actors anticipate, prepare for, and overcome the expected forces of resistance to reforms.

We now discuss in greater depth the specific elements of the analytical framework.

Analyzing a Country's Governance and Operating Environment

This is the core premise of our proposed analytical framework: anticorruption policies and programs need to be crafted on the basis of a careful analysis of the nature of governance and the patterns of corruption in a country. This premise is straightforward enough but it is not a practice in many countries. Various governments have overlooked or hardly conducted thorough research in developing and implementing anticorruption efforts. This is not to say that such thorough research will ensure success, but that it can enhance the prospects that chosen anticorruption instruments will have some impact on the problem.

When conducting research, be aware not only of its possibilities for making future programs more effective, but also of its limitations. The nature of governance and the drivers of corruption are complex, presenting interactions among each other that are not easily detectable, much less immediately manipulable by public policy. This is, in fact, a key lesson from the past and present failures of many existing anticorruption efforts. Thus, it is all the more important to be methodical in the matter. Institutional change—or the change of incentive structures that make corruption more costly (and, conversely, make noncorruption less costly)—is what anticorruption action seeks to achieve, and it is a dynamic and uncertain process (North 2003).

To know what strategies and tools might work in a particular governance environment it is important to understand that environment in the first place. The country governance setting is a key determinant of the likely effectiveness or ineffectiveness of any anticorruption measure. For example, although there is growing consensus that media have a role to play in any anticorruption program, the effectiveness of investigative journalism in China will differ from that in the Philippines. In this regard the nature of governance must be factored in assessing the weight and efforts devoted to particular anticorruption approaches.

There are a number of diagnostic instruments for assessing governance and operating environment at national or subnational levels. They may be viewed as an inverted pyramid of categories, providing, as it were, first a broad view of the forest and eventually a close-up view of the trees. Beginning at the broadest point these categories are:

1. Comparative cross-country surveys of governance (see appendix 2.1)
2. Country-focused diagnostics (such as the World Bank's institutional governance reviews)
3. Within-country surveys (such as report cards and enterprise or business climate surveys)
4. Sector-focused surveys (such as the World Bank's public expenditure tracking surveys).

Policymakers and key actors have found the diagnostics in the first category to be useful because of their comparative appeal and because they provide benchmarking information to assess performance. The second category lists forms of country case studies conducted to gain an in-depth understanding of the nature of governance in a country, with close attention paid to country-specific factors in politics, economics, social conditions, and the like. The third category offers in-country surveys that cover sectors or areas perceived to be most affected by corruption and poor governance. The fourth category describes studies that focus on governance and corruption conditions in particular sectors, such as health, education, or customs. In sum, this range of categories presents a systematic and sequential way of using diagnostic instruments. [2]

In drawing insights from diagnostic studies, the analysis of country governance should focus on a country's drivers of corruption. Such a review needs to be comprehensive and to encompass political, legal, economic, and social dimensions. All of those dimensions are important, but a special mention must be made of politics and incentives. Incentives and constraints faced by politicians strongly influence the nature and extent of corruption, so developing a good understanding of this landscape is extremely important in designing an anticorruption program. Among other things, a comprehensive framework analysis would include the following factors:

- Political system governing how state power is exercised, decisions are made, and accountability is enforced
- History and lessons of the country's anticorruption efforts
- Constitutional and legal framework concerning corruption
- Media freedom and civil liberties
- Regulations governing disclosure of information
- Activism of civil society and polling organizations
- Size, behavior, and values of the private sector

- Public awareness and sociocultural attitudes toward corruption
- Independence and integrity of the judiciary
- Effectiveness of anticorruption agencies, prosecutorial agencies, supreme audit institutions, and the like
- Quality and incentives of civil servants
- Local anticorruption champions and advocates in government, civil society, and the private sector
- Extent of political corruption.

Understanding a country according to each of the dimensions listed above would be a formidable task if done from scratch, but starting from square one is not necessary. One way of telescoping the process is to look at a country's governance indicators using existing comparative studies and surveys. The number of indicators available for a wide range of countries is growing (see appendix 2.1). [3]

These indicators provide data for developing a rating of a country's governance environment that may then be used to assess the potential impact of a particular anticorruption measure. Determining an overall rating of governance (or other aggregate measures of rating the key components of a country's governance environment) is necessary because the number of governance indicators can be large. For example, in the work of the World Bank the indicators used are based on several hundred individual variables measuring perceptions of governance that are drawn from 25 separate data sources and constructed by 18 different organizations (see Kaufmann, Kray, and Mastruzzi 2003). Thus, an aggregate rating becomes useful in providing a sense of the prospective effectiveness of anticorruption strategies and instruments in different governance settings, as we shall explain shortly. In this matter we draw heavily on the work of researchers who have tried to delineate the relationships between the effectiveness of various strategies and instruments and the governance environment. In the following section, we will discuss two pioneering studies to illustrate this analytical relationship.

Typology of Country Governance Environments: Two Approaches

There are two typologies that help explain the importance of selecting anticorruption instruments appropriate to a country's governance environment. The first typology deals with a country's "quality of governance." Jeff Huther and Anwar Shah (1998) developed a governance quality index based on four subindexes:

1. A citizen participation index (an aggregated measure using indexes of political freedom and political stability)

2. A government orientation index (an aggregated measure using indexes of judicial efficiency, bureaucratic efficiency, and lack of corruption)
3. A social development index (an aggregated measure using indexes of
   human development and egalitarian income distribution)
4. An economic management index (an aggregated measure using indexes of outward orientation, central bank independence, and inverted
   ratio of debt to gross domestic product).

This governance quality index is three-tiered: "good," "fair," or
"poor." Huther and Shah applied the index to 80 countries, as shown in
table 2.1, so the index provides a snapshot of the nature of a country's
governance relative to that of other countries. Certainly the index is not
meant to be deterministic or static because a country's governance quality can and does change over time, for better or for worse.

Concerning the countries covered by the case studies in this volume,
in table 2.1 we see that the Republic of Korea is rated as having "good
governance," the Philippines and Thailand have "fair governance," and
Indonesia has "poor governance." (Since Huther and Shah's study was
published in 1998 the governance situation in each of those countries has
more or less changed for the worse or for the better, as the case studies
will show). Generally speaking, the case studies illustrate how the ratings
of country governance can help in the design and improvement of anticorruption programs and policies.

The second typology tackles the different patterns of corruption
among countries. In a study on corruption in transition economies in
Europe, the World Bank (2000a) created a two-dimensional matrix of corruption. The two dimensions are *state capture* and *administrative corruption*,[4] as shown in figure 2.1.

State capture refers to "...shaping the formation of the basic rules of
the game (that is, laws, rules, decrees, and regulations) through illicit and
non-transparent private payments to public officials" (Hellman, Jones,
and Kaufmann 2000, p. 2).[5] In Asia this practice is also known as crony
capitalism (Kang 2002). Administrative corruption, also known as petty
corruption, refers to the "...private payments to public officials to distort
the prescribed implementation of official rules and policies" (Hellman,
Jones, and Kaufmann 2000, p. 2).[6] Variance in these two types of corruption presents different kinds of challenges and likewise poses different
prospects for the effectiveness of anticorruption policies.[7]

In developing this typology, the authors explained that "...an anti-corruption strategy should be designed not only in response to the level of
either state capture or administrative corruption alone in a given country
but to the interaction of these forms of corruption as well" (World Bank
2000a, p. 58). This is important because strategies and tools to combat

Table 2.1. Quality of Governance Ranking of Countries

Country	Quality index	Country	Quality index
Good governance			
Switzerland	75	Czech Republic	60
Canada	71	France	60
Germany	71	Belgium	58
Netherlands	71	Malaysia	58
Austria	70	Israel	57
United States	70	**Republic of Korea**	**57**
Finland	68	Trinidad and Tobago	57
Australia	67	Greece	55
Denmark	67	Spain	55
Norway	67	Costa Rica	54
Sweden	67	Hungary	54
Ireland	66	Uruguay	54
United Kingdom	66	Chile	53
Singapore	65	Italy	53
New Zealand	64	Argentina	52
Japan	63	Jamaica	52
Fair governance			
Panama	50	Tunisia	47
Romania	50	Brazil	46
South Africa	50	Russia	46
Venezuela, R.B. de	50	Turkey	46
Poland	49	Paraguay	45
Ecuador	48	Sri Lanka	45
Jordan	48	**Philippines**	**44**
Mexico	48	Zimbabwe	44
Oman	48	India	43
Peru	48	**Thailand**	**43**
Saudi Arabia	48	Côte d'Ivoire	42
Colombia	47	Papua New Guinea	41
Poor governance			
Egypt	40	Togo	29
Morocco	40	Zambia	29
China	39	Senegal	28
Kenya	39	Uganda	28
Cameroon	38	Yemen	28
Honduras	38	Iran	26
Indonesia	**38**	Malawi	26
Nicaragua	37	Sierra Leone	26
Nepal	36	Zaire	25
Pakistan	34	Rwanda	22
Nigeria	33	Liberia	20
Ghana	32	Sudan	20

Country names in boldface: subject of case studies in this volume.
Source: Huther and Shah 1998.

Figure 2.1. Stylized Typology of Corruption Conditions

	High/Medium	High/High
State capture	(High state capture/medium administrative corruption)	(High state capture/high administrative corruption
	Medium/Medium	Medium/High
	(Medium state capture/medium administrative corruption	(Medium state capture/high administrative corruption)

Administrative corruption

Source: World Bank 2000a.

administrative corruption may be compromised by state capture and vice versa. Of course, like the ratings on quality of governance, the snapshots of state capture and administrative corruption are meant to reflect conditions at the time of their taking. Thus they should be assessed in relation to current realities. In fact, as the authors said, "...it might be more useful to know in which direction a country is moving within the typology rather than its position at any given time" (World Bank 2000a, p. 58).

Reviewing the Global Menu of Anticorruption Instruments

Given the history of anticorruption efforts worldwide, the list of measures that have been tried is likewise long and varied. Since their founding, nation-states have wrestled with issues of balancing accountability and power. For example, in the United States the very structure of government was, to some of its founders, a measure to ensure accountability among powerful institutions through mutual checks and balances. [8] Thus, anticorruption measures broadly include instituting checks and balances in the political system (for example, strengthening the judiciary and promoting government decentralization), expanding civil society (for example, fostering a freer press and freedom of information and association), increasing accountability among political officials (for example, establishing asset disclosure regimes and campaign finance rules), injecting greater competition into the economy (for example, breaking up monopolies and enhancing regulatory institutions), and improving public administration and public finance (for example, developing a meritocratic civil service and fiscal discipline) (Kaufmann 2000). Other measures include raising public awareness, promoting public participation, establishing "watchdog" agencies, involving the private sector, and joining international initiatives (Stapenhurst and Kpundeh 1999; Langseth, Stapenhurst, and Pope 1997).

For its part the World Bank uses an anticorruption strategy framework with five components: (1) increasing political accountability, (2) strengthening civil society participation, (3) creating a competitive private sector, (4) establishing institutional restraints on power, and (5) improving public sector management. [9] Each of these components contains various tools and instruments. Of particular relevance to Asia is the comprehensive menu of anticorruption measures outlined in the Asian Development Bank (ADB) and Organisation for Economic Co-operation and Development (OECD) Anti-Corruption Action Plan for Asia and the Pacific (see table 2.2).

The importance in compiling anticorruption measures used globally is in being able to come up with an "anticorruption menu." In this regard, we made a preliminary compilation to create such a menu of measures (see appendix 2.2). We researched information from various secondary sources, including Web sites that have data on measures in use around the world.[10] The list is varied but it does not say much about the efficacy of the measures included. We recommend as a next step that a fact sheet be developed for each measure, which includes (a) information on the problem that the measure was designed to address, (b) how the measure would work to reduce corruption, and (c) what prerequisites or enabling conditions are necessary for the measure to be effective. This recommendation requires further research, which is beyond the scope of this project. At present it is sufficient to say that a global menu of anticorruption measures can be developed and used as a basis from which country-relevant measures may be drawn.

Crafting Anticorruption Measures Based on a Country's Governance Environment

Equipped with understanding about a country's governance environment and its patterns of corruption, policymakers can choose from the global menu of anticorruption measures the instruments that are likely to be appropriate and effective in their country. An anticorruption strategy does not have to be a comprehensive one in all cases. In some countries there may be enough resources, political commitment, and civil society support to launch an attack on all fronts. More often, however, this may not be the case, so a more focused approach may be very advisable. The analysis of a country governance environment is crucial for making that choice because the effect of anticorruption measures depends in part on

(*Text continues on page 33.*)

Table 2.2. Recommended Measures in the ADB-OECD Anti-Corruption Action Plan for Asia and the Pacific

Pillar 1 *Developing effective and transparent systems for public service*	Pillar 2 *Strengthening antibribery actions and promoting integrity in business operations*	Pillar 3 *Supporting active public involvement*
Establish systems of government hiring of public officials that ensure openness, equity, and efficiency, and promote the hiring of people with the highest levels of competence and integrity through: • Development of systems for compensation adequate to sustain appropriate livelihood and according to the level of the economy of the country in question • Development of systems for transparent hiring and promotion to help avoid abuses of patronage, nepotism, and favoritism; help foster the creation of an independent civil service; and help promote a proper balance between political and career appointments • Development of systems to provide appropriate oversight of discretionary decisions and of personnel with authority to make discretionary decisions	Take effective measures to actively combat bribery by: • Ensuring the existence of legislation with dissuasive sanctions that effectively and actively combat the bribery of public officials • Ensuring the existence and effective enforcement of anti-money-laundering legislation that provides for substantial criminal penalties for laundering the proceeds of corruption and crime consistent with the law of each country • Ensuring the existence and enforcement of rules to ensure that bribery offenses are thoroughly investigated and prosecuted by competent authorities; these authorities should be empowered to order that bank, financial, or commercial records be made available or be seized and that bank secrecy be lifted • Strengthening of investigative and prosecutorial capacities by fostering intera-	Take effective measures to encourage public discussion of the issue of corruption through: • Initiation of public awareness campaigns at different levels • Support of NGOs that promote integrity and combat corruption by, for example, raising awareness of corruption and its costs, mobilizing citizen support for clean government, and documenting and reporting cases of corruption • Preparation and implementation of education programs aimed at creating an anticorruption culture.

• Development of personnel systems that include regular and timely rotation of assignments to reduce insularity that would foster corruption.	gency cooperation, by ensuring that investigation and prosecution are free from improper influence and have effective means for gathering evidence, by protecting those people helping the authorities in combating corruption, and by providing appropriate training and financial resources • Strengthening bi- and multilateral cooperation in investigations and other legal proceedings by developing systems that, in accordance with domestic legislation, enhance (a) effective exchange of information and evidence, (b) extradition where expedient, and (c) co-operation in searching for and discovering forfeitable assets as well as prompt international seizure and repatriation of those forfeitable assets.	Ensure that the general public and the media have freedom to receive and impart public information (particularly information on corruption matters) in accordance with domestic law and in a manner that would not compromise the operational effectiveness of the administration or, in any other way, be detrimental to the interest of governmental agencies and individuals, through:
Establish ethical and administrative codes of conduct that proscribe conflicts of interest, ensure proper use of public resources, and promote the highest levels of professionalism and integrity through: • Prohibitions or restrictions governing conflicts of interest	Take effective measures to promote corporate responsibility and accountability on the basis of existing relevant international standards through: • Promotion of good corporate governance that would provide for adequate internal company controls such as codes of conduct, the establishment of	

(Table continues on the following page.)

Table 2.2. (continued)

Pillar 1 Developing effective and transparent systems for public service	Pillar 2 Strengthening antibribery actions and promoting integrity in business operations	Pillar 3 Supporting active public involvement
• Systems to promote transparency through disclosure and monitoring of, for example, personal assets and liabilities • Sound administration systems to ensure that contacts between government officials and business services users, notably in the areas of taxation, customs, and other corruption-prone matters, are free from undue and improper influence • Promotion of codes of conduct that take due account of the existing relevant international standards as well as each country's traditional cultural standards, and regular education, training, and supervision of officials to ensure proper understanding of their responsibilities	channels for communication, the protection of employees reporting corruption, and staff training • The existence and the effective enforcement of legislation to eliminate any indirect support of bribery, such as tax deductibility of bribes • The existence and thorough implementation of legislation requiring transparent company accounts and providing for effective, proportionate, and dissuasive penalties for omissions and falsifications for the purpose of bribing a public official, or hiding such bribery, in respect of the books, records, accounts, and financial statements of companies • Review of laws and regulations governing public licenses, government procurement contracts, or other public undertakings, so that access to public sector contracts could be denied as a sanction for bribery of public officials.	• Establishment of public reporting requirements for justice and other governmental agencies that include disclosure about efforts to promote integrity and accountability and to combat corruption • Implementation of measures providing for a meaningful public right of access to appropriate information.

- Measures to ensure that officials report acts of corruption and which protect the safety and professional status of those who do.

Safeguard accountability of public service via effective legal frameworks, management practices, and auditing procedures through:

- Institution of measures and systems to promote fiscal transparency
- Adoption of existing relevant international standards and practices for regulation and supervision of financial institutions
- Adoption of appropriate auditing procedures applicable to public administration and the public sector, and measures and systems to provide timely public reporting on performance and decisionmaking
- Adoption of appropriate transparent procedures for public procurement that promote fair competition and deter corrupt activity, and establishment of adequate simplified administration procedures

Encourage public participation in anticorruption activities, in particular through:

- Cooperative relationships with civil society groups, such as chambers of commerce, professional associations, NGOs, labor unions, housing associations, the media, and other organizations
- Protection of whistleblowers
- Involvement of NGOs in monitoring of public sector programs and activities.

(Table continues on the following page.)

Table 2.2. (continued)

Pillar 1 *Developing effective and transparent systems for public service*	Pillar 2 *Strengthening antibribery actions and promoting integrity in business operations*	Pillar 3 *Supporting active public involvement*
• Enhancement of institutions for public scrutiny and oversight • Adoption of systems for information availability, including information on issues such as application-processing procedures, funding of political parties, and electoral campaigns and expenditures • Simplification of the regulatory environment by abolishing overlapping, ambiguous, or excessive regulations that burden business.		

Source: Adapted from the ADB-OECD Anti-Corruption Action Plan for Asia and the Pacific, November 30, 2001.

the governance environment in which they are applied. Without sufficient knowledge of conditions policymakers are more likely to make mistakes in committing to ill-informed and poorly advised projects.

Table 2.3 presents the effect of specific anticorruption measures assessed relative to the quality of a country's governance environment, and suggests that the choice of measures must be calibrated according to that environment.[11] A particular policy that is effective in one setting may be ineffective if not counterproductive in another. Huther and Shah (2000) explained that some well-known anticorruption policies or programs are unlikely to have much impact in "weak" to "fair" governance environments. Those policies and programs would include approaches such as conducting seminars to raise public awareness, creating anticorruption agencies and ethics offices, and increasing public sector wages. By themselves those measures are likely to have little effect because they are not suitable to the governance conditions. Policies and programs such as instituting economic reforms, improving media and judicial independence, reducing the size of the public sector, and strengthening the rule of law would have greater effects against corruption in "weak" to "fair" governance environments. In such circumstances a targeted approach focused on promising areas (that is, where leadership, resources, and means for collective action are available) may be more effective.

However, it is not sufficient simply to base the choice of anticorruption instruments on broad assessments of the quality of governance. It is also critical to look at the nature of corruption in the country. The degree and combination of state capture and administrative corruption affect the ability of officials to implement certain anticorruption measures effectively. That is because the depth of corruption problems is a good indicator of the likely strength and capacity of the opposition to reformers. The more serious state capture and administrative corruption are, the more formidable vested interests are in countering reforms. Here again a targeted approach in promising areas would be more effective.

For example, a country governance environment with intermediate levels of state capture and administrative corruption presents less daunting conditions. In such a context the World Bank recommends strengthening political accountability and transparency through deepening institutional reforms in civil service, public finance, procurement, and the judiciary; introducing greater transparency into political financing; and building strong partnerships with civil society. Those are the kinds of broad measures that have reasonable prospects of being implemented because the state retains some autonomy and can leverage the relative strengths of its institutions in pursuing change.

In contrast, where the governance environment is characterized by high levels of state capture and administrative corruption the challenge

Table 2.3. Assessment of Selected Anticorruption Instruments

Anticorruption instrument	Quality of governance			Comments
	Weak	Fair	Good	
Raising public aware-ness of corruption through seminars	n.r.	Low	Med.	In countries with weak gover-nance, corrupt practices and agents are generally well-known.
Raising public officials' officials' awareness of corruption through seminars	n.r.	Low	Med.	Public officials may be aware of corruption but unwilling or unable to take action because of incentive problems in coun-tries with weak governance.
Establishing anti-corruption agencies/ombudsman position	n.r.	Low	Med.	With endemic corruption, anti-corruption agencies or ombuds-man may actually extort rents. Positive influence if precondi-tions for good governance exist.
Establishing ethics office	n.r.	Low	Med.	Positive influence may be limit-ed to societies with good gover-nance.
Raising public sector wages	...	Low	Med.	May have positive impact on on petty corruption but little impact on grand corruption. Negative impact if part of the problem is excessive public employment.
Reducing wage compression	...	...	...	More relevant as an incentive mechanism for career develop-ment. May increase corruption if the public sector is viewed as a lucrative career option by greedy elements of society.
Establishing merit-based civil service	Low	Med.	High	May be derailed by bureaucratic processes in highly corrupt societies.
Conducting public opinion surveys	Low	Med.	Med.	Public opinion surveys have served as a useful tool in articu-lating citizens' concerns (e.g., Bangalore scorecard).
Demanding financial accountability	Low	Low	Med.	Appropriate when democratic accountability and a substantial accounting/bookkeeping infra-structure with some integrity are in place.
Establishing parliamen-tary oversight	Low	Med.	Med.	Parliamentary oversight can be helpful but parliamentary micro-management is not an effective form of governance.

Anticorruption	Quality of governance			Comments
instrument	Weak	Fair	Good	
Reducing public employment	Med.	Low	Low	May reduce opportunities for corruption.
Decentralization	Med.	Low	Low	May improve accountability and may increase sense of social purpose for public officials.
Promoting client-client-based civil service/ bureaucratic culture	Med.	Med.	Low	Success depends on service delivery orientation of public service, reinforced by accountability for results.
Pursuing economic policy reform	High	Med.	Low	Reduces potential corruption by shifting decisionmaking to the private sector.
Promoting media and and judicial independence, citizen participation	High	Med.	Low	Allows for detection, followed by accountability.
Reducing size of the public sector	High	Med.	Low	By reducing the number of government activities, officials can focus on the primary objectives of the state.
Strengthening the rule of law	High	Med.	Low	Is essential for any progress.

n.r.   Not relevant
...   Negligible
Med. Medium
Source: Huther and Shah 2000.

is tougher because the forces of corruption are stronger relative to the state. In such cases the World Bank recommends reforms that focus on deconcentrating economic interests through restructuring, competition, and enhanced entry; building accountability and oversight mechanisms; and promoting collective action among countervailing interests. Those types of measures are intended to weaken vested interests by reducing the scope for corruption and increasing the risks of detection, investigation, and prosecution.

In our analytical framework we consider both the broader ratings of governance and the particular assessments of patterns of corruption in choosing and crafting anticorruption strategies (see table 2.4). We use the governance quality ratings with state capture and administrative corruption assessments as guiding indicators to select and prioritize anticorruption instruments. In this regard we differentiate countries beyond a broad three-tiered categorization of governance. The approach allows us to capture some of the complexity among countries within the same category of governance quality.

For example, state capture afflicts countries with different qualities of governance. Each of the four countries studied in this book have been stricken with relatively high levels of state capture. Even so-called good-governance countries, such as Korea, have not been immune. And Korea's case is not unique. The experiences of Italy and, to some extent, France likewise suggest that state capture is an insidious problem that can strike seemingly good governance environments (see Heidenheimer, Johnston, and LeVine 1989). With regard to administrative corruption, however, it appears to strike mainly poor- to fair-governance countries.

There are serious implications for policymaking when one considers both governance quality and particular patterns of corruption. For example, dealing with state capture in a poor governance environment demands a different strategy than does tackling state capture in a good governance context. The former situation will certainly be a more formidable task than the latter because the capacity of governmental institutions, civil society, and the private sector to combat corruption is likely to be less robust in a poor governance context than in a good governance environment. The forces of resistance in settings with state capture and poor governance are likely to be strong because of the resources they have accumulated from corruption. In such situations emphasis may be on reducing opportunities for corruption.

For example, a country that demonstrates poor governance, with unsurprisingly high levels of state capture and administrative corruption, calls for a judicious approach to combating corruption. Its conditions would not necessarily be mitigated by establishing anticorruption agencies or the office of an ombudsman. Because those agencies have been shown to be relatively effective in good-governance countries, they are often recommended as necessary institutions for poor-governance countries. In fact, setting up such agencies in poor-governance countries with high state capture and petty corruption may serve only to broaden corruption and increase the price of illicit transactions. In short, such putative solutions could worsen the problem because the anticorruption agency may easily get entangled in embedded corruption. Thus, effective anticorruption instruments must be crafted to reflect the quality of a country's governance environment and the degree of its state capture and administrative corruption.

We suggest in table 2.4 policy priorities that are likely to be effective in different country governance environments with particular corruption patterns. Our approach is more amenable to a targeted program than to a comprehensive program. In the table we show that countries with high levels of state capture and administrative corruption are likely to suffer

Table 2.4. Crafting Anticorruption Strategies According to Governance Quality and Corruption Patterns

State capture	Petty corruption	Governance quality	Recommended anticorruption strategies	Rationale
High	High	Likely poor governance	Primary emphasis on political and economic reforms to inject greater political and economic competition across governmental levels and key economic sectors; focus governmental reforms to limit state economic involvement and minimize regulations and interventions.	Under these conditions, the strategy should focus on reducing the scope and opportunities for corruption; measures to increase risks are initially likely to be ineffective because governance institutions (civil society, police, and the judiciary) are still weak and corrupt interests are relatively strong.
High	Medium	Mainly poor-governance countries (some fair- and good-governance countries also)	Focus remains on broad institutional reforms to make politics and business competitive across the board, to foster a strong party system, and to promote market-driven economic measures.	Depending on governance quality, a "high/medium" pattern needs to focus on the state's susceptibility to capture; thus the strategy should be to lessen state economic involvement (because administrative corruption is not severe; this would be secondary focus).
Medium	High	Mainly poor-governance countries (some fair-governance countries also)	Streamline bureaucratic systems and procedures to reduce petty corruption; emphasis on major governmental reforms to reduce bureaucratic economic involvement.	Depending on governance quality, a "medium/high" pattern requires prioritizing strategy to cut administrative opportunities for corruption; a broad-based coalition is needed to exert external pressure because of high petty corruption.
Medium	Medium	Generally fair- to good-governance countries	Pursue reforms to strengthen state institutions and the bureaucracy; continue cutting down corruption-prone activities, and enhance exposure and enforcement mechanisms.	With a "medium/medium" pattern, anticorruption strategy should focus on insulating the state and bureaucracy; efforts should target lowering corruption incentives and incidence, and intensifying penalties and the risks of being penalized.

Source: Authors' assessments.

from poor governance quality. But, as noted earlier, high state capture by itself does not necessarily mean poor governance. Korea, a good-governance country that has joined the ranks of the OECD, has eliminated petty corruption but has not been spared instances of state capture.

Administrative corruption would seem to be easier to tackle than state capture, arguably because the people who partake in and benefit from petty corruption are the broad transacting public, which is generally dispersed, not organized, and lacking in resources. The opposite is true for state capture whose beneficiaries are elite groups and powerful individuals who are generally concentrated in the capital and urban areas, are organized, and certainly endowed with political and economic resources.

That distinction has implications for the choice and crafting of strategies to fight corruption. Looking at countries with high degrees of administrative corruption and state capture, the reforms that are likely to be effective are those that reduce the scope of and rewards for corruption. That suggests, for example, the need for calibrated liberalization and deregulation of an economy because those actions reduce prospects for corruption by removing the state from direct economic activities. The fewer the prospects, the lesser the chances for corruption. As the cases in this book show, those reforms can be implemented with relative success in a poor to fair governance context. Measures to enhance enforcement and punishment, although critical, are of somewhat lesser priority in poor governance environments. Enforcement-oriented measures that can increase risks for corruption are unlikely to be effective in poor governance countries because the enforcement institutions themselves (that is, police and the judiciary) are weak and often part of the problem.

In cases of medium administrative corruption and high state capture, the focus of anticorruption measures should be less on the bureaucracy itself than on the major economic interests that have penetrated the state and purchased preferential treatment. The strategy should be to lessen state economic involvement and reduce the number and scale of projects that can be magnets for corruption. Because administrative corruption is not severe, bureaucratic reforms would be a secondary focus. With fair to good governance conditions, civil society may be tapped to combine forces with reformist bureaucratic actors. They can band together to pass measures that will introduce greater political and economic competition in the country. Such steps would reduce the size and gains of corruption opportunities even as they enhance the risks of prosecution and conviction.

In poor- to fair-governance countries with high petty corruption and medium state capture, the key challenges are streamlining and strengthening the capacity of bureaucracy to deliver public services in a transparent and accountable manner. Doing so narrows the scope for and prospects of administrative corruption. With only moderate state capture, some state support for bureaucratic anticorruption measures may be found. But clearly the ability of top officials to execute the state's policies and programs will depend in great part on their finding fulcrums for leverage within a corrupt bureaucracy.

Countries that are moderate in terms of state capture and administrative corruption are likely to be fair- to good-governance countries. In such cases the prospects for fighting corruption are more propitious because the state and bureaucracy, on balance, have some capacity to counter corrupt forces. Anticorruption thus needs to focus on insulating further both the state and the bureaucracy by reducing opportunities for corruption and increasing the penalties and the risks of being penalized. Under those conditions there is reason to emphasize enforcement and accountability mechanisms.

* * *

In summary, the discussion of the first three elements of the analytical framework has focused on designing or improving anticorruption strategies based on international experience and on adapting them to the specific conditions of the governance environment in which the measure will be applied. We believe that approach can help practitioners arrive at a better technical design for anticorruption programs that have the potential to be more effective. We have argued that a choice needs to be made regarding a comprehensive program versus a targeted one and that choice should be based on an analysis of the country's governance environment. In the next three sections we explain how a sound technical design needs to be followed by three other elements that are essential for effectiveness and results. Those elements are a broad coalition of supporters, effective leadership and management structures, and regular monitoring and reporting by independent and credible sources.

Building Broad Anticorruption Coalitions

Developing an anticorruption agenda, no matter how technically sound, needs a broad coalition to ensure it goes beyond the drawing board. The importance of such a coalition is a function of the quality of governance of the country and its patterns of corruption. The poorer the governance and the worse the corruption, the more critical coalition-building becomes because the resources, organization, and concentration of corrupt interests in the more corrupt countries far outweigh those of the broader transacting public.

As one analyst-practitioner put it, "those who suffer the consequences of corruption and thus who stand to benefit from reducing it (usually the general public) are spread out across many civil society groups or are even unorganized."[12] The challenge, thus, is to surmount the problem of collective action: bringing together the dispersed, pooling their resources, and building a movement that can outsmart, if not outweigh, the formidable forces of corruption.

Scanning the situation in many poor- to fair-governance countries, we see that there are varying levels of development and capacity of civil society and the private sector. Some groups appear to have spread themselves thinly as they try to combat corruption on various fronts, whereas others are geared toward particular problem areas, such as tax collection or customs administration. In both cases, anticorruption groups find themselves unable to advance their cause because they are "outgunned" by the purveyors and beneficiaries of corruption. This is why a more strategic focus on coalition-building is needed (Gonzalez de Asis 2000). Only when the various anticorruption groups are able to coalesce as a cohesive force can they have realistic prospects of neutralizing or countering the organizational and financial advantages of corrupt elements.

If coalition-building becomes more critical depending on the governance and patterns of corruption in a country, it becomes all the more so depending on the nature of the anticorruption reforms being pushed. The more significant and sweeping the reforms, the more serious the resistance will be and thus the more crucial coalition-building is to the endeavor. Therefore, a coalition-building strategy needs to be calibrated with the anticorruption strategy.

In mobilizing a coalition against corruption, it is crucial to find and draw the support of reformist officials. Even in environments with poor governance and high levels of state capture and administrative corruption, there are pockets of reform. Sometimes the search is not too difficult, as when there are visible officials who have displayed reformist goals. As one observer wrote, "Many public institutions may be afflicted by corruption, yet within them are caring and honest officials—including some in high positions—who, with the right encouragement and support, are prepared to address the corruption in their midst" (Kaufmann 1998, p. 143).

In other instances the quest for political allies will be tough because there are no visible proponents of reform. In many poor-governance countries it is not surprising that there are fewer public officials who expressly take on anticorruption issues. Because the beneficiaries of corruption are formidable politically and economically, public officials face a situation where the costs of reform are immediately daunting. In fact, in those environments where there is a low risk of being punished for corruption, there is conversely a high risk in pushing reforms. The challenge for the anticorruption coalition is not just to increase the risk of being penalized for corruption, but also to lower the risk of backlash for anticorruption advocates.

In finding and nurturing political leaders who are supportive of anti-corruption efforts, remember that the higher the official involved, the better. That is because there is a cascading effect when high office is involved. Those officials will have greater resources and more networks that can be converted to support reform. A cascading impact can lead to a so-called bandwagon effect where those people who previously sat on the fence will jump into the anticorruption coalition. For example, as is discussed in the Thailand case study in this volume, in 1997 the involvement of former Thai prime minister, Anand Panyarachun, and other notables in a social movement for good governance helped create a broad coalition that produced what is perhaps the world's most expressly anticorruption constitution.

In seeking the support of reformist officials for an anticorruption coalition, it is important to understand their concerns and criteria. If they are elected incumbents, they likely will worry about votes and reelection. In a poor governance environment where political corruption is part of the problem, politicians will naturally weigh the tradeoffs between the potential electoral benefits of an anticorruption platform and a strategy of playing politics-as-usual. In this regard the mood of the public is critical to shifting the calculus of politicians. If the public has demonstrably turned against corruption, politicians will appreciate that an anticorruption campaign can be appealing to the electorate. If the public has not embraced the fight, the anticorruption coalition needs to help raise public awareness and support.

Whatever the situation, it is crucial that officials and other stakeholders have access to information to make the case for anticorruption efforts. That can be done by making materials available on the Internet. Technical assistance may be provided to the officials. For example, research papers and memoranda about the problem of corruption can be used as the basis for speeches and seminars by executive officials that could help shape the public's mood and propel anticorruption alternatives. In the legislative branch policy research can become the basis for bill sponsorship and public hearings. The process of getting an anticorruption bill sponsored and read on the floor of the assembly is a significant move by itself. Public hearings on the bill can educate both legislators and the public about the costs and consequences of corrupt practices and the attendant benefits of more transparent and accountable systems. Naturally, if the anticorruption platform of reformist politicians is vindicated in the polls, it is likely that this platform will help shape their governing agendas.

Working with nongovernmental actors is a crucial component to broadening an anticorruption coalition. In countries with poor- to fair-quality governance where there is an increasingly strong civil society and a developing free press, an anticorruption agenda cannot do without the support of nongovernmental organizations (NGOs) and the mass media (see Stapenhurst 2000). Civil society groups, such as NGOs, academic institutions, and research organizations, have proven themselves in various cases to be powerful partners in counter-corruption coalitions. The more an institution is perceived as politically nonpartisan and impartial, the more significant its contribution to the coalition can be. The work and findings on anticorruption by researchers, analysts, and other scholars may become the bases for investigation by government agencies, hearings by the legislative assembly, social mobilization by NGOs, and may draw the spotlight of media coverage. For example, in the Philippines the Philippine Center for Investigative Journalism helped start the ball rolling on the formation of a broad coalition that eventually toppled the corrupt government of President Joseph Estrada. Its series of exposés on the sudden and unexplained wealth of the president and his associates led to a public outcry, an impeachment trial, and eventually Estrada's removal from office.[13]

To be sure, in poor-governance countries academic institutions and research entities are generally weak, with scant resources and few incentives to take on state actors from which many derive their budgets. The media in those countries are likewise not quite independent and therefore cannot be counted on to be a singular catalyst for reform. In this context, international organizations and external support can play a crucial role. Their skills and resources can be pivotal in helping build demand for change and mobilizing a broad reform coalition. At the request of the Philippine government, for instance, the World Bank (2000b) conducted a wide-ranging study of corruption there and recommended a nine-point agenda for reforms (see also World Bank 2001). It is important to emphasize, however, that international involvement must be nonpartisan and actually must be seen as such because accusations of partisanship can divide the anticorruption coalition and quickly undermine reform efforts.

In short, the challenge in seeking partners for a broad coalition for reforms is to assemble sufficient players and stakeholders in government and civil society whose reach and weight can shift the balance of forces that heavily favors corrupt interests. Shifting this balance means the coalition can gain maneuvering room to work at changing people's and policymakers' values about corruption. An encompassing and nonpartisan coalition will have greater credibility in reframing the problem of corruption and proposing policy options. Having shifted the balance, it is no less important that the anticorruption coalition can then be more effective in ensuring that policy reforms are prioritized in the government's agenda, that they are decided on and allocated resources, and that the policies and programs implemented are appropriate and effective.

Establishing Accountable Anticorruption Leadership and Management

The leadership and management structures of anticorruption programs are varied. Many of them actually are modeled on the institutions and practices of Western countries. The ombudsman, for example, originated in Scandinavia; the Independent Commission against Corruption was started in British-ruled Hong Kong. Therefore, various existing anticorruption leadership and management structures worldwide originally were based on the experience of good-governance countries.

There are other kinds of structures and arrangements that more or less emanated from good-governance countries. Some are constitutionally independent of the executive branch and others are set up by the executive branch to serve either in an advisory role or with the authority to investigate and help prosecute public officials of all ranks. Apart from the ombudsman and independent commissions, there are the presidential commissions, multisectoral advisory groups, institutions to administer ethical codes of conduct, regulations for financial disclosures by public officials, appointment of special authorities or commissions to handle or investigate specific corruption allegations, and parliamentary committees to oversee codes of conduct and campaign finance issues.

The variety of leadership and management structures for combating corruption is reflected in the different countries in Asia (see table 2.5).

The wide variety of leadership and management structures indicates the diverse approaches to combating corruption in different countries. It also suggests that some countries have modeled their structures on the successful experience of other countries. It is unfortunate in many cases that only the structures have been copied, not the accomplishments. Generally the performance record of these different organizations has left much to be desired, marked more often by failure than success. For example, the Philippine Office of the Ombudsman, which combines the powers of its Scandinavian namesake and the investigative authority of independent commissions against corruption, only achieved a conviction rate of 6 percent in 2001. This pales in comparison with the 79 percent conviction rate of the Independent Commission Against Corruption in Hong Kong, China, in the same year. [14]

This divergence in performance illustrates the difficulties of trying to transplant leadership and management structures from good-governance countries to fair and poor governance environments. In poor-governance countries, the network of political, economic, and social institutions in general is weak, which hinders the ability of anticorruption agencies to be effective. At the very least, an anticorruption agency must have the following attributes:

Table 2.5. Examples of Anticorruption Institutions in the Asia-Pacific Region

Economy	Anticorruption agency
Australia (New South Wales)	Independent Commission Against Corruption
China	Supreme People's Procuratorate, Central Disciplinary Inspection Committee
Hong Kong, China, Special Administrative Region	Independent Commission Against Corruption
India	Central Bureau of Investigation, Central Vigilance Commission, Election Commission
Indonesia	KOPKAMTIB (Operational Command for the Restoration of Security and Order), Financial Auditing Body, Financial and Development Auditing Body, National Commission to Investigate State Officials' Wealth, and National Ombudsman Commission
Republic of Korea	Korean Independent Commission Against Corruption, Board of Audit and Inspection, Public Prosecutors Office, and the Ombudsman
Macao	Independent Commission Against Corruption
Malaysia	Anticorruption Agency
Pakistan	National Accountability Board
Philippines	Office of the Ombudsman, Civil Service Commission, Presidential Antigraft Commission, and Commission on Audit
Singapore	Corrupt Practices Investigation Bureau
Taiwan, China	National Counter-Corruption Commission
Thailand	National Counter-Corruption Commission, State Audit Commission, Ombudsman, and Electoral Commission.

Source: Quah 2000.

- Political support from the head of state and broader political leadership
- Political and operational independence to investigate the highest levels of government
- Access to documentation and power to question witnesses
- Leadership with great integrity (Pope and Vogl 2000).

Even with those attributes the ability of anticorruption agencies to raise the risks and reduce opportunities for corruption is contingent on the quality of governance in a country. An anticorruption agency in a good governance environment will likely be more potent than an agency in a poor governance environment. In a good-governance country the agency can collaborate with other institutions that are more or less effective in their jobs, such as the police, the prosecutors, and the courts. In a poor-governance country those institutions are more likely to be poorly staffed, ill equipped, and weakly motivated. Worse, those institutions are often corrupt themselves. So an anticorruption agency in a poor governance environment can face enormous resistance and opposition. If poorly monitored and not held accountable, the agency can become infected with precisely the problem it was created to solve.

Determining the leadership and management structures for anticorruption programs is not an easy task, especially in poor governance environments. It is not sufficient to model the structures on the institutions and programs of other countries. In our view that has been a recipe for failure. Transplanted structures find themselves in very different grounds, and thus yield different results. It is crucial in the crafting of leadership and management structures, therefore, to consider the circumstances of a country's governance and operating environment.

What makes the task more difficult in poor to fair governance environments is the quality of officials who assume leadership and management positions. The recruitment process is often fraught with political corruption, which compromises the kinds of officials who are elected or hired from the highest office of the land to the lowest position. Even good-governance countries are not immune to falling short in the officials who lead anticorruption drives. In Korea former president Kim Dae-Jung's efforts to leave a legacy of effective anticorruption were tarnished by the corruption prosecution and conviction of his two sons.

The problem surely is most acute in poor to fair governance contexts. In the Philippines former president Estrada's initiative to tackle corruption was an example of how the messenger can mix up the message. Because of allegations of corruption swirling around Estrada himself, many in the media, civil society, business, and other sectors greeted the initiative with skepticism, if not scorn. The president's actions backfired in the face of evidence of presidential corruption and ironically helped propel the building of a successful anticorruption effort against his government.

In summary, the task of selecting leadership and management structures for a battle against corruption requires paying attention not just to the design of the institutions but also to the quality of recruited officials. Merely transplanting structures that worked well elsewhere can produce a familiar façade but not necessarily the needed internal workings of the structure. Those institutions must be designed to withstand the likely attacks of vested interests that will naturally try to destroy or sabotage the structures. Such design requires creating the institutions with a sufficiently strong combination of incentives and disincentives for its officials to behave and perform as mandated. Creating those institutions often requires resources that poor-governance countries lack. It is here that international and bilateral sources can be of help. Given the firepower of corrupt interests in countries with high levels of state capture and administrative corruption, international and bilateral support can help make the structures as "bullet-proof" as possible.

Monitoring and Evaluating Policy and Program Feedback

Many anticorruption reforms have fallen short after they have become policy because officials and stakeholders failed to effectively monitor and assess feedback about the implementation.[15] The anticorruption policy may be technically sound and have a broad coalition behind it, including appropriate leadership and management structures, but still it may falter. The failure to foster and listen to feedback from implementation results in the fatal error of not knowing the nature, location, and strength of corrupt elements that are naturally opposed to reforms. With monitoring and evaluation mechanisms, anticorruption reformers are able to assess information from implementation and accordingly to adjust policy reforms.

Opposition in implementation can occur in several ways. Key actors may defy the policy directly. In the Philippines, for example, the effort of the government of President Gloria Macapagal-Arroyo to corporatize the Bureau of Internal Revenue saw its employees use the courts and the streets to prevent the passage of legislation. The defiance may be less confrontational or overt, but no less effective. For instance, in Indonesia, as described in the case study later in this book, the attempt by an anticorruption team to investigate alleged corruption in the Supreme Court was cut short when the regulation that created the team was declared unconstitutional. In other cases noncompliance with the policy may delay the implementation in different ways that circumvent, if not cripple, the policy.

Monitoring and evaluating implementation can help overcome opposition to policy by providing critical information to officials about where, when, and how they might be able to adapt, calibrate, or sequence the policy. Broadly speaking, this step requires collecting and disseminating empirical information on the state of corruption, using various indicators. It entails qualitative analysis to assess levels of resistance and to foster cooperation and compliance among key actors and stakeholders. In monitoring it is critical to anticipate the location, organization, and strength of potential opposition *and* potential support for reforms.

Anticorruption coalitions need to be supported with an ongoing supply of empirical information and analysis to counter the opposition mounted against them. It helps to have this empirical information on the nature and magnitude of corruption (collected by credible institutions using sound methodologies) prominently and widely disseminated through media outlets because the resistance can sometimes be strong enough to cause the slow or sudden death of reforms unless public opinion and outrage against corruption are formed and sustained over many years.

As noted earlier in the chapter, there is a growing set of governance indicators being compiled at the country level by various groups and organizations. Although these cross-country compilations are extremely useful and influential in the international arena, many developing countries appropriately are collecting indigenous sources of information on corruption. Some of these information sources go to subnational levels. Such indigenous as well as international monitoring and reporting systems on indicators of corruption and governance are an essential component of the analytical framework for improving the effectiveness of anticorruption policies and programs.

Various diagnostic instruments are being pioneered around the world to collect micro-level information on corruption and on public service deliveries in developing countries. A sample of those instruments is presented in table 2.6.

Although these empirical monitoring tools are indispensable to making anticorruption policies and programs more effective, they must be supplemented by qualitative sociopolitical analysis of the vested interests that will passively or actively oppose the anticorruption policies and programs.

Strategic considerations have to contend with resistance within government or in the public at large (Grindle and Thomas 1991). To be sure, combined resistance is more formidable than is resistance from either the public or bureaucrats alone. The nature of the resistance generally corresponds to the nature of the reform being pursued—that is, the one who will be hurt by the reform is the one who will likely resist. Conversely, whoever benefits is likely to be a supporter. Of course, the world of costs and benefits can be more or less immediate, depending on the immediacy and impact of a reform. For example, the pain of abolishing an agency will be immediately felt by bureaucrats, whereas the expected rewards of a corporatized agency are likely to be felt by the public only in the future. Therefore bureaucratic resistance will be more immediate, and public support less forthcoming.

Opposition to reform will likely emerge in the bureaucracy if the policy means more costs than benefits to the officials and employs weak coercive or remunerative instruments to ensure and enforce compliance. The

Table 2.6. Examples of Anticorruption Survey Instruments

Diagnostic survey instrument	Developer
Public Officials Survey—The purpose of this survey is to identify different practices inside the public sector related to the management of personnel, the budget, and the delivery of public services. In particular the survey investigates corrupt and improper practices in (a) personnel management, (b) budgeting, (c) project planning, (d) information management, and (e) performance of the public sector. It also investigates (a) public officials' opinions about state reforms, (b) the performance of the public sector, and (c) the capacity of official institutions to undertake the battle against corruption.	World Bank Institute (www.worldbank.org/ wbi/governance)
Enterprise Survey—The purpose of this survey is to gain a better understanding of the obstructions and limitations to business development. In particular the survey examines (a) the perceived obstacles to business development, (b) analysis of the corruption problem, (c) the different faces of corruption, (d) transparency in public services in the judicial system, (e) bureaucratic costs, and (f) tax evasion and the informal sector.	World Bank Institute (www.worldbank.org/ wbi/governance)
Household Survey—The purpose of this survey is to find out how households perceive the services they receive in their homes and the ways to improve them. Among other things the survey focuses on (a) perceived dishonesty in various public institutions (for example, the judicial system, educational system, health system) as well as in public service providers (for example, customs office, tax payment offices, water works, police, transit authorities, licensing, public registry, schools, telecommunication providers, post office, power companies, public hospitals, social security, trash collection) and (b) the efficiency of anticorruption agencies.	World Bank Institute (www.worldbank.org/ wbi/governance)
Citizen Report Cards—According to the developers of this instrument, report cards are an aggregate of public ratings on different aspects of service quality, built on specific random surveys of users of different public services (that is, utilities in a city). The report cards include information on corruption encountered.	Public Affairs Center, Bangalore, India (www.pacindia.org)

Diagnostic survey instrument	Developer
Public Expenditure Tracking Surveys (PETS)— These surveys focus on collecting micro-level data on the characteristics of the service facility, the nature of financial flaws from facility records, output, and accountability arrangements. In this process PETS also help uncover where and to what extent corruption and abuses are leading to breakdowns in future delivery systems.	Uganda, with assistance from the World Bank (www.worldbank.org/ poverty/empowerment/ toolsprac)
Transparent Accountable Governance Surveys— Pioneered in the Philippines, these surveys cover businesses to deepen understanding of public and private sector perceptions of the roots and realities of corruption.	Social Weather Stations (www.sws.org.ph and www.tag.org.ph)
*Social Accountability Mechanisms—*These are featured in a number of recent loans financed by the World Bank. They include the accountability of governments to their citizens through collection and disclosure of information on expenditures and performance.	World Bank (www.worldbank.org/ poverty/empowerment/ toolsprac)

costs to bureaucratic entities can come in different forms—such as if the policy is seen as eradicating the bureaucracy, impinging on its turf, reducing its personnel, adding more administrative work, or placing an additional drain on its budget.

Resistance will come from the public sphere if the programs mean more costs than benefits to the public, with no significant incentives or disincentives for cooperation. The high costs and low benefits can be varied. The policy, for instance, may result in some inefficiency in governmental procedures, as the government adds measures to increase transparency and accountability. This is in many ways a concern among those who contend that anticorruption projects can sacrifice efficiency and effectiveness in the name of control (see Anechiarico and Jacobs 1996). Or the policy may be seen as making use of resources at the expense of other programs perceived to warrant a higher priority.

A situation in which combined and coordinated resistance emerges from inside and outside government can constitute the most serious challenge to the implementation of reforms. At the extreme this resistance can be expected in poor-governance countries under high state capture conditions because the anticorruption agencies of the state often have been influenced by corrupt elements and are unable to respond effectively (Hellman and others 2000). In that context, the close monitoring and evaluation of anticorruption policies is critical.

In monitoring and evaluating, it is important to be on the lookout for ways and means to calibrate or modify policies to make them more effective. Reformers have to watch for the impact of the policy on the existing power structures and networks within and outside the state. They should be prepared to balance incentives and disincentives in the reforms to ensure that there are sufficient rewards for cooperation and adequate instruments for compliance. As noted earlier, the failure of many reforms has been their inability to prepare for opposition from beneficiaries of corruption who are often more organized and more resourceful than the officials and groups promoting reform.

Monitoring and evaluation include paying attention to arrangements that can mobilize additional resources to counter resistance that will likely be powerful in poor- to fair-governance countries with medium to high levels of state capture. The more organized and economically endowed the expected opposition might be, the more the anticorruption agenda should be accorded substantial political and economic resources. And it is important to consider tinkering with the policy itself, recalibrating its parts, resequencing its approach, and so forth to modulate the action and mollify the opposition.

Monitoring and evaluation should also pay attention to how anticorruption policy is understood by stakeholders and the public. Vague provisions can result in diverging interpretations, which would make noncompliance inevitable. Unless reforms are on solid constitutional and legal grounds, the implementation can be obstructed by court challenges or weakened by policy inconsistencies.

Finally, monitoring and evaluation must take into account the resources required and available to them. The resources required depend on the nature of the reform and the implementation approach taken. These resources can be technical, administrative, and managerial measures. They can be bureaucratic and organizational means. They can also be more properly legal moves and political forces. They may also include international actors and foreign aid. [16] These courses of action are most critical when we are dealing with poor governance and high levels of state capture and administrative corruption. In those environments resources are expectedly in short supply and often may not be accessible right away. Whatever limited resources there are, they must be deployed effectively. There is, therefore, less margin for error in such contexts than in good governance contexts where the state has sizable resources to spare to overcome resistance and ensure implementation.

Summary

Because the quality of governance and the patterns of corruption among countries differ, a country's anticorruption strategy must be appropriate to its conditions. A strategy that is not reflective of the governance and corruption realities of the country environment is unlikely to work and may even help worsen the problem. The analytical framework we propose is akin to six building blocks that can strengthen the foundation of anticorruption. We are not saying that this approach will guarantee success—no one can guarantee that—but that it can increase the chances that the strategy will be effective.

The first element of the framework is an analysis of a country's quality of governance and patterns of corruption. A governance quality review should include studying a country's various dimensions of governance, such as rule of law, regulatory capacity, government effectiveness, voice and accountability, and control of corruption. One dimension—incentives or constraints faced by politicians—deserves special mention because it is a key determinant of the nature and extent of corruption. Such an analysis of governance environment can draw on growing comparative governance research and can help provide a well-founded assessment of a country's quality of governance and its patterns of corruption.

The second element involves compiling a menu of anticorruption policies and programs being practiced internationally. We suggest developing fact sheets about specific anticorruption measures in terms of their effects on officials' cost-benefit calculations—that is, the impact of measures on reducing corruption opportunities, narrowing corruption gains, raising penalties, and increasing risks. Such fact sheets could also identify the prerequisite conditions that must be in place for the anticorruption measure to be effective.

The third analytical effort is to select from the global menu of anticorruption measures those policies and programs that would constitute an appropriate corruption-fighting agenda in relation to a country's quality of governance and patterns of corruption, particularly its conditions of state capture and administrative corruption. The agenda may be comprehensive or targeted at a few areas, depending on resources, political will, civil society support, and implementation capacity. The fact sheets on particular anticorruption measures are useful in this analytical application, helping reformers not only to identify relevant anticorruption measures but also to prioritize their implementation.

The fourth element of the framework is building a broad anticorruption coalition that spans reformist elements from different sectors of society, of sufficient size and credible leadership to shift the balance of forces in favor of change. An anticorruption agenda, no matter how technically sound, will likely crumble without a solid coalition behind it. This is particularly the case in poor-governance countries, where high levels of state capture and administrative corruption produce powerful opponents to change. Mobilizing an anticorruption coalition in such a context is complicated but utterly necessary.

The fifth aspect of our analytical framework is establishing leadership and management structures and systems that are appropriate to a country's governance and operating environment, equipped with the necessary authority, powers, and resources to implement the reform program. Transplanting institutions and organizations that have worked elsewhere without taking context into consideration can be problematic. In poor-governance countries the need for authoritative and accountable leadership and management is acute. This is, all too often, the Achilles heel of anticorruption efforts.

Monitoring and evaluating feedback from the implementation of anticorruption policies and programs is the sixth aspect of the framework. It enables reformers to anticipate the opposition's location, strength, and resources and accordingly to mobilize resources in response. Nowhere is this effort more important than in a poor governance environment where the struggle against corruption carries with it significant risks in the form of powerful beneficiaries of corruption. There are various methods for monitoring and evaluating that enable officials and stakeholders to assess where, when, and how they can adjust and calibrate their efforts to ensure compliance and implementation.

To conclude, this analytical framework builds on the growing contributions of research in governance and corruption. Although much work remains to be and is being done, some progress has been made in identifying measures that would be effective in certain governance environments and particular corruption conditions. In that regard, this six-part framework is presented as one strategic approach to developing a multidimensional reform strategy appropriate to a country's governance environment and patterns of corruption.

The need to be focused and targeted in anticorruption efforts cannot be overemphasized because of the complex and resistant nature of the problem. Combine that with the relatively weak position that governments and other reform advocates find themselves in, particularly in poor to fair governance contexts, and it becomes all the more imperative to ensure that scarce political and economic resources are deployed effectively to fight the problem. Opponents of anticorruption policies and programs, more often than not, are operating from a position of strength that is enhanced by poor policy design and coordination, lack of public support, and inadequate resource mobilization, among other things. We hope that the analytical framework we recommend here can help shift the balance between corrupt and reform forces in favor of the latter.

Appendix 2.1. Selected Sources of Governance Indicators

Source	Aspects of governance assessed[a]	Specificity	Method of data collection	Coverage across countries	Coverage over time	Reliance on subscribers	Use in published studies
Asia Intelligence, Political and Risk Consultancy	Corruption in the legal system, police, and the judiciary	Medium	Survey of business managers	Low	Low	Yes	Low
Business Environment Risk Intelligence (BERI)	Bureaucratic delays, contract enforceability, nationalization risk, and policy stability	Low	Experts (many)	Low	High	Yes	Medium
Country Risk Review, Standard and Poor's, DRI/McGraw-Hill	Political stability, regulations, contract enforcement, and corruption	Medium	Experts	High	High	Yes	Low
Country Risk Services, Economist Intelligence Unit	Political, economic, policy, and financial aspects	Low	Experts	High	Medium	Yes	Low
Freedom House	Political freedoms and civil liberties	Low	Experts (few)	High	High	No	High
Gallup Millennium Survey, Gallup International	Civil liberties, government accountability, and corruption	Low	Survey of individuals	Medium	Low	No	Low
Global Competitiveness Report (GCR), World Economic Forum	Civil service independence from politics, competence of public sector personnel, tax evasion, and effectiveness of police force	Medium	Business survey	Low	Low	No	Low
Heritage Foundation/ Wall Street Journal	Property rights, black market, and regulation	Low	Experts (few)	High	Low	No	Low

Source	Concepts measured							
International Country Risk Guide (ICRG), Political Risk Services	Corruption in government, law and order, tradition, and bureaucratic quality	Low	Experts (few)	High	High	High	Yes	High
Kaufmann, Kraay, and Zoido-Lobatón of World Bank's Governance Matters II	Graft, rule of law, voice and accountability, political instability and violence, government effectiveness, and regulatory burden	Low	Aggregation	High	Low	Low	No	Low
Latinobarómetro	Democracy, social fraud, and civic culture	Low	Survey of individuals	Medium	Medium	Medium	No	Low
Opacity Index, PricewaterhouseCoopers	Transparency, corruption, contract enforcement, and regulation	High	Survey of experts	Medium	Low	Medium	No	Medium
Transparency International, State Capacity Project, Columbia University	Corruption Perceptions Index	Low	Aggregation	Medium	Low	Medium	No	Medium
World Business Environment Survey, World Bank	Corruption, state capture, political stability, regulation, and rule of law	High	Survey of private enterprises	High	Low	High	No	Medium
World Competitiveness Yearbook (WCY), International Institute for Management Development	Bribing and corruption, tax evasion, public service exposure to political interference, personal security, and private property	Medium	Business survey	Low	Low	Low	No	Low
World Development Report 1997 (private sector survey), World Bank	Policy unpredictability, quality of government services, corruption and red tape, and judicial unpredictability	Medium	Business survey	Medium	Low	Medium	No	Low

a. Partial list only for some sources.
Source: Adapted from World Bank information available at www1.worldbank.org/publicsector/indicators.htm.

Appendix 2.2. A Selective Global Review of Anticorruption Instruments

Anticorruption instruments	OECD	Non-OECD countries	Quality of Governance Weak	Fair	Good	Remarks
A.						
Requirements imposed by law						
A.1 Statements of general duties, obligations, and values of public office; standards of public behavior; rules and procedures for public procurement	Belgium Czech Republic France Germany Hungary Ireland Italy Japan Rep. of Korea Mexico Poland Sweden Switzerland	Most countries	Low	Low, D	Medium, A, D	Success depends on service delivery orientation of public service, reinforced by accountability for results, especially for weak- to fair-governance countries. If combined with appropriate legal safeguards and rule of law, such strategies may lead to an increase in the magnitude of penalties (D). As standards are identified, so are the appropriate penalties. For countries with good governance, improving bureaucratic culture may lead to a decline in corrupt transactions (A).
A.2 Requirements for public officials to declare assets and financial interests; rules on conflict of interest, including receiving gifts, concurrent office holdings, and financial and political activity	Belgium Czech Republic France Germany Greece Hungary Ireland Italy	Most countries	Low, D	Low, D	Medium, A, B, D	Appropriate when accountability and a substantial accounting/bookkeeping infrastructure with some integrity are in place. For weak- and fair-governance countries this strategy may increase probability of paying penalties (D) only when matched with legal safeguards and upholding the rule of law (which are present in countries with good gover-

nance). Hence, for such countries, this strategy may decrease corrupt transactions (A), decrease expected gains (B) because of transparency, and increase penalty (D).

Japan
Rep. of
  Korea
Mexico
Poland
Spain
Sweden
Switzerland

		High, A, C, D	Medium, A, C, D	Medium, A, C, D
A.3[a]	Laws to deal with political corruption (Public Officers Disqualification Order 1959; Holders of Representative Office [Punishment for Misconduct], and so forth)	Pakistan		

Needs adequately trained, qualified, and professional work force for satisfactorily investigating corruption crimes. May decrease number of corrupt transactions (A), increase probability of paying penalty (C), and increase magnitude of penalty (D) provided preconditions are present. Lack of good governance requirements should be addressed, such as freedom of information, transparent administrative procedures, internal system for redressing grievances.

(Appendix continues on the following page.)

Appendix 2.2. (continued)

Anticorruption instruments	OECD	Non-OECD countries	Quality of Governance Weak	Fair	Good	Remarks
B. *Specialized corruption services/agencies*						
B.1 Under the commissariat police, the *Office Central pour la repression de la corruption*, the *Office Central de lutte contre la deliquance economique et financiere organisee* (specializing in financial organized crime), and the *Brigade Nationale* (specializing in serious crime) can inquire into corrupt public sector activities.	Belgium	Most countries	Not relevant	Low, C	Medium, A, C	With endemic corruption, anticorruption agencies or ombudsman may actually extort rents. Positive influence if preconditions exist. With minimal preconditions, anticorruption agencies or ombudsman may contribute toward increasing probability of paying penalty (C). For countries with good governance, this anticorruption instrument may also reduce the number of corrupt transactions.
B.2 *Le Ministere public de la Confideration* investigates misconduct implicating public officials	Switzerland					
B.3 The Service for Detecting Corruption and Serious Economic Criminality exists with the police. It has intel-	Czech Republic					

ligence and international functions.

B.4   France   *Le Service Central de prevention de la Corruption, la Commission centrale des marches, la Cour des comptes, la Mission interministrelle d'enquete sur les marches, la Commission centrale des marches, Commission des comptes de campagne et des financements politiques, la Commission pour la transparence financiere de la vie politique* have independent authority.

B.5   Germany   Audit offices can investigate within their jurisdictions. Some branches have independent bodies to investigate suspected corruption.

B.6   Greece   The Body of Inspectors-Controllers of Public Administration oversees the functioning of the administration, local authorities, and entities established under public law.

(Appendix continues on the following page.)

Appendix 2.2. (continued)

	Anticorruption instruments	OECD	Non-OECD countries	Quality of Governance			Remarks
				Weak	Fair	Good	
B.7	The Government Control Office controls financial management and waste, and investigates and recommends government action.	Hungary					
B.8	The Public Offices Commission can investigate matters concerning public officials and ministers that may involve corruption.	Ireland					
B.9	Special judicial agencies, the General Finance Inspectorate (Treasury Ministry), the General State Accounting Service, the Public Service Department Inspectorate, and administrative investigation institutions.	Italy					
B.10	Presidential Secretary for Corruption Inspection; Board of Audit and Inspection; Prime Minister's Administration Co-coordinator for Anti-Corruption; the Meeting of	Rep. of Korea					

		Ministers on Anti-Corruption; the individual government agencies conduct internal investigation; the 15-member Special Commission on Anti-Corruption (consisting of lawyers, professors, members of the private sector, civic and religious groups) serves as an advisory body to the president.
B.11	Mexico	The Secretariat of Comptrollership can investigate all irregularities involving public officials.
B.12	Poland	Departments established within the Ministry of Justice for investigating organized crime also investigate public sector corruption in that context.
B.13[a]	Papua New Guinea the Philippines	National Government Contracts Review Committee

(*Appendix continues on the following page.*)

Appendix 2.2. (continued)

Anticorruption instruments	OECD	Non-OECD countries	Quality of Governance Weak	Fair	Good	Remarks
B.14[a] Independent anticorruption commissions/bodies		Hong Kong (China) the Philippines Kenya				For Hong Kong, China, ICAC is not the strategy itself, but a mechanism to implement a broader strategy of rule of law and to mobilize popular support. Anticorruption agencies in situations with high incidence of corruption and poor governance may not work. In these cases, its operations may be stopped once it starts to be effective. A case in point is the Kenya Anti-Corruption Authority (KACA) established in 2000. KACA started its work focusing on middle-ranking offenders, but when it investigated a minister and a wife of another minister, the High Court stepped in and declared the KACA unconstitutional.[c]
C. *Human resources management controls*						
C.1 Disciplinary action up to and including dismissal	France Germany Greece Hungary Ireland	Most countries D	High D	Medium C, D	Low C, D	Highly relevant for countries with weak governance because this will contribute to strengthening the rule of law. Success of implementation depends on the existence of other preconditions, e.g., posi-

Code	Instrument	Countries				Comments
		Italy Japan Rep. of Korea Mexico Poland Spain Sweden				tive culture of the bureaucracy. May also increase the probability of paying penalty (C).
C.2	Standardized recruitment and selection of officials	France Germany Greece Hungary Ireland Japan Rep. of Korea Poland	Most countries	Low	Medium A	Medium A	For countries with weak governance, this instrument may not be useful because corrupt elements usually have full decision power on hiring and selection. May decrease number of corrupt transactions if some preconditions exist.
C.3	Processes for preventing or detecting conflicts of interest (including the declarations of interest and employment restrictions)	Belgium Czech Republic France Germany Hungary Ireland Italy Japan	Most countries	Low, D	Medium, A, B, D		Appropriate when accountability and a substantial accounting/ bookkeeping infrastructure with some integrity are in place. For weak- and fair-governance countries this strategy may increase probability of paying penalties (D) only when matched with legal safeguards and upholding the rule of law (which are present in countries with good gover-

(Appendix continues on the following page.)

Appendix 2.2. (continued)

Anticorruption instruments	OECD	Non-OECD countries	Quality of Governance			Remarks
			Weak	Fair	Good	
	Rep. of Korea Mexico Poland Spain Sweden Switzerland					nance). Hence, for such countries this strategy may decrease corrupt transactions (A), decrease expected gains (B) because of transparency, and increase penalty (D).
C.4 Enhancing the responsibility and quality of senior managers	Germany Greece Italy Sweden		Low	Medium	High	May worsen corruption if corrupt officials will be given more responsibility. This instrument should be matched with a positive bureaucratic culture, rule of law, and transparency.
C.5 Regular redeployment of officials in positions susceptible to corruption	Germany Greece Japan Italy		Low	Medium A	Medium A	Outcome depends on the governance environment. May not have a significant impact for countries with weak governance. With minimal preconditions this may decrease the number of corrupt transactions.
D. *Transparency mechanisms*						
D.1 Standardization and transparency in public procurement	Belgium Czech Republic France Germany	Philippines	High A, C	High A, C	Medium A, C	Essential for bringing down the number of corrupt transactions. Greatest impact when matched with rule of law, decentralization, financial accountability, and positive bureaucratic culture.

64

		Greece Hungary Ireland Italy Rep. of Korea Mexico Poland Sweden Switzer- land	Most countries	Low, D	
D.2	Declarations of financial interests of public officials	Czech Republic France Greece Hungary Ireland Italy Japan Mexico Rep. of Korea Poland Sweden	Medium, D	Medium, A, B, D	Appropriate when accountability and a substantial accounting/ bookkeeping infrastructure with some integrity are in place. For weak- and medium-governance countries this strategy may increase probability of paying penalties (D) only when matched with legal safeguards and upholding the rule of law (which are present in countries with good governance). Hence, for such countries this strategy may decrease corrupt transactions (A), decrease expected gains (B) because of transparency, and increase penalty (D).

(Appendix continues on the following page.)

Appendix 2.2. (continued)

Anticorruption instruments	OECD	Non-OECD countries	Quality of Governance			Remarks
			Weak	Fair	Good	
D.3 Procedures for dealing with conflicts of interest	Czech Republic Germany Hungary Ireland Rep. of Korea Mexico Poland Spain Sweden Switzerland	Most countries	Low D	Medium D	Medium A, B, D	Appropriate when accountability and a substantial accounting/ bookkeeping infrastructure with some integrity are in place. For weak- and fair-governance countries this strategy may increase probability of paying penalties (D) only when matched with legal safeguards and upholding the rule of law (which are present in countries with good governance). Hence, for such countries this strategy may decrease corrupt transactions (A), decrease expected gains (B) because of transparency, and increase penalty (D).
D.4 Right of access to public information	Belgium Greece Hungary Ireland Italy Rep. of Korea Spain Sweden	Most countries where substantive democracy exists	High A, C	Medium A, C	Low A, C	Allows transparency and detection. Highly relevant for weak-governance countries. Should be matched with rule of law and positive bureaucratic culture. May reduce number of corrupt transactions and increase probability of paying penalty.

No.	Measure	Countries					Comments
D.5	Independent body for receiving complaints about corruption	France Germany Ireland Rep. of Korea Mexico	Hong Kong, China	High, A, C	Medium, A, C	Low, A, C	For Hong Kong, China, community-based anticorruption offices were established to receive complaints directly. Supports transparency (see D.4).
D.6	Disclosure of political party funding	Belgium France Greece Ireland Rep. of Korea		Low	Low	Low	May not have any impact at all when corruption is rampant and where elections are not fair.
D.7	Law requiring provision of reasons for administrative decisions	Belgium France Greece Ireland Italy		Low	Low	Low	Corruption may be discouraged by clarifying penalties.
E.	*Guidance and training for public officials or politicians*						
E.1	Codes of conduct or statements of standards or expected behavior	Belgium France Germany Greece Hungary Ireland Italy	Most countries	Medium, C, D	Medium, C, D	Low, A	Success depends on service delivery orientation of public service, reinforced by accountability for results, especially for weak- and fair- governance countries. If combined with appropriate legal safeguards and rule of law, such strategies may lead to an increase in the magnitude

(Appendix continues on the following page.)

Appendix 2.2. (continued)

Anticorruption instruments	OECD	Non-OECD countries	Quality of Governance			Remarks
			Weak	Fair	Good	
	Japan Rep. of Korea Mexico Spain Switzer- land					of penalties (D). For countries with good governance, improving bureaucratic culture may lead to a decline in corrupt transactions (A).
E.2 E.2ª Training or other methods of raising awareness on corruption (including those for the private sector)	France Germany Greece Hungary Japan Mexico Poland Spain Sweden Switzer- land	Hong Kong, China	Not relevant	Low	Medium	In countries with weak governance, corrupt practices and agents are generally well known.
F *Types of evaluation* F.1 Periodic assessment as part of the routine work of a government department, office, or a parliamentary body	Hungary Ireland Italy Japan	Most countries	Low, A	Medium, A	Medium, A	May be a deterrent (A) when there is a positive culture in the bureaucracy and rule of law. Parliamentary oversight can be helpful but parliamentary microman-

		Rep. of Korea Switzerland				agement is not an effective form of governance.
F.2	Assessment by a dedicated or specialized body	France	Low, A	Medium, A	Medium, A	May be a deterrent (A) when there is a positive culture in the bureaucracy and rule of law.
G	*New actions being considered*					
G.1	Enhancing or establishing offenses and penalties	Belgium Czech Republic Germany Greece Hungary Japan Rep. of Korea Switzerland	Low, D	Medium, D	Medium, D	May only work if necessary preconditions exist, e.g., rule of law, positive bureaucratic culture, and so forth.
G.3	Introduction or enhancement of powers held by specialist bodies	Belgium France Germany Ireland Italy Switzerland	Low	Low	Medium, A, C, D	Good-governance countries may benefit through a reduction in the number of corrupt transactions (A), increased probability of paying penalties (C), and increased magnitude of penalty (D).

(Appendix continues on the following page.)

Appendix 2.2. (continued)

	Anticorruption instruments	OECD	Non-OECD countries	Quality of Governance				Remarks
				Weak	Fair	Good		
G.4	Organizational effectiveness and improved performance	Germany Hungary Ireland Italy Mexico	Most countries	Low	Medium	High		Should be matched with incentives. May increase sense of social purpose for public servants and officials.
G.5	Review of regulations	Italy Rep. of Korea Mexico Switzerland		Medium, D	Medium, D	Medium, D		Supports the enhancement of the rule of law.
G.7	Review of the interaction of domestic and international law	Czech Republic Greece Ireland Sweden Switzerland		Medium, D	Medium, D	Medium, D		Supports the rule of law, particularly corruption with transnational characteristics.
G.8	Reviews of high-risk areas	Germany Switzerland		Medium, D	Medium, D	Medium, D		Supports enhancing the rule of law.

H. Unclassified initiatives

H.1.[b]	Public awareness campaigns, corruption prevention studies for public bodies and private sector companies, including	Hong Kong, China	Not relevant	Low	Medium	In countries with weak governance, practices and agents are generally well known.
H.2.[a]	use of real cases and commercials. Public management reforms leading to a definition of a new "corporate culture" characterized by greater autonomy, and deregulation to encourage innovative practices and reduce regulation and controls	Papua New Guinea	Low	Low	Medium	For countries with weak governance this may reduce accountability of high-ranking officials (ministers) to corrupt practices of other public servants under him or her. Without appropriate systems and procedures, innovative behavior may increase temptation for corruption. Systems and accountability structures should keep pace with devolution.
H.3.[b]	Money-laundering laws (activities that have the purpose of disguising the origin of and preserving proceeds of crime, and include concealing, converting, disposing of, transferring, or using those funds to acquire other property).	Hong Kong, China	High, A, C, D	High, A, C, D	Low, C, D	Necessary for weak- and fair-governance countries to decrease corrupt transactions (A), increase probability of paying penalty (C), and increasing penalties (D).
H.4.	Integrating issues on bribery and corruption into the elementary and secondary curricula	Rep. of Korea	High	High	High	Long-term intervention. Should be matched with other preconditions. Leadership by example, especially for the youth, is of high importance.

(Appendix continues on the following page.)

Appendix 2.2. (continued)

Anticorruption instruments	OECD	Non-OECD countries			Remarks
		Quality of Governance			
		Weak	Fair	Good	
H.5. Peer-review mechanism	All OECD countries	Not relevant	Not relevant	Medium	This intervention assumes a high degree of existence of preconditions and therefore is only applicable to countries with good governance.
H.6. Addressing the supply side: laws against bribery	All OECD countries	High, A, C, D	High, A, C, D	Low, C, D	Necessary for weak and fair governance countries to decrease corrupt transactions (A), increase probability of paying penalty (C), and increasing penalties (D).
H.7. Ethics and corruption-prevention plans	All OECD countries	Medium, A, B, C, D	Medium, A, B, C, D	Medium, A, B, C, D	Crucial assumption here is that the plans contain the specific strategies to combat and prevent corruption by having the necessary preconditions.
H.8. Ensuring consistency of ethics and anticorruption policies	All OECD countries	Low, A, B, C, D	Medium, A, B, C, D	High, A, B, C, D	Code of Ethics and corruption strategies should go hand in hand. Consistency in poor governance countries will not achieve much without critical preconditions.

Note: A = decreases the number of corrupt transactions; B = decreases gross gains from corruption; C = increases probability of paying penalties; D = increases magnitude of penalties.

Source (unless otherwise noted): Organisation for Economic Co-operation and Development 1999.

a. Asian Development Bank 2000; OECD 2000.

b. United Nations Development Programme 1998.

c. *Economist* 2001; Kuther and Shah 2000; Bolongaita and Bhargava 2001.

Notes

1. Although we refer to country as the domain for analysis, the analytical framework proposed can be applied at the subnational level and can be used to analyze and improve effectiveness of either a program or a particular anticorruption measure.

2. We thank Ed Campos for this helpful perspective on the categories of diagnostic instruments.

3. See www1.worldbank.org/publicsector/indicators.htm.

4. In these countries, anticorruption is particularly complex as political, economic, and social institutions are restructured to faciliate the shift toward market-driven processes.

5. The authors made a distinction between state capture and state influence, the latter being the ability to shape the rules of the game without the need for private payments because of factors such as firm size, ownership ties to the state, and frequent interactions with state officials. We think this is not necessarily a black-and-white distinction because influence can include exchanges that are preferential to firms deriving from nonmonetary rewards. For example, the payoffs of firms might be in the form of political support, business opportunities, and so forth. Such payoffs are arguably even more difficult to measure than is state capture.

6. For example, for a country with high state capture there is commensurately a high degree of insecurity of property rights because captor firms compete to use the state for their protection. Although specific advantages can accrue to firms that engage in capture activities, the costs to the economy are serious.

7. For example, Hellman, Jones, and Kaufmann (2000) estimated that the overall growth rate of the enterprise sector would be 10 percent lower in a three-year period compared with growth in a noncapture economy.

8. As James Madison memorably put it: "If men were angels, no government would be necessary. If angels were to govern men, neither external or internal controls on government would be necessary. In framing a government which is to be administered by men over men, the great difficulty lies in this: *You must first enable the government to control the governed, and in the next place, oblige it to control itself*" (*The Federalist* no. 51).

9. See www1.worldbank.org/publicsector/anticorrupt.

10. See, for example, the Corruption Online Research and Information System (CORIS) of Transparency International (www.corisweb.org), the World Bank's anticorruption Web site (www1.worldbank.org/publicsector/anticorrupt), and the Anti-Corruption Ring Online (AnCorR Web) of the OECD (www1.oecd.org/daf/nocorruptionweb/index.htm).

11. See appendix 2.2 for a comprehensive list of anticorruption instruments, with our preliminary comments about the link between the effectiveness of anticorruption instruments in relationship to characteristics of the governance environment.

12. J. Edgardo Campos, personal communication, May 21, 2003. We are grateful to Ed Campos for his insights on coalition-building.

13. See the Web site of the Philippine Center for Investigative Journalism at www.pcij.org.

14. It should be noted that under the leadership of the new Philippine ombudsman, Simeon Marcelo, who took over the post in November 2002, remarkable progress is being made in prosecution. For example, the conviction rate from January to May 2003 has risen to 19 percent.

15. A dearth of information and analysis prevails in this area and it would be a fruitful arena for further research.

16. Although external aid is a critical resource, high levels of aid without accountability may promote aid dependency, rent-seeking, and inefficiency (see Knack 2000).

References

Anechiarico, Frank, and James B. Jacobs. 1996. *The Pursuit of Absolute Integrity: How Corruption Control Makes Government Ineffective*. Chicago: University of Chicago Press.

Asian Development Bank. 2000. "Combating Corruption in the Asian and Pacific Economies." Available at www.adb.org/documents/conference/combating corruption/default.asp.

Bolongaita, Emil, and Vinay K. Bhargava. 2001. "Making National Anti-Corruption Policies and Programs More Effective: An Analytical Framework." Paper prepared for the World Bank's Global Distance Learning Program on Combating Corruption in the Asia-Pacific Region.

Gonzalez de Asis, Maria. 2000. "Coalition-Building to Fight Corruption." Paper prepared for the Anticorruption Summit. Washington, D.C.: World Bank Institute.

Grindle, Merilee S., and John W. Thomas. 1991. *Public Choices and Policy Change: The Political Economy of Reform in Developing Countries*. Baltimore: Johns Hopkins University Press.

Heidenheimer, Arnold J., Michael Johnston, and Victor T. LeVine, eds. 1989. *Political Corruption: A Handbook*. New Brunswick, New Jersey: Transaction Publishers.

Hellman, Joel S., Geraint Jones, and Daniel Kaufmann. 2000. "Seize the State, Seize the Day: State Capture, Corruption and Influence in Transition." World Bank Policy Research Working Paper 2444. Washington, D.C.

Hellman, Joel S., Geraint Jones, Daniel Kaufmann, and Mark Schankerman. 2000. "Measuring Governance, Corruption, and State Capture: How Firms and Bureaucrats Shape the Business Environment in Transition Economies." World Bank Policy Research Working Paper 2312. Washington, D.C.

Huther, Jeff, and Anwar Shah. 1998. "Applying a Simple Measure of Good Governance to the Debate on Fiscal Decentralization." World Bank Policy Research Working Paper 1894. Washington, D.C.

———. 2000. "Anticorruption Policies and Programs: A Framework for Evaluation." World Bank Policy Research Working Paper 2501. Washington, D.C.

Kang, David. 2002. *Crony Capitalism: Corruption and Development in South Korea and the Philippines*. Cambridge, U.K.: Cambridge University Press.

Kaufmann, Daniel. 1998. "Challenges in the Next Stage in AntiCorruption." In *New Perspectives on Combating Corruption*. Washington, D.C.: Transparency International and the Economic Development Institute of the World Bank.

———. 2000. "Governance and Controlling Corruption Is Central for Socio-Economic Development and Growth: New Reports and Evidence." Presentation to the International Center for Policy Studies Roundtable, November 6, Kyiv.

Kaufmann, Daniel, Aart Kraay, and Massimo Mastruzzi. 2003. "Governance Matters III: Governance Indicators for 1996–2002." World Bank Policy Research Working Paper 3106. Washington, D.C. Paper and data available at http://www.worldbank.org/wbi/governance/gov data2002/index.html.

Knack, Stephen. 2000. "Aid Dependence and the Quality of Governance: A Cross-Country Empirical Analysis." World Bank Policy Research Working Paper 2396. Washington, D.C.

Langseth, Petter, Rick Stapenhurst, and Jeremy Pope. 1997. "The Role of a National Integrity System in Fighting Corruption." World Bank Institute Working Paper 18868. Washington, D.C.

North, Douglass C. 2003. "Understanding the Process of Economic Change." Paper presented at the Forum Series on the Role of Institutions in Promoting Economic Growth. June 24, Mercatus Center, George Mason University, Arlington, Va.

OECD (Organisation for Economic Co-operation and Development). 1999. *Public Sector Corruption: An International Survey of Prevention Measures.* Paris.

————. 2000. *Trust in Government: Ethics Measures in OECD Countries.* Paris.

Pope, Jeremy, and Frank Vogl. 2000. "Making Anticorruption Agencies More Effective." *Finance and Development* 37 (2). Available at www.imf.org/external/pubs/ft/fandd/2000/06/pope.htm.

Quah, Jon S. T. 2000. "Accountability and Anticorruption Agencies in the Asia-Pacific Region." In *Combating Corruption in the Asian and Pacific Economie.* Manila: Asian Development Bank.

Stapenhurst, Rick. 2000. "The Media's Role in Curbing Corruption." Developmental Working Paper 21024. Washington, D.C.: World Bank Institute.

Stapenhurst, Rick, and Sahr J. Kpundeh, eds. 1999. *Curbing Corruption: Toward a Model for Building National Integrity.* Washington, D.C.: World Bank.

United Nations Development Programme. 1998. "Corruption and Integrity Improvement Initiatives in Countries." Available at magnet.undp.org/Docs/efa/corruption/Corrupti.htm.

World Bank. 2000a. *Anticorruption in Transition: A Contribution to the Policy Debate.* Washington, D.C.

————. 2000b. *Combating Corruption in the Philippines.* World Bank Philippine Country Management Unit, East Asia and Pacific Region, Manila.

————. 2001. *Combating Corruption in the Philippines: An Update.* World Bank Philippine Country Management Unit, East Asia and Pacific Region, Manila.

3

Anticorruption Initiatives in the Philippines: Breakthroughs, Limits, and Challenges

Corruption wastes public resources, greatly affecting the delivery of public services and holding back the growth and progress necessary to lift people out of poverty. Cognizant of that truth, every administration has made its fair share of attempts to combat corruption. Some breakthroughs have occurred and more are possible but under only a fair-governance environment anticorruption policies and programs in the Philippines cannot go too far. Many anticorruption measures are subject to an upper threshold imposed by the frailties of Philippine institutions. Our thesis in this chapter is that the effectiveness of anticorruption programs is dictated by the strengths or weaknesses of a country's governance structure. The prospects for implementation of a policy are either helped or hindered by the nature of governance. What works for a good-governance country may not necessarily work in a fair-governance country. Therefore, serious challenges remain.

Mindful of those challenges and limits, we will try to unbundle the varied practices of corruption to identify and compare different patterns of the problem, to evaluate the effectiveness of anticorruption policies and programs in the Philippines with a view to rationalizing them, and to contribute to the growing policy dialogue on developing practical strategies for combating corruption.

This chapter draws on a number of sources of recent research and lessons of experience, including the World Bank's work in the Philippines. Because of space and time constraints, we will cover only recent anticorruption initiatives. Our assessment uses heuristic devices

This chapter was contributed by Eduardo T. Gonzalez and Magdalena L. Mendoza. Both authors are affiliated with the Development Academy of the Philippines, Pasig City. Gonzalez is president; Mendoza is managing director of the Center for Governance.

supplied by the World Bank, the Asian Development Bank (ADB), and the Organisation for Economic Co-operation and Development and relies on some documented cases and other anecdotal evidence.

The chapter is organized as follows. The first section describes the country's governance environment, the role of political structures (including restraints and veto points), the historical origin of failings, and the track record in governance. The second section characterizes the degree of state capture, political and bureaucratic corruption, grand and petty corruption, "policies for sale," international bribe-paying, and changes in corruption perception over time. Anticorruption policies and programs discussed in the third section include measures to develop effective and transparent systems for public service to strengthen anti-bribery actions and promote integrity in business operations, and to support active public involvement. Anticorruption strategies are outlined in five key areas: public sector management, institutional restraints, political accountability, competitive private sector, and civil society participation. The fourth section addresses coalition-building and the nature of forces and their resources that can be mobilized in the fight against corruption. In section 5 are the answers to the question, can anticorruption institutions and agencies successfully and credibly lead the fight? The final section makes the argument for a strong institutional design.

Country Governance

The Philippines is widely held to be the oldest democracy in Southeast Asia. The authoritarian regime of Ferdinand Marcos disrupted this democratic tradition. But since the popular overthrow of that regime in 1986, the Philippines has managed to redemocratize, although in fits and starts. The government of Corazon Aquino restored and maintained formal democratic institutions that survived a series of coup attempts by renegade military officers and Marcos loyalists. During the administration of Fidel Ramos, political stability increased and economic growth improved as domestic and international business confidence returned. The ensuing government of Joseph Estrada, however, faced widespread accusations of high-level corruption, cronyism, and collusion, which eventually led to its downfall in the wake of popular protests and withdrawal of military support. President Gloria Macapagal-Arroyo assumed power with high expectations that she would control corruption and alleviate the poverty that persists in the country. The difficult conditions that face the current government include a sizable budget deficit and the lukewarm attitude of international investors in the wake of persistent concerns about global terrorism amid a worldwide recession. Despite the potential for escalation of conflict in southern Philippines, peace and order generally hold sway.

Governance has been defined as the exercise of authority through formal and informal institutions in the management of a country's resource endowment. In the Philippines it is crucial to understand this in the context of a political economy characterized by relatively weak institutions for which vested private interests compete for control. As suggested by De Dios and Ferrer (2001) as well as A. Mendoza (2001), these political contests for control of resources are quite intense because the state has disposition over a significant amount of resources and exercises discretion over a wide sphere. It will be noted that Philippine institutions, although not working like clockwork, are not as weak as those found in the transition states in Southeast Asia. Democratic institutions such as separation of powers, judicial independence, and rule of law had good foundations, but they were eroded during the years of martial law. Weakened institutions in both national and local governments also weakened accountability and served to support rent-seeking activities by exploiting government rules and resources. Discretion substituted for ambiguous rules. This discretionary power in a context of brittle accountability supplies the basic incentives for corruption.

From the perspective of a principal–agent relationship, the agents (in this case, the politicians and bureaucrats) are able to abuse the advantages offered by such discretionary power in the wake of the incoherent interests of the principal (in this case, the electorate or the public at large). According to De Dios and Ferrer (2001) this incoherence of public interest stems partly from social divisions (resulting from ethnic-linguistic dimensions, religion, and urban–rural distinctions) and the gap between rich and poor. Moreover, large segments of Philippine society do not necessarily believe that institutions of government represent values that are superior to those of smaller groups, such as clan or family, and that contributes to a split-level set of acceptable public behaviors. In that context, as De Dios and Ferrer put it, "where the notion of what constitutes public interest is either vague or disputed, reward and penalty mechanisms are unlikely to function smoothly" (p. 9).

Assessment of Governance in the Philippines

On many counts of governance the Philippines has received fair marks, suggesting that the country is reasonably managed, although serious challenges remain. In a 1998 ranking of countries by quality of governance, the Philippines was rated "fair," with an index of 44 on a scale of 0 to 100 (100 being the highest score) (see figure 3.1). Governance quality in this case is a composite index of four subindexes: citizen participation, government orientation, social development, and economic management (Huther and Shah 1998).

Figure 3.1. Fair Governance Marks for the Philippines

Score

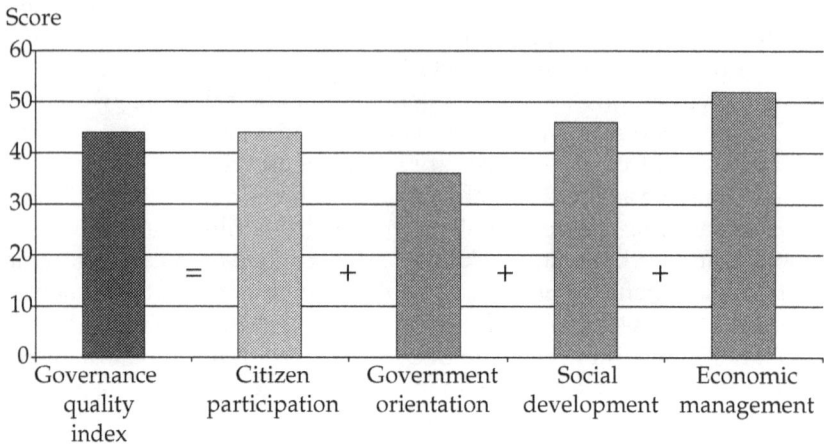

Note: The higher the score, the better.
Source: Huther and Shah 1998.

There is a fair degree of political freedom and political stability in the
Philippines. Elections are regular and relatively free and open, although
generally only the moneyed and landed families contest and win them.
Other forms of political participation are comparatively high—for example, nongovernmental organizations (NGOs) register a powerful presence as a voice mechanism—but they encounter the problem of collective
action, as the cost of organizing coalitions that represent broader interests
can be quite frustratingly great.

In part because of strong popular participation and the natural
demands of democracy, lately there has been a surge of public sector
reform initiatives. The Philippine government, however, remains inade-
quately oriented toward providing public goods. Bureaucratic inefficiencies are fairly pronounced. Allegations of corruption in the judiciary are
widespread. The courts are especially important because the judiciary
needs to enforce accountability through timely and fair decisions.
Otherwise, corruption and a weakened judicial system are likely to be
partners in crime, so to speak, feeding on each other to erode a country's
institutional defenses (Mauro 1998) and to inflict harm that falls lopsidedly on the nation's poor people.

The country's fair governance marks are corroborated by the World
Bank's research on governance indicators (http://www.worldbank.org/
wbi/governance/govdata2002), which surveyed NGOs, commercial risk-
rating agencies, and think-tanks from 1996 to 2002. The Philippines has the

following percentile ranks (on a scale of 0 to 100): voice and accountability, 54.0; political stability/no violence, 29.7; government effectiveness, 55.7; regulatory quality, 57.7; rule of law, 38.1; and corruption, 37.6 (figure 3.2). The percentile rank indicates the percentage of countries worldwide that rate below the selected country. In other words, the Philippines ranks poor in rule of law, corruption, and political stability; and average in government effectiveness, regulatory quality, and voice and accountability.

The Price of Weakened Institutions

When administrative capacities are weak and principal interests are not well articulated, governments respond or compensate by overregulating. Excessive regulations, however, undermine trade and business development. Wage and price controls, anticompetition policies, barriers to entry in major economic sectors, and weak antitrust policies combine in diverse ways to discourage the flow of investments and thus to hinder growth and development.

In a fair governance environment stricter regulation can bring about sharply higher levels of corruption (figure 3.3). In public choice theory, more procedures and longer delays make possible bribe extraction or make

Figure 3.2. Fair Marks for the Philippines in New World Bank Indicators

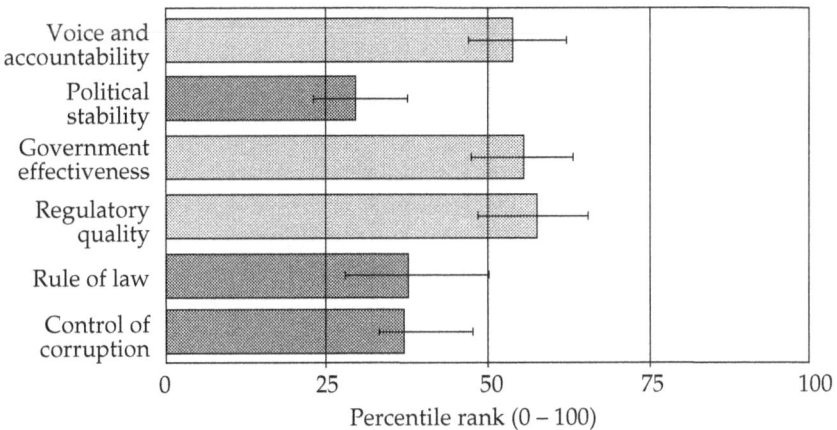

Note: The governance indicators presented here reflect the statistical compilation of responses by a large sample of enterprise, citizen, and expert survey respondents in industrial and developing countries, as reported by a number of survey institutes, think tanks, nongovernmental organizations, and international organizations. See note to table 7.4, p. 245.
Source: Kaufmann, Kraay, and Mastruzzi 2003.

Figure 3.3. More Corruption Comes with More Regulation

Corruption index, 1997

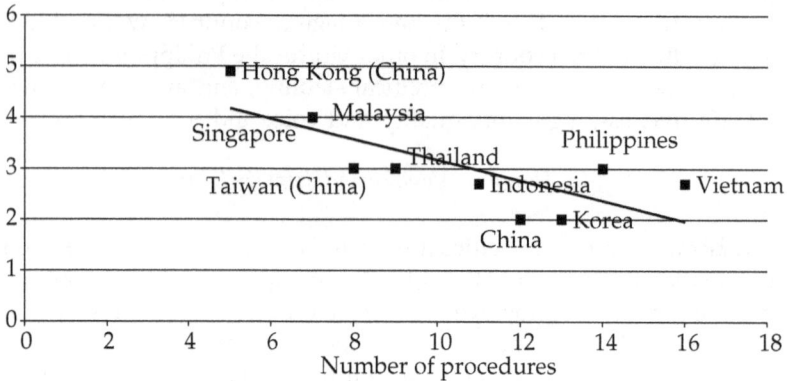

Note: The lower the corruption index, the worse.
Source: University of Maryland, IRIS Center data, 2000; Djankov and others 2002.

entry less appealing to potential competitors (Djankov and others 2002). Regulation becomes an instrument to create rents for bureaucrats, incumbent firms, or both. Stricter regulation is thus associated with greater corruption and less competition (Claessens, Djankov, and Lang 1999).

Feeble institutions can also lead to state capture, which "refers to the capacity of firms to shape and affect the formation of the basic rules of the game (that is, laws, regulations, and decrees) through private payments to public officials and politicians" (Hellman, Jones, and Kaufmann 2001, p. 6). Corporate clout may come in the form of ownership concentration, which can put a country's legal institutions in harm's way. In empirical tests using assorted measures of ownership concentration, Claessens, Djankov, and Lang (1999) found that a relatively small number of families had a strong effect on the economic policy of governments. In the Philippines a single family (the Ayalas) had ultimate control over 17.1 percent of the total market capitalization (p. 3).

Such wealth concentration and the interlocking links among owners and government officials cast doubt on the independence of legal institutions in the country. According to Claessens, Djankov, and Lang, it raises the prospects that the legal system may be endogenous to the variety and strength of control over the corporate sector. In a situation of state capture, legal institutions are subverted and less likely to evolve in a manner that promotes transparent and market-based activities. In figure 3.4 the greater the share controlled by the top 15 families, the lower the level of judiciary efficiency, the weaker the rule of law, the higher the judicial cor-

Figure 3.4. Are Asian Judicial Systems Endogenous?

Score

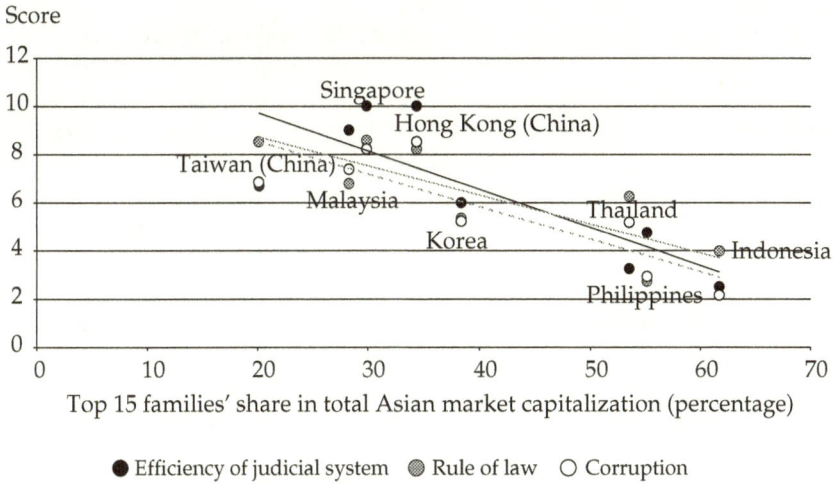

Top 15 families' share in total Asian market capitalization (percentage)

● Efficiency of judicial system   ◉ Rule of law   ○ Corruption

Note: The higher the score, the less the ownership concentration.
Source: Claessens, Djankov, and Lang 1999.

ruption, or any combination of the three. Indonesia, the Philippines, and Thailand seem to have the lowest levels of legal institutional growth because of heavy ownership concentration in the corporate sector.

The Role of Political Structures

The Philippines has a presidential system of government,[1] with three distinct sets of powers: the legislature (which makes the law), the executive (which implements the law), and the judiciary (which interprets and applies the law). This separation of powers creates "veto points" that are deemed necessary to check arbitrary exercise of power. Veto points ensure that no policies are adopted and implemented by one party without undergoing scrutiny by another party. The wider the separation of powers, the greater the number of veto points needed to reverse any rule-based commitments (World Bank 1997).

In form, the Philippines has a powerful chief executive. The Philippine president, directly elected by voters, possesses veto powers over laws passed by the legislature. But the system of checks and balances in a U.S.-modeled setup somewhat ties down the Philippine president. Judicial oversight is present in several tiers, from local courts handling "first instance" cases to appeals court and the Supreme Court. But the effectiveness of the judiciary is often compromised by its own weaknesses and its vulnerability to executive pressure.

Elections are another veto point. Short electoral cycles give the voters more opportunities to replace the legislature (lower house). But there is a tradeoff: Philippine legislators, to bolster their reelection chances, often favor government programs with visible short-term results that may not be appropriate but only politically expedient. Moreover, elections are expensive: estimates suggest that a successful presidential campaign needs US$80 million and a congressional campaign US$2.6 million. It is not surprising that, once they are elected, politicians are expected to pay back financiers either through large contracts or juicy appointments (Coronel 1998). Ironically, frequent electoral vetoes have not stopped the country from ousting presidents through extraconstitutional means.

Figure 3.5 shows the sense of equilibrium in the country's political structure since independence. The data were compiled by Djankov and others (2002). The high degree of autonomy of the Philippine president is constrained by a good number of veto points that include a bicameral legislature and an independent judiciary. Effectiveness of the legislature, the last index, shows a fairly responsive Philippine Congress.

There is a caveat, however. By and large the congress does not mediate differing interests; its policies, laws, and resource priorities are seen by some as directly favoring powerful constituencies. The judiciary, widely perceived to be corrupt, is said to be unable to uphold the rule of

Figure 3.5. An Autonomous Executive and Veto Points Complement Each Other

Score

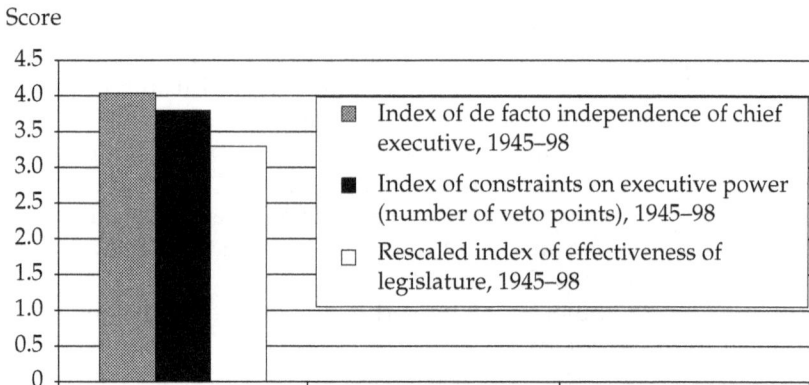

Index of de facto independence of chief executive, 1945–98

Index of constraints on executive power (number of veto points), 1945–98

Rescaled index of effectiveness of legislature, 1945–98

Note: The higher the score, the better.
Source: Djankov and others 2002.

law consistently, thus bringing insecurity and unpredictability to social, political and economic relations. (Judicial reforms are under way, as discussed in a later section.) Nevertheless, without the checks and balances provided by the political structure, already frail institutions would further weaken and decline.

To be sure, it should be noted that despite the frailty of its institutions, the Philippines has managed to maintain a delicate balance between rights and rules. After its experience with authoritarianism, the country's weakened institutions have prevented a return to the arbitrary exercise of state power. Filipino citizens have realized more the value of their political rights and freedom and of the institutions that have self-determination or an extremely high degree of autonomy. Figure 3.6 suggests that autocracy and political rights are polar opposites in the Philippines. The yearning of Filipinos for political freedom remained high during the period under study (1972–98) even though more than half of the period was spent under martial rule.

Their yearning found its most intense articulation in EDSA I and EDSA II.[2] "People Power" has become an established way to counter the weaknesses of the country's political structures and the lack of maturity of government institutions. It has its inherent risks, not the least of which is the unpredictability of its outcomes, being grounded on extraconstitutional means. But it testifies to the strength of civil society participation

Figure 3.6. Autocracy and Political Freedom Are Polar Opposites

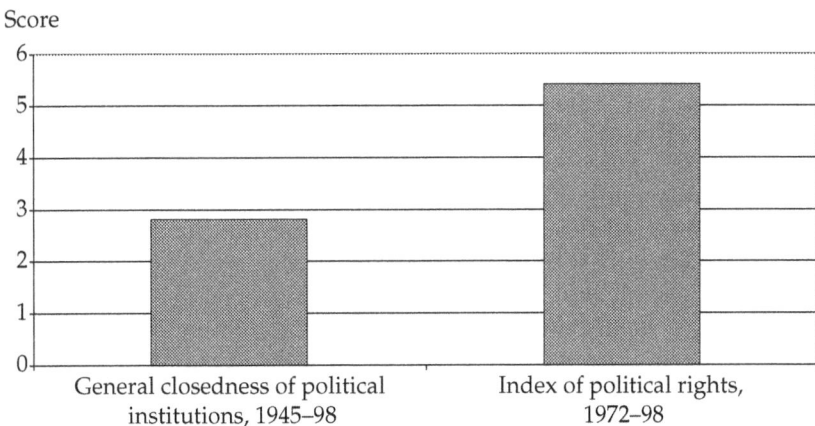

Note: The higher the score, the better.
Source: Djankov and others 2002.

and its ability to overcome collective action hurdles. After martial rule civil society has emerged as a "fourth" institutional structure that mediates between the state and the public. It must be stressed that an activist civil society is a good pressure point although it has its own accountability problems. Note, however, that *such activism is not the answer to the failure of government institutions, which must be confronted on its own terms.* Vigilance is not a substitute for efficiency and effectiveness.

Social Dysfunctions

The fragile nature of state institutions has meant that Filipinos have continued to rely on nongovernment institutions, primarily the family or extended kinship ties. The more basic, informal rules of behavior that North (1990) acknowledged are the default mode in traditional societies. As regards corruption, it means that the sanctions against corruption have always existed merely as formal governmental rules that did not necessarily carry weight in the more private or family spheres whose main criterion is overwhelmingly pragmatic and individual (De Dios and Ferrer 2001).

Filipino society emphasizes the centrality of the family, which takes precedence over both the individual members and the community. In fact, in community decisionmaking, the unwritten rule is that it is the influential family, not individual members of the community, that decides on the resolution of important matters. There is more: "familism" combines with reciprocity to open the door to corruption for individual family members. This congruence between what is accepted as legally "correct" (although ethically questionable) and what is felt to be culturally "right" in actual life has given rise to many of the current difficulties in combating corruption and enforcing transparency and accountability in government (M. Mendoza 2001).

Postwar Origins of Failings

Over the last 50 years there has been a mixed record of government actions in managing the country's resources and promoting development. During the 1950s and 1960s nationalist sentiments led to policies that favored import substitution through imposition of high tariff rates and protection of local companies from foreign competition (Saldaña 2001). Around that time an industrial elite composed mostly of families previously in trading businesses emerged to influence industrial policies. Nevertheless, until the 1960s the Philippines was ranked second to Japan in terms of economic growth.

The country's protectionist policies often promoted rent-seeking among the elite and diverted resources from people who needed them most. The

1970s and early 1980s were characterized by heavy government interventions in the guise of master planning for economic and social development. Furthermore, 14 years of authoritarian rule, from 1972 to 1986, saw the surge of cronyism, the enfeebling of congress, and the deterioration of the judiciary. It was characterized by economic mismanagement and corruption at the highest levels. By the 1980s the Philippines lagged behind most East Asian nations that pursued more purposive policies of growth with equity. The outcome for the country had been slow growth, persistent poverty and inequality, and environmental degradation.

A Mixed Record in Governance

In a context of fair governance quality, the position of government as a virtual monopolist makes it susceptible to rent-seeking activities. But in the 1990s throughout the Ramos administration, deregulation and privatization of some public enterprises shifted decisionmaking to the private sector. This somewhat reduced the scope of government and made it more focused.

Reforms in public sector management and increased autonomy of local governments also fostered greater transparency and accountability. Devolution of delivery of basic services brought decisionmaking closer to the frontline and increased participation of civil society and peoples' organizations in local policymaking.

Even as these reforms were being undertaken, the government struggled with its frail accountability structures and restrained ability to enforce the law against errant officials and against an incoherent expression of public interest in anticorruption. Poor incentives such as noncompetitive pay, and recruitment and promotion practices that are not based on merit, have given officials the excuse not to play by the rules. The World Bank's 1997 *World Development Report* (World Bank 1997) concluded that higher-level staff in the civil service were significantly underpaid relative to their private sector counterparts. Civil service reforms have been crafted to address those issues, although some have produced unintended consequences. The Early Retirement Program and the Attrition Law, for example, prevented the public sector from retaining qualified people. Another serious concern of the civil service is the historical concentration of political patronage in the presidency because the chief executive holds the power to appoint more than 3,000 political and career officials from the cabinet level down to regional and district levels.

Contours of Corruption

The postcolonial years beginning in 1946 saw virtually every Philippine government administration contending with allegations of corruption—

post war reparations, back pay and foreign currency corruption in the 1950s, the Harry Stonehill scandal[3] and rampant smuggling in the 1960s, Marcos's crony capitalism in the 1970s, the so-called *Kamag-anak, Incorporated*[4] during the Aquino years, and charges of land scams and kickbacks involving major projects during the Ramos administration.

Between 1977 and 1997 the government lost an estimated US$48 billion (Office of the Ombudsman 1997).This amount could have wiped out most of the country's total external indebtedness, which stood at US$52.4 billion in 2001.[5] In tax collections alone, losses from 1993 to 1995 were estimated at PhP 210 billion (about US$8 billion at that time), compared with the potentially collectible revenue of PhP 493 billion (US$19 billion). This means for every tax peso collected, 43 centavos went to private pockets (Talisayon n.d.).

On the expenditure side the Philippine Center for Investigative Journalism (PCIJ) has listed instances of corruption involving the so-called pork barrel[6] of members of Congress (Coronel 1998). The current chair of the House Appropriations Committee, Congressman Rolando Andaya, said that about PhP 21 billion of the government's PhP 104 billion procurement budget in 2001 was lost to graft and corruption resulting from collusion, lack of competition and transparency, and delays in the implementation of government projects. The procurement budget, which includes the pork barrel of senators and members of the House of Representatives, covers goods and services, civil works, and infrastructure projects (Javellana 2002). Log-rolling and pork-barrel legislation, as well as patronage politics, paved the way for socially costly tradeoffs that compromise development programs and projects.

The judiciary has not been of much help in fighting corruption. Apart from their slow dispensation of justice, many judges are widely perceived to be corrupt themselves. A survey conducted in 1999 by the Philippine public opinion polling organization Social Weather Stations (SWS) showed that 62 percent of respondents perceived significant levels of corruption within the judiciary. Many or most judges could be bribed according to 57 percent of those polled. In the June 2000 SWS survey, the judiciary ranked third as the most notorious branch of national government in terms of corruption, close on the heels of the executive branch and the legislature, which ranked first and second, respectively.

Economic Sources of State Capture

There has been no rigorous analysis of how firms in the Philippines use their political influence to distort both the legal framework and the policymaking process in an effort to gain concentrated rents. But significant family control and interlocking shareholdings among affiliated firms are said to leave insiders with excessive power to pursue their own interests (Saldaña 2001) and raise the possibility that some institutions may be predisposed to forms and concentration of control over the corporate sector.

The top 15 families in the Philippines control more than 50 percent of total market capitalization in the country (Saldaña 2001). An Asian Development Bank study similarly found high ownership concentration among Philippine firms.[7] According to the ADB study, the largest shareholder owned 33.5 percent, the top 5 owned 60.2 percent, and the top 20 owned 69.0 percent of the total outstanding shares of an average nonfinancial publicly listed company in 1997 in the Philippines. In three-fourths of the listed companies the top 5 shareholders owned more than 50 percent of voting shares. In one-third of the listed companies the largest controlling shareholder owned at least a majority of shares (Saldaña 2001).

Political versus Bureaucratic Corruption

Public sector corruption may involve either politicians or bureaucrats. Political corruption is distinct from bureaucratic corruption, partly because of differences in goals. Bureaucrats and administrators are thought to be primarily seeking pecuniary gain, whereas politicians are thought to have both pecuniary and political interests. Hence, for instance, few bureaucrats would find it appealing to peddle influence beyond the confines of the public agency. On the other hand, politicians would have no second thoughts about buying votes, corrupting the electoral system, or harassing opponents to secure political advantages (De Dios and Ferrer 2001). Political corruption thus weakens the bonds of control and monitoring between the principals (society at large) and those who serve them (politicians and bureaucrats).

It is political corruption that is awesome in terms of scale and level, according to De Dios and Ferrer (2001). Instances of padding registered voter rolls and manipulating election outcomes, and of campaign finance scandals are too obvious to be ignored. They are symptomatic of wide discretion, vague mandate, and weak controls in the political selection process. The Best World (BW) scandal is another example of political corruption in which weak market institutions allowed the head of state to extend his authority beyond his traditional spheres of influence (Pascual and Lim 2001).

Political corruption intertwines with state capture in two ways when high ownership concentration encourages corrupt trading practices. First, management and large shareholders expropriate company assets for their private benefit. Control of the stock exchange by family-controlled firms works against the transparency of transactions and the fair price formation essential to the growth of capital markets. Second, poor market governance and weak regulatory capacity encourage a relaxed attitude that enables a political regime to influence transactions, such as when the Best World[8] scam went on unchecked. What was new in the BW case was the capture of the stock market by a president and his cronies so as to leverage assets for greater profits (Pascual and Lim 2001).

A clear indication of how political connections skew formal rules and regulations in favor of vested interests was the track record of government in recovering the ill-gotten wealth and assets of the Marcos regime and its cronies. The Marcoses and their allies were able to go into compromise deals, retain or recover their assets and corporations (in what many consider to be corrupt deals), and return to their public careers (M. Mendoza 2001).

Bureaucratic corruption is clearly of subordinate importance and may in fact be a handmaid to politicians who can easily intervene in bureaucratic decisions. According to De Dios and Ferrer (2001), obvious examples of bureaucratic action having been influenced by politicians include the exemption of the former president's housing project from building and environmental regulations, the dropping of tax cases facing a presidential crony, and the use of pork-barrel funds by elected politicians to earn corruption rents (which may have been facilitated with the knowledge and consent of at least some bureaucrats in the public works agencies). In that regard, De Dios and Ferrer contended that "it is difficult to imagine that any serious move to limit the regular forms of corruption in the bureaucracy can succeed without first demonstrating a credible commitment to drastically reducing political corruption" (2001, p. 15).

Grand versus Petty Corruption

Corruption in the Philippines happens in all levels of government. The higher the level, the bigger the scale, because discretion over the use of resources goes up with the bureaucratic ladder. It is useful to make a distinction between petty corruption and grand corruption. Rose-Ackerman (1999) defined grand corruption as "a substantial expenditure of funds with a major impact on a government budget and growth prospects" (p. 27). Petty corruption, on the other hand, involves routine government transactions, such as tax payments, allocation of permits, and regulatory enforcement, typically overseen by middle- and lower-level bureaucrats (Elliott 1997).

Grand corruption involves the transfer of large economic resources to private firms and individuals through procurement contracts, award of concessions, and sale of public assets. Bribes are offered and accepted to ensure the capture of these resources; in turn, these bribes transfer monopoly rents to private interests. In the process, corrupt officials and private vested interests distort public choices and decisions (A. Mendoza 2001). Petty corruption occurs in closed and routine bureaucratic contexts, such as in the Bureau of Internal Revenue and Bureau of Customs, and in the police, where bribery and extortion are predominant forms. While not always involving large amounts, this form of corruption is often the kind that is known to ordinary citizens (A. Mendoza 2001).

Grand corruption fudges the distinction between genuine exercise of discretion and corrupt practices. Hence, the Estrada Administration's decision to partially scuttle the open-skies policy to favor Philippine Airlines was rationalized (to some, credibly) as a valid defense of national interest rather than an instance of cronyism, whereas the purchase of shares of speculative stocks by the Social Security System and the Government Service Insurance System was seen as valid risk-taking by management because it could not immediately be regarded as a behest purchase. In addition, creative practices in grand corruption have also been attempted in conjunction with large public policy shifts. Recent instances are the sale of government guarantees, stock price manipulation, and behest stock acquisitions (A. Mendoza 2001).

As the scale of corruption increases, acts assume a more distinctly political character, and the yardsticks for evaluation become more amorphous, owing to the limited information on such deals that is available to the public. Agents (that is, politicians and bureaucrats) are better informed about prospective policy changes that offer new rent opportunities (for example, privatization initiatives during liberalization episodes) (A. Mendoza 2001).

Policies for Sale

Another type of corrupt transaction is the sale of policies or rules. Examples of policies that can be "sold" are industrial priorities, fiscal policies, regulatory rules, judicial decisions, and electoral rules, among others (De Dios and Ferrer 2001). Changes in regime or policy environment can provide opportunities to secure illicit gains from policies for sale. The most recent visible example of this has been the distortion of aviation rules under the Estrada administration to favor Philippine Airlines (Pascual and Lim 2001).

International Bribe Paying

Corruption is not just a domestic problem. Bribery by multinational firms remains an important issue in the Philippines. It is widely held that foreign companies pay bribes to do business in developing countries, resulting in mounting distortions in fair international commerce. The bribe-payers' survey conducted from April to July 1999 by Transparency International (www.transparency.org) provided a disturbing picture of the degree to which leading exporting countries are perceived by private sector leaders in 14 emerging market economies (including the Philippines) to be using corrupt practices. The 14 account for more than 60 percent of the imports of all emerging market economies.

The Bribe Payers Index ranks leading exporting countries in terms of the degree to which their companies are perceived to be paying bribes in developing economies. The biggest bribe givers are Asian exporting countries, led by China. European Union nations are less likely to pay bribes to win business in the subject countries. But firms based in Great Britain do accept what are known as "facilitation payments" made to expedite routine business needs, such as clearing customs and obtaining permits, although they profess never to offer, solicit, or accept bribes *in any form* ("The Short Arm of the Law" 2002). Expectedly, bribes are great-est in public works and construction, defense, power, mining, health care, telecommunications, and banking and finance, in descending order. Low public sector salaries, immunity of public officials (that is, they can secure bribes and chances of being discovered are low), secrecy in government, worsening public procurement practices, the privatization process, and financial liberalization are the reasons given for why bribes are accepted.

Changes in Perception of Corruption over Time

Over time, despite the prevalence of corruption in the country, there have been improvements in reducing opportunities for corruption through policy and regulatory reform. This can be gleaned, for instance, from the time series of Transparency International's Corruption Perceptions Index (CPI) for the Philippines (figure 3.7). During 1980–85, the index, calcu-lated retrospectively, was at a low of 1, and in 1999 it rose to 3.6 (on a scale of 1 to 10, a higher number meaning a lower perception of corruption). By 2000, however, the CPI had dropped to 2.8. It improved slightly in 2001 but slid to 2.6 in August 2002. As the World Bank observed, "though encouraging in the sense that progress has been made, the low score also means that there is a lot to go" (World Bank 2000b, p. vii).

Analysts have found that policy and regulatory reforms toward greater economic freedom lead to less bribery and corruption (Gwartney and Lawson 2001). Thus it may be instructive that during the period in which the Philippines's CPI improved from 1 in 1980–85 to 3.6 in 1999, there was also a parallel increase in summary ratings of economic free-dom in the country: from 5.0 in 1985 to 5.6 in 1990 to 7.2 in 1995 to 7.6 in 1999.[9] By 2000, however, the CPI had dropped to 2.8. The CPI had gone

Figure 3.7. Corruption Perceptions Index, Philippine Scores, Selected Years, 1980–2002

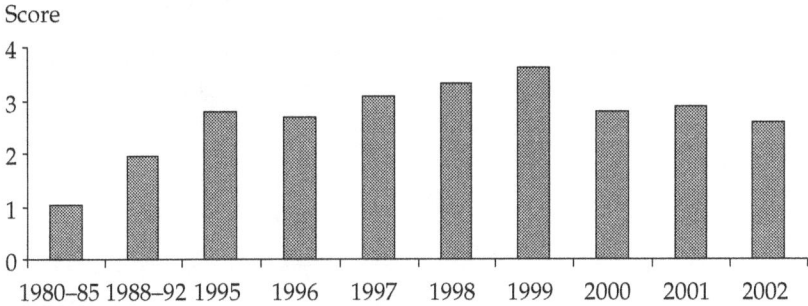

Source: Transparency International, www.transparency.org.

up slightly to 2.9 by 2001. This decline in perception ratings is arguably tied to the impact of the widespread reports of corruption during the short-lived presidency of Joseph Estrada.

The Political and Economic Risk Consultancy noted a "marked improvement" in the Philippines after President Macapagal-Arroyo took over from Estrada, but stressed that Manila's score remained well below the average grade of 5. In a scale of 1 to 10, with 1 being the best possible score, Singapore was graded 0.90, followed by Japan (3.25) and Hong Kong, China (3.33) ("Philippine Corruption Rating Improves Slightly" 2002).

Since 1987, when SWS began charting the Filipino people's satisfaction with the way Philippine governments have been combating corruption, each administration has received negative marks, except at the beginning of each term, as figure 3.8 indicates. The Aquino administration, coming to power right after the Marcos regime, initially garnered quite high positive net satisfaction ratings,[10] but those easily dissipated. On average, Filipinos of all income classes rated each Philippine government below zero, suggesting great displeasure with the way in which the fight against corruption was conducted.

Between 1998 and 2001, 38 to 49 percent of Filipinos indicated that a great deal of corruption existed in the public sector (figure 3.9). Another 29 to 36 percent were certain about some degree of corruption prevailing in government. It was also the second time that the number of those saying there was no corruption was at its lowest, thus underscoring its severity. Government's performance in eradicating graft and corruption has been stagnant and continues to be consistently lower than its "overall performance."

Figure 3.8. Net Satisfaction with the National Administration in Eradicating Graft and Corruption, by Income Class

Net satisfaction

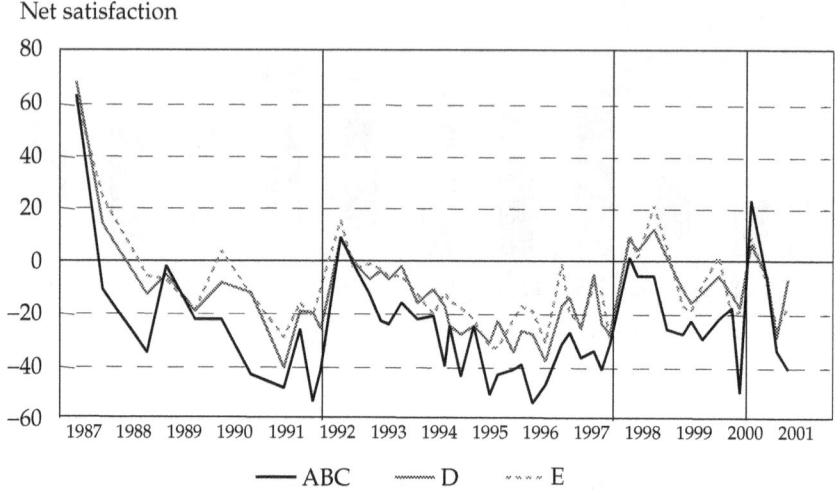

Legend: ——— ABC   ~~~~~~ D   ~ ~ ~ E

Note: 0 = neutral. Letters indicate self-rated income class: A = very rich; E = very poor.
Source: Social Weather Stations, national surveys, 1997–2001.

Figure 3.9. Perceived Extent of Public Sector Corruption

Percent

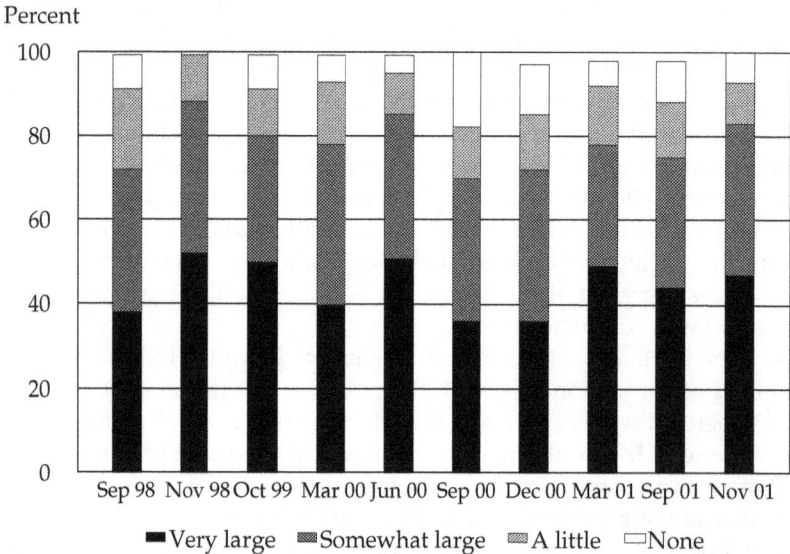

Legend: ■Very large   ▦Somewhat large   ▨A little   ▢None

Source: Social Weather Stations, national surveys, September 1998 to November 2001.

Enterprise managers surveyed by SWS in October 2000 saw corruption equally prevalent in government spending and revenue collection. Of those who perceived corruption in the public sector, half said most/all companies in their sector of business bribe the government, with median bribes amounting to 15 to 20 percent of contracts.

Corruption in the private sector was also a serious concern. According to SWS national surveys, three-tenths of Filipinos in September 2001 said there was "a great deal" of corruption in the private sector and another 35 percent said there was "some" corruption. About a tenth (11 percent) said there was "none." The perceived amount of corruption in the private sector in 2001 was the worst since October 1999 when 30 percent said it was very large. A quarter of the same enterprise managers who were surveyed in 2000 thought in 2001 that most/all companies in their sector of business bribed other private companies, with (median) bribes amounting to 10 percent of contracts.

Corruption continued to be seen more as an economic development issue than as a moral issue. A large majority of Filipinos (79 percent) in September 2001 thought corruption was wrong "because it hurts national development"; those who thought it was wrong "due to its immorality" totaled 21 percent.

On the bright side, Filipinos continued to be hopeful rather than cynical that government could be run without corruption. A large majority (68 percent) of Filipinos surveyed by SWS in September 2001 thought that "the government can be run without corruption," whereas 31 percent said corruption was "part of the way things work." That sentiment has been practically the same since September 1998 (59 percent), but split in June 2000. The caveat, however, is that the public was more often than not undecided on how to rate the sincerity of selected institutions in fighting public sector corruption.

Anticorruption Policies and Programs

How have the country's anticorruption efforts fared with respect to the following pillars of action: (1) developing effective and transparent systems for public service, (2) strengthening antibribery actions and promoting integrity in business operations, and (3) supporting active public involvement? These pillars, crafted by the ADB-OECD as an anticorruption template for Asia-Pacific countries,[11] underlie a set of strategies that include enhancing state capacity and public sector management, strengthening political accountability, enabling civil society, and increasing economic competition. They are considered in the context of a fair governance environment.

Incidentally, the pillars and the strategies are consistent with the nine-point approach[12] proposed by the World Bank to the Philippine government in 2000 and the subsequent National Anti-Corruption Plan[13] prepared by the Development Academy of the Philippines (DAP) at the direction of the Philippine government.

Philippine efforts to address administrative corruption have largely focused on reforms in the management of public resources and administration. The Philippine public sector has been bombarded with reforms aiming to instill meritocracy, eliminate organizational dysfunctions, promote improved service delivery and accountability through decentralization, and rein in agencies to achieve financial discipline, among others. So far, although significant strides have been made, the reforms run the risk of backstepping because of weak institutionalization, high internal resistance to change, and inadequate resources to sustain the changes.

Meritocratic Civil Service with Adequate Compensation

Formally the Philippines has long had a meritocratic system for appointment, promotion, and performance evaluation through the establishment of an independent civil service oversight body, a Commission on Appointments that screens top political appointees, and a career executive development program for officials at the public manager level. But form hides inherent weaknesses: persistent inability to address poor pay, especially for career officials; vulnerability of political appointees to congressional favors to win confirmation; and inadequate funding to launch a demand-driven career development program.

The qualification standards required by the Civil Service Commission (CSC) serve as deterrents to political patronage but that has not been enough to depoliticize appointments. Under the CSC chair, Karina Constantino-David, a legislative measure is in the offing—the revision of the Civil Service Code. It proposes to limit the appointing powers of the executive branch and transfer the function to the CSC. The downside of this proposal is that it might encourage political capture of the CSC. Another key feature of this proposed code is career progression through rank rather than through designation. That progression is similar to an academic structure where individuals progressively advance in their professorial career (for example, from assistant professor to full professor) but may be designated to managerial positions (for example, department chair or dean) from time to time.

Success in this regard greatly depends on the service delivery orientation of the public service, reinforced by accountability for results. Also, developing service delivery standards requires a high degree of competence and a high level of participation within the bureaucracy.

More than 10 years after passage of the Salary Standardization Law, fixed wage rates have not helped curb corruption, despite the fact that the salaries of low-ranking public sector employees now match those of the private sector. Although by itself there is merit in raising wages, some impact would be felt if salary increases were in the nature of pay decompression. Studies show that middle managers and top-ranking officials in the public sector get only a third of what their counterparts in business receive. Decompression is not easy to implement given the government's budget constraints. To support it financially will require streamlining an oversized bureaucracy. But the payoffs are greater because it can reduce the vulnerability of middle managers and top officials to high-level corruption.

The Ethics Office

Many organizations in the Philippines continue to conduct seminars on ethics although their effects on reducing corruption remain to be proven. Worth mentioning are moral recovery programs and values orientation workshops (VOWs) conducted by CSC, the Office of the Ombudsman, and DAP. In the 1990s VOWs proliferated but generated no concrete results. Any ethics program must be run alongside changes in incentives. Huther and Shah (2000) argued that the positive influence of an ethics office may be limited to societies with good governance.

That observation suggests in no way that codes of conduct are unimportant. Codes set the norm for good behavior but they have to be deployed to be effective. At the moment, the bureaucracy is too dependent on a CSC code of ethics that is not widely disseminated and does not take account of the peculiarities of each agency.

When President Macapagal-Arroyo assumed office, one of her first directives was the prescription of a code of conduct for relatives and friends of top officials. A preferred situation would be one in which there is automatic adherence to the norms without need for the president to keep reminding public officials that conflicts of interest are prohibited.

Financial Accountability

Financial accountability is said to be appropriate when democratic accountability and substantial accounting and bookkeeping infrastructure with integrity are in place. Greater parliamentary and public oversight is likewise crucial as are strong budget execution processes. In the past, the lack of a medium-term perspective in expenditure projections of government agencies, compounded by unrealistic revenue forecasts, lead to ad hoc and nontransparent adjustments during the budget execution process. A major change introduced by the government under the leadership of Budget and Management Secretary Emilia Boncodin, is the Medium-Term Expenditure Framework (MTEF), which links planning and budgeting beyond the typical one-year budgeting cycle to ensure sustainability of the government's economic plan and eliminate adjustments during budget execution. Another feature of the program is the Organizational Performance Indicators Framework (OPIF) that forces government agencies to focus on outcomes and the delivery of priority programs. The MTEF and OPIF, however, are in "compliance" stage. Strong capacity building is needed to deploy these measures in all agencies of government, both national and local.

The Department of Budget and Management also initiated major reforms in government procurement in 1999. A critical step undertaken was the amendment of basic regulations related to government procurement of goods and services to increase competition, reduce delays, and limit the discretion of bids and awards committees. An electronic procurement system was launched in 2000, and it includes (1) a public tender board, an electronic bulletin board where all government bid opportunities and decisions are posted; (2) a suppliers registry, where all accredited suppliers of agencies are listed; and (3) an electronic catalog, a virtual store for supply requirements of agencies.

Initial results have shown declining procurement costs (for example, textbook costs have declined by an estimated 40 percent, and drug costs by an estimated 27 percent), faster supplier verification (from three weeks to one hour), and faster processing of expressions of interest (from seven months to 30 minutes by e-mail) (World Bank 2001, pp. 20–21). The Bureau of Internal Revenue (BIR) also claimed that it was able to slash procurement spending when the agency shifted to electronic bidding because it was easier to locate local and global suppliers online.

An omnibus bill on government procurement reform, which was approved by the lower house of congress during the Estrada Administration, has been reintroduced in the new congress to solidify the changes. Reforms in procurement cast a wide net in the bureaucracy because it is mandated. It requires moderate technical competence and is relatively easy to implement—factors that enable this measure to show quick results.

On the revenue collection side, reforms were revived under then-Commissioner Rene Banez. Banez addressed the problem of tax administration through reform of the tax system; reengineering of tax processes to make them simpler, more efficient, and transparent; and redesign of human resource policies and of systems and procedures to transform the work force. But his short-lived stint seems to have put these reforms on hold, although newly installed Commissioner Guillermo Parayno vowed to continue the reforms. The country is in dire need of a more innovative strategy to fight corruption in tax collection—one that will attack the incentive structure in these agencies. As the World Bank noted, reforms in the BIR still lack a comprehensive anticorruption strategy (World Bank 2002).

Through the Commission on Audit (COA) the government is also pursing accounting and auditing reforms, which include value for money audit, participatory audit involving civil society, government-wide and sectoral performance audits, the team audit approach as an alternative to residency auditing, and an accrual accounting–based financial management information system via computerization. The team audit approach is expected to give the COA a more streamlined audit structure, increase the number of audits, and eliminate collusion between resident auditors and agency personnel.

Because COA actions are always after-the-fact, they are more useful as lessons learned than as preventive actions. The commission thus needs to be more proactive and consistent in investigating and publishing reports on procurement, management of public assets, and diversions of public funds.

Efficient and Client-friendly Bureaucratic Culture

As part of the government's anticorruption drive, President Macapagal-Arroyo directed all agencies to cut by half the number of signatures involved in government transactions (for example, for applications for passports, birth certificates, housing, environmental permits, professional licenses, and the like). Local government units are likewise implementing a signature reduction project (for example, in the issuance of business permits, building permits, and clearances). The CSC complemented this drive with a directive to all government offices—especially frontline service agencies—to post flowcharts, documents required, fees, processing times, and officials responsible for the evaluation and approval of licenses and permits. Reducing the number of signatures and steps reduces the opportunities for illicit transactions. This plan could also address the problem of information asymmetry between the service providers and the transacting public, and eventually eliminate fixers if the proposed program on publishing a citizen handbook on government services can be activated.

The government has also recognized the capability of information and communications technology not only to speed up processes but also to make government transactions more transparent and to minimize direct interface between the revenue collectors and the transacting public. In addition to electronic bidding, information and communication technology applications are being pursued in filing of taxes (electronic filing and payment system), posting of budget releases, vehicle registrations, authentication of birth certificates, issuance of passports, and automation of elections. Progress generally has been sporadic.

The e-Commerce Act, passed in 2000, requires all public agencies to automate processes and transactions and to network among themselves for purposes of information sharing and knowledge management. The deadline for compliance has passed and only a few agencies have been able to automate their internal operations and are still far behind in computerizing frontline transactions. Progress along these lines is expected to be slow because of the high level of financial resources and technical competence required.

Decentralization

As an anticorruption tool, decentralization has had an ambiguous record. Comparative analyses of fiscal decentralization suggest a negative correlation between decentralization and corruption: the greater the decentralization, the lesser the corruption (Huther and Shah 1998). In the Philippines a decade of decentralization has increased the accountability of local governments in health, local public works, and agricultural development, among other areas. Blair (1996), citing the Philippines' more recent experience with decentralization, concluded that decentralized democratic governance has a positive impact on the quality of governance, especially in reorienting government from a command-and-control to a service provider role. Anecdotal evidence has shown that decentralization increases productive efficiency in the Philippines by limiting the leakage of funds and other sources (Azfar and others 2000).

But decentralization also has its downside. In some instances, localization worsens corruption, especially when vested private interests control local governments. Potential losses from decentralized procurement can also be staggering. With less oversight local governments could be more susceptible to capture or collusion with local contractors (Gonzalez and Mendoza 2002). The Local Government Code, with its grant of new powers and responsibilities to local executives, brought new players into the corruption game without requiring them to take their lead from national officials. Localization has widened opportunities to capture rent (A. Mendoza 2001).

There are pockets of success stories on decentralization in the Philippines, however. What the government is doing, with the support of the donor community, is to strengthen the accountability and capacity of local governments. The pilot testing of the report card surveys, a joint effort of ADB and DAP among local government units is an initial step to raise the accountability of local officials for the services (garbage collection, traffic management, public safety, public market management, and licensing) that they ought to deliver to their constituencies. The institutionalization of report card surveys for local government units, together with strong local capacity in financial management and audit, is thus vital to raising service standards and eliminating corruption at the local level. Overall, decentralization has great promise in reducing corruption because it entails lower monitoring costs and encourages more accountability for local expenditures.

Reduced Public Employment and Public Sector Size

For eight years now, the Philippine Government has been pushing for the passage of the reengineering bill that would give the president the power to streamline and reorganize the entire executive department. Meanwhile, it is the privatization of a number of government-owned and -controlled corporations, especially in the oil industry and utilities sector, that has actually reduced public employment, although to a limited extent.

Pending the passage of the reengineering bill, administrative streamlining has proceeded in various agencies under the executive department. The biggest restructuring effort took place in the Department of Health (DOH) when it tried to localize many of its remaining functions.[14] The DOH restructuring was not an easy task. A year after it, the agency faced a case in court filed by resisting employees. It has also recentralized some functions under the new administration.

In 2002 President Macapagal-Arroyo abolished about 77 ad hoc bodies created by executive fiat during the last three administrations (per Executive Order 72). More bodies are slated for abolition. Although no evaluation has been made so far on the impact of these streamlining efforts, they are expected to reduce prospects for corruption.

Institutional Restraints

The institutional design of the state can be an important mechanism in checking corruption. In particular, the development of institutional restraints within the state is thought to be most effectively achieved through some degree of separation of powers and the establishment of cross-cutting oversight responsibilities among state institutions. Effective constraints can diminish opportunities for the abuse of power; abuses easily can be penalized if they occur (World Bank 2000a). It is thus ironic that Philippine institutions are not as effective at ensuring accountability because their design, patterned after the U.S. presidential system, is precisely intended to foster accountability.

The Philippine Constitution provides for the separation of powers of the executive, legislative, and judicial branches of government. Institutional pathologies of these three branches enervate the system of checks and balances. Instead of being co-equal, congress, particularly the lower house, is not too effective at checking the presidency in great part because of the weakness of the party system and the electoral vulnerability of individual politicians to the incentives and disincentives that the president can employ. Moreover, congress, which has the "power of the purse," is itself saddled by allegations of corruption—for instance, those associated with the use of the congressional development fund, commonly referred to as the pork barrel.

Rule of Law

The Philippines has numerous anticorruption laws. These include the Antigraft and Corrupt Practices Act, the Unlawfully Acquired Property Forfeiture Act, the Disclosure of Assets and Liabilities, the Plunder Act, the Code of Conduct and Ethical Standards, and recently the Anti-Money-Laundering Act. All these laws provide stiff penalties, but their poor enforcement—the low probability of being detected, prosecuted, and punished—make some public officials not fearful of paying the penalties. With a weak judiciary it is not surprising that convictions are rare. A comparison between the Philippines and Hong Kong, China, suggested that the probability that an official in the Philippines would escape prosecution for corruption is 35 times greater than in Hong Kong.[15] When the most important veto point—the judiciary—cannot perform its functions, the credibility of other state institutions is diminished.

Reforming the Philippine police is also a crucial ingredient of the anticorruption campaign. The Philippine National Police was reorganized in 2000, with increased benefits for the rank-and-file. But it needs stronger measures to rid itself of corrupt law enforcers.

It takes time to develop groundbreaking enforcement approaches. Despite its high benefits for the anticorruption drive, the rule of law is stalled by low public participation and loose and unjust application.

Judicial Independence

The Philippine judiciary was set up on good institutional foundations during the American period. Before martial rule was imposed the judiciary had a good reputation as the "last bastion of Philippine democracy." Today the judiciary has not fully recovered from the assaults on its independence and integrity during its debilitating experience under the Marcos authoritarian regime. The judiciary is also weighed down with problems of case congestion and delay, and politicized appointments. The good news, though, is that the judiciary has begun an ambitious campaign for reform. The Supreme Court's Action Program for Judicial Reform seeks to restore public trust and confidence in the country's justice system, promote judicial independence, and enhance effectiveness. Those reforms are being implemented under the aegis of the chief justice himself.

The Supreme Court has partnered with an NGO, Bantay Katarungan, to monitor court proceedings and applicant screenings for positions in the lower courts and courts of appeals. It has intensified disciplinary actions against corrupt judges. Between November 30, 1998, and April 2001, the Supreme Court disciplined 230 judges either by dismissal or by administrative sanctions on corruption charges (Initorio 2001).

Parliamentary Oversight

Congress exercises its oversight functions prominently during the annual budget hearings that lead to the enactment of the general appropriations law. It has also been active in the investigations of graft cases through the Senate Blue Ribbon Committee. Although the Senate investigation of the *jueteng* (illegal numbers game) case and other allegations of presidential wrongdoing were among the crucial events that led to the impeachment trial of Joseph Estrada, congressional investigations are too episodic to substitute for regular oversight of executive functions.

Political Accountability

In view of the country's various institutional constraints and weaknesses, political accountability has been minimal. Accountability refers to the restraints placed on the behavior of public officials by organizations and constituencies that have the power to place sanctions on them. As political accountability increases, the costs to public officials of making decisions that benefit their private interests at the expense of the broader public interest also increase (World Bank 2000a).

Political Competition

Effective sanctions on politicians can be enhanced through a meaningful degree of political competition in the electoral process. Such competition increases the likelihood that alternative candidates and parties will seek to expose corruption in government or hold politicians accountable for the poor performance associated with high levels of corruption (World Bank 2000a).

Of course political competition exists in the Philippines. But is it genuinely competitive? The Constitution calls for the development of a free, open, multiparty political system. There are nominally many parties, but only two or three count when it comes to legislation and party politics itself. Hardly any party commands the kind of party discipline common in strong party systems. Periodic party switching, often after presidential elections, testifies to the weakness of parties and party competition. The Philippine party system has been evolving according to the free choice of the elite, organized to perpetuate their economic interests by constantly seizing hold of political office (Gonzalez 2001). Party switchers join the incumbent administration to seek political favors. In such a case, the degree of political competition is not meaningful enough to penalize erring politicians. Rather, the "artificial" competition creates conditions conducive to administrative corruption and state capture.

Transparency in Party Financing

The Philippines also has rules requiring transparency in party financing. Political parties often resort to corporate and private donations to raise campaign funds, but that can become a venue for corruption because politicians and political parties may give those donors improper favors in return for their contributions (Gonzalez 2001). The country's election code sets guidelines and prohibitions on financial contributions to political parties, but the rules (for example, a low ceiling on election expenses) are too unrealistic and tend to provide incentives to hide rather than declare fund sources. The Commission on Elections (COMELEC), which is tasked to oversee these matters, lacks the capability to investigate the contributions that reach political parties. Its monitoring mechanism is very weak. Even worse is the fact that when violations occur, COMELEC rarely applies sanctions (Rocamora 1998).

Asset Declaration and Conflict of Interest Rules

Measures to foster transparency of public officials include opening the sessions of the legislature and judiciary to the public, periodic government reporting, better laws on disclosure of assets and conflict of interest, and public access to information. Unfortunately many of those measures have had little impact on curbing corruption. For instance, although filing a statement of assets and liabilities is mandatory for all public officials, the reports are not verified effectively. Misdeclaration of assets by public officials is also not penalized. On its own initiative the PCIJ has begun focusing on some high-ranking officials. Another example is the current divestment law that requires public officials to dissociate from their private business activities while in office. The law has many loop-holes, making it easy for public officials to make use of dummies to sat-isfy the requirement.

Competitive Private Sector

State capture has somewhat been constrained by a number of measures, such as economic policy liberalization, greater competition especially in concentrated sectors, and regulatory reform. But weaknesses abound when it comes to establishing a stronger and more transparent frame-work for corporate governance and creating instruments of voice for small business and trade unions.

Privatization

Beginning with the Aquino administration and accelerating during the Ramos years, liberalization was pursued in the fields of telecommunica-tions, banking and insurance, energy, air and sea transportation, and con-struction. The privatization program involved the full or partial sale of "big-ticket" items under the Asset Privatization Trust, such as Metro Manila's water supply system, Philippine Airlines, the state oil firm, and the Philippine National Bank. These moves encouraged more players to come in, widened consumer choices, and allowed government to focus on vital public services. The most recent privatization attempt of the gov-ernment targeted the National Power Corporation (NPC), but it has been mired in controversy because the cost of NPC's inefficiency in managing resources is being borne by the taxpayers.

Privatization must be accompanied by a good regulatory framework. As documented by Virtucio and Lalunio (2001), the privatization process can also prove susceptible to manipulation, enabling vested interests to gain control of a substantial part of the economy. In the Philippines a number of government monopolies were privatized in the absence of sufficient regu-latory framework. For example, Virtucio and Lalunio argued that the pri-vatization of the North Harbor merely amounted to the transfer of a gov-ernment monopoly to a private monopoly of cargo-handling operations.

Integrity in Business and Banking Operations

In September 2001 the Philippines passed the Anti-Money-Laundering Act. The Philippines was earlier included in the Financial Action Task Force (FATF) list of 19 countries and territories that were not cooperative in addressing money laundering. The law gives the implementing coun-cil the power to freeze accounts, institute forfeiture proceedings, file criminal complaints, and cooperate with other countries in going after money launderers. The FATF, however, has decided that the content of the law is inadequate and that the country still has to do more to prove its commitment to counter money laundering before it can be removed from the Non-Cooperative Countries and Territories list (see the Makati Business Club, www.mbc.com.ph).

Corporate Governance

The Philippine corporate sector has its own share of governance weaknesses. The 1997 financial crisis highlighted several corporate governance issues: ownership concentration, weak supervision, relatively few publicly listed firms, insider trading, limited minority shareholder rights, and cozy relationship of corporations with external auditing firms.

In recent years corporate governance reforms have been high on the government's agenda in the wake of the Estrada corruption scandals. Spurred in part by the BW stock market manipulation case, the Philippines passed the Securities Regulation Code (RA 8799) in August 2000. The code strengthened the regulatory powers and independence of the Securities and Exchange Commission and incorporated antifraud provisions.

Some business groups have launched anticorruption projects. The Makati Business Club, an elite formation of big business, has waged its initial anticorruption effort on behalf of private sector interests. Its initiatives in fighting corruption include Project Simplification, which aims to simplify transactions in licensing and real estate permits, and the Transparency and Accountability in Governance Project,[16] which surveys firms on the extent of corruption in the private sector. More recent initiatives are being undertaken by the Governance Advisory Council (GAC), a private sector–led body created in 2001 by President Macapagal-Arroyo under Executive Order 25. The GAC has prepared a new corporate governance reform agenda that covers guidelines on the roles and responsibilities of corporate boards, a code of proper practice for directors, and a code of ethics for enterprises. There are, however, long-term structural measures that also need to be addressed—raising the independence and qualifications of directors, appointing outsiders to boards, publicly disclosing crossholdings, protecting minority shareholder rights, setting stiffer penalties for insider trading, promoting strong enforcement of ethical standards, and the like.

Notwithstanding those initiatives, integrity pacts, which commit public procurement agencies and private contractors of goods and services to bribery-free contracting, are yet to be realized. Other major issues concerning the private sector are tax evasion, bribery of tax agents, and facilitation payments for regulators.

Active Public Involvement

An effective anticorruption program cannot succeed without the intense vigilance and active involvement of the general public. In the Philippines, mounting public involvement has included (a) instilling public awareness about corruption, (b) formulating and advocating action plans to fight corruption, and (c) monitoring government's actions and decisions. Greater civil society activism is one of the key ingredients that can crack the country's institutional barriers wide open.

Elevated Public Awareness of Corruption

Seminars, conferences, and workshops conducted by civil society organizations (including academia and international agencies) have helped disseminate information about the patterns and severity of corruption and have raised public awareness of its ills. But this measure has low impact in an environment where there is a culture of tolerance to corruption. Huther and Shah (2000) argued that in countries with less than good governance, corrupt practices and agents generally are well known. The more important measure for a country with fair governance like the Philippines would be giving citizens a voice in exacting accountability and engaging them to actively participate in monitoring government actions and decisions—for example, public expenditure, revenue collection, and regulation.

In that regard the Philippines has made a number of strides in the right direction. To raise public awareness, NGOs have used opinion surveys, which have helped shape public opinion about corruption. The surveys also serve as a useful tool not just as a check on the performance of public officials, but as a means to articulate citizens' concerns. The report card, as suggested earlier, serves this purpose.

Media Independence and Participation

The Philippines has the freest press in Asia. An independent media helps check the level of corruption through exposés. It is a necessary anticorruption tool, especially in a context of fair governance. By disseminating information and analysis, media helps alleviate the information asymmetries that worsen the collective action problem. Specifically, exposés lend a hand in raising public awareness and action. For example, the Philippine Center for Investigative Journalism's investigation of President Estrada paved the way for the filing of impeachment charges against the president.[17] The PCIJ also conducted and published damning investigative reports on the misuse of pork-barrel funds, textbook procurement scams, and shady business deals involving a telephone monopoly. To be sure, the Philippine media is not immune from allegations of corruption. It is widely held that many reporters are "on the take."

Public Access to Information

The Philippine constitution provides for the right of people to information on matters of public concern.[18] In principle it is the duty of officials to provide information to the public. To that end, the judiciary has tended to rule in favor of the citizens' right to know, and thus a legal atmosphere has developed that makes it easier for both journalists and citizens to assert their right to information. In addition, a tradition of openness and discussion that has roots in the country's longer experience with democracy and a free press provides for wider access than in most other Southeast Asian countries.

Access to information, however, has yet to be institutionalized and is often subject to constraints. Many state agencies have not recognized that providing access is part of their functions. Despite strides toward greater transparency in government, citizens still come up against a culture of secrecy. The inclinations and agenda of public officials also determine whether and to what extent information will be released (Chua 2001).

Citizen Participation

Citizen participation in the fight against corruption was made prominent in the Philippines by the popular ouster of Joseph Estrada in January 2001, and previously that of Ferdinand Marcos in 1986. On a more limited scale, there are other notable anticorruption programs that harness civil society participation. These are the participatory audit initiated by the COA and the formation of civil society watchdogs such as Procurement Watch Inc. (PWI) and Bantay Katarungan (judicial watch). Nominally the Ombudsman has also accredited some 361 NGOs and peoples' organizations as corruption prevention units and 1,074 student and community-based youth organizations as junior graft-watch units (Office of the Ombudsman 2001, p. 14).

Among local NGOs, the Concerned Citizens of Abra for Good Government (CCAGG), a community-based watchdog organization, has been noted for uncovering corruption in local public works, which resulted in the conviction of the construction engineers involved. CCAGG also teamed up with the state audit agency for a participatory audit of the Abra provincial government. PWI, an NGO organized by a group of economists, lawyers, and policy analysts, helps monitor on demand the major procurement activities of the government. Aside from being a watchdog,

PWI conducts studies, promotes e-procurement, and assists in streamlining procedures that govern procurement of goods, supplies, materials, services, and infrastructure projects of the national government.

Lesser known is the 1,000-member Fellowship of Christians in Government (FOCIG), which has fellowship groups in 50 government agencies. FOCIG has quietly made its presence felt by publishing a booklet on how to transact business with various government agencies.

In 2001, civil society organizations, led by the Transparency and Accountability Network (TAN), have taken the first steps toward developing a civil society anticorruption action agenda. The agenda consists of action plans for preventing corruption, prosecuting offenders, and promoting a corruption-intolerant culture. In that regard, part of the strength of civil society involvement stems from the optimism of many Filipinos that things can get better. TAN is composed of 19 academic institutions, media, and NGOs.

See appendix 3.1 for a summary evaluation of anticorruption policies and programs.

Improving Organizational Coherence and Filling in the Gaps

The scattered reforms mentioned above clearly imply several major weaknesses. First, the effort suffers from lack of organizational coherence. Furthermore, there is no overarching anticorruption framework. The challenges are to address decisively the diffusion of effort within the bureaucracy and to achieve focus through a sustained anticorruption campaign.

Second, there are gaps in the wider executive action needed to complement initiatives intrinsically focused on combating corruption. These discontinuities include a lack of consistency in applying conflict of interest rules, inadequate audit procedures and inactive case referral systems (for example, the COA is not compelled to submit its audit findings to the ombudsman if corruption is uncovered), weak enforcement of the e-Commerce Act, and lack of any regulatory framework for civil society organizations (hence, those organizations remain unaccountable for their actions).

Third, parallel legislative remedies are not moving fast enough in certain cases. There are no vigorous moves to amend the salary standardization law in favor of pay decompression that can stimulate managerial efficiency in the bureaucracy. More innovative strategies that can attack the entrenched incentive structure at the Bureau of Internal Revenue would depend on the passage of an important measure to corporatize BIR (through the creation of the Internal Revenue Management

Authority). Right now, objections from BIR employees threaten to stymie that bill. Recent moves to lessen the depth of presidential power to appoint have found expression in a proposed measure in the new civil service code, which is yet to be passed by congress. Other measures needing congressional fast-tracking include rationalizing privatization by crafting a good regulatory framework, strengthening the anti-money-laundering legislation to comply with international standards, implementing the constitutional right to information through passage of an information accessibility law, improving transparency in party financing by revising COMELEC rules, and making the private sector more accountable through corporate governance laws.

Filling the gaps to combat corruption might appear overwhelming because doing so entails significant changes in the structure of political institutions in the context of relationships within government and among government, civil society, and the private sector, and changes in the existing policy and program practices of the Philippine Government. But a determined leadership can overcome the difficulties and create virtuous circles of reform.

Toward a Unified Leadership and Management of the National Anticorruption Plan

At present, the anticorruption effort of the government is diffused among several agencies, with major mandates and overlapping jurisdictions, as indicated in appendix 3.2. Lack of coordination among those agencies is exacerbated by the episodic nature of the government's anticorruption efforts. Since the 1950s Philippine presidents, from Elpidio Quirino to Gloria Macapagal-Arroyo, have created their own antigraft and corruption investigation units and agencies (appendix 3.3). Most of those efforts have been short-lived, and because they were executive creations, their powers often were not sufficient to deal with hard corruption cases.

The creation of the Office of the Ombudsman in 1986 represented a clear departure from intermittent anticorruption initiatives. A constitutional body, it was designed to be an effective anticorruption body independent of pressures from the executive branch. In principle it would seem it has all the powers needed.[19] After more than 10 years in operation, however, it has little to show in terms of reducing corruption in the country. Because of its poor conviction record the office is suffering from a credibility problem. It is also criticized for putting too much emphasis on prosecution and lacking a proactive stance on corruption prevention.

The formulation of a National Anti-Corruption Plan (NACP) in 2000 underlined the weak spot of the Ombudsman. After consultations with various stakeholders, DAP proposed an anticorruption blueprint. The plan adopted a programmatic approach, looking at the whole cycle of investigation, prosecution, and prevention. It also featured a long-term sequencing of anticorruption actions and a centerpiece 10-point jump-start program for immediate execution. Its proposal for a broad civic coalition was especially appealing to civil society. Like Hong Kong, China's Independent Commission Against Corruption, NACP had corruption prevention and community relations components. It was its emphasis on prevention and education that made NACP distinct from other anticorruption plans. Unfortunately, NACP floundered partly because it was housed under another presidential creation—the National Anti-Corruption Commission (NACC)—and partly because of opposition from legal circles. As a result, Executive Order 268 creating NACC was frozen by Estrada himself.

Apart from the Office of the Ombudsman, there are a few more important anticorruption bodies in the Philippines, a fact that accentuates the diffusion of effort in the anticorruption campaign in the country.

Following the People Power revolution in 1986, then–President Aquino created the Presidential Commission on Good Government (PCGG), charged with recovering the ill-gotten wealth of the Marcoses. Sixteen years later the PCGG has not been successful in its task. The recent appointment of lawyer Haydee Yorac, a well-known graftbuster, has raised hopes for a better effort.

In 2001 President Macapagal-Arroyo reenergized an old antigraft body, renaming it the Presidential Anti-Graft Commission (PAGC). Like its precursor, PAGC investigates corruption cases against presidential appointees. It inherited the weakness of the old commission: it does not adjudicate but merely recommends action to the president. The bright spot is that the new commission can conduct its own studies on new transparency and accountability measures at all levels of the bureaucracy. Recently the commission has been quite active in issues of corruption prevention. In partnership with TAN, the Presidential Committee on Effective Governance, and DAP, PAGC is coordinating the formulation of a transparency and accountability agenda for the government. The partnership has also adopted many features of the NACP.

The Presidential Committee on Effective Governance (PCEG), created in October 1999, is a cabinet-level body responsible for formulating an agenda to strengthen and streamline the public sector and is taking the lead in enacting legislative and administrative reforms. At present the PCEG is spearheading the signature reduction project, a commitment of the Macapagal-Arroyo Administration to cut red tape and reduce corruption in critical government services.

The Sandiganbayan, the main antigraft court, adjudicates criminal cases brought to it by the Office of the Ombudsman. Only the cases pertaining to high-level officials (director level and above) are referred to this body. It has a bench of 15 judges. Because the role of the judiciary is to decide on the basis of evidence presented, this institution does not have a proactive role in anticorruption. As an agency, however, it is reputed to be relatively free from corruption (World Bank 2000b).

To unite the disparate initiatives on combating corruption, a first and necessary step is to strengthen the Office of the Ombudsman. It is the only body capable of consolidating all anticorruption reforms. To secure its independence, competence and integrity would be critical—the ombudsman must provide credible leadership. Additionally, efforts must be made to ensure that its work is grounded on corruption prevention, community relations, and international cooperation as much as on prosecution. Adopting the major elements of NACP could lead to significant strides in the ombudsman's anticorruption drive.

A credibly committed ombudsman, along with the development of a broad anticorruption coalition, will also ensure that the anticorruption program is not a hostage to the vagaries of the political process, including frequent changes in leadership. Even the World Bank (2000a) noted that any strategy that relies only on high-level leadership will be vulnerable to the many uncertainties of the political process.

PAGC must be of a temporary nature. Once the Office of the Ombudsman is able to exercise its authority more fully, PAGC must wither away. On the other hand, the Office of the Ombudsman must partner with the PCEG, which has proved quite effective in enforcing discipline in the executive branch. With PCEG a part of the broad coalition, the Office of the Ombudsman could establish its own credibility in corruption prevention (for example, in devising agency-specific anticorruption measures such as the reduction of red tape and the institutionalization of corruption vulnerability assessments). On the investigation and prosecution side, interagency coordination (say, among the National Bureau of Investigation, the Department of Justice, the CSC, and COA) will be helped by a strengthened ombudsman.

A complementary step is to strengthen the judiciary and enhance the integrity, especially of the lower courts. It is pointless to quicken the pace of action in many areas, especially the Office of the Ombudsman, when the judiciary itself may need reform.

For both the Office of the Ombudsman and the Sandiganbayan, a necessary but insufficient step is to fast-track the resolution of corruption cases. That requires inventorying for speedy resolution all the anticorruption cases filed against top government officials and prominent businesspeople and citizens—tax evaders, and bribe givers and takers. Fast-tracking high-profile cases seeks to demonstrate that anticorruption laws can be enforced in equal measure to all citizens, government officials, and personnel, regardless of position and stature. This is another process that involves the collaboration of investigative and prosecutorial bodies to vigorously pursue corruption cases in the courts. It requires neutralizing undue pressures to delay, suspend, or stop the settlement of these cases.

Along those lines, statistics on backlogs can be published, and inaction by the courts and anticorruption bodies can be highlighted in the media. Immediate studies can be done on how to simplify lengthy and unwieldy procedures being practiced by anticorruption bodies, and how to enhance interagency cooperation to tighten cases and increase chances for their successful prosecution.

Designing a Coherent Anticorruption Strategy: Focus on Prevention

Undeniably, given a fair governance environment the Philippines will not have the capacity to pursue reforms in all of these areas at the same time. A selection and sequencing of reform priorities dovetailed to the particularities of corruption in the country is needed. The anticorruption campaign is like a group of long-distance relay runners passing the baton: many activities provide the impetus for the next set of activities and each successive phase is dependent on the outcomes of preceding actions.

The preparatory stage entails foundation-building activities. Government buy-in is a first requisite to the campaign. Key government officials must demonstrate unequivocal political commitment. Credible leadership will eliminate fragmentation. No additional anticorruption may be needed as long as the existing setup can be made to deliver.

A detailed diagnosis is also a preliminary act because not much information on the extent of corruption is available. So far, the campaign depends mostly on surveys. Adequately funded medium-term programs that can dig deeper into the underlying causes of corruption and build institutions that can resist it would be helpful. Furthermore, an assessment of the political culture would reveal the incentives and disincentives and the level of trust that people have in their institutions. As the World Bank (2000a) stated, trust is an effective determinant of social capital and the capacity of community to coordinate their efforts.

It is also necessary at this point to start generating interest in the campaign among civil society groups, which will provide the key players in such projects as citizen watchdogs and report card surveys. Civil society groups must be encouraged to take an active role and eventually assume leadership in monitoring and evaluation.

At the same time, improving the accountability systems of civil society groups is necessary. Because of the come-and-go nature of many NGOs— a contrast to the long shelf-life of government agencies—it is difficult to make them answerable for their actions. To be sure, this last point may be less about the nature of NGOs than about the ability of Philippine institutions to make them accountable.

Keeping an eye on the anticorruption effort would mean a number of things:

- Establishing new performance indicators for anticorruption efforts. The governance indicators that have been developed do not adequately address the issue of corruption. Baseline data on corruption will have to be collected as well; existing indicators will have to be cross-referenced for a start. An annual anticorruption report would be a crucial guide for decisionmakers in generating successive rounds of reforms.
- Creating a monitoring and evaluation structure designed specifically for the anticorruption program. It must be based on a framework for which there is consensus among government, the private sector, and civil society.
- Interacting with international monitoring bodies, such as the World Bank, Transparency International, the Political and Economic Risk Consultancy, and the Center for Institutional Reform and the Informal Sector (IRIS Center) of the University of Maryland, among others.
- Ensuring open access to information to enable media to continue the investigative reporting of corruption cases.

Progress along these lines would mean the use of analytical tools, such as comparison and trending and benchmarking.

As envisioned in the NACP, several jump-start programs can provide momentum for the first phase. These programs would include agency transactions reengineering, corruption vulnerability assessment, open public documents, lifestyle checks, anticorruption vanguards, public ethics, and civil society watchdogs.

Reengineered Transactions in Selected Agencies

Many Philippine government agencies make for easy targets in the anticorruption campaign because their scope of work is relatively well-delineated and confined and can be examined readily. In most cases, however, their procedures are either cumbersome or ill-defined. Quick fixes involve (a) short-circuiting the process using fixers, forcing the public to resort to bribery to complete the transaction speedily, or (b) using discretion arbitrarily to extort money from, say, contractors, suppliers, lessees, or taxpayers.

Streamlining agency rules and regulations, as well as systems and procedures, will make them less vulnerable to corrupt practices.

Priority action is needed in agency functions where corruption is perceived to be most rampant: revenue collection, procurement, registration, and licensing.

A companion program to transaction reengineering is the citizen charter. Agencies can lessen information asymmetry by disclosing the streamlined procedures. The program requires specific government agencies to publish handbooks or guidebooks for the transacting public on how to access particular services. The program assumes that those who need them most are least informed of these services. Disseminating complete, accurate, timely, and reader-friendly information about what government goods and services are available, who is entitled to them, and from whom, when, where, and how they can be obtained, is very important in giving each citizen a fighting chance to access the services without paying grease money or having to deal with fixers.

Assessment of Vulnerability to Corruption

Every agency is vulnerable to corruption. Broad discretion, weak sanctions for corrupt behavior, cumbersome procedures, lack of service standards, poorly disseminated rules, weak checks and balances—all have the potential to induce mischief.

Assessment of vulnerability to corruption pinpoints the likely areas where corruption might occur. That suggests analysis of the agencies' supervision and control systems, policies and procedures, penalty systems, and high-risk transactions (especially those that heavily involve dealing in cash). The assessment also checks whether safeguards that can forestall wrongdoing are in place.

The corruption vulnerability index, a rough measure that ranks agencies on the basis of their susceptibility to misbehavior, can precede the assessment of vulnerability. That indicator can be the basis for selecting and targeting priority agencies. In turn, the assessment can determine what kind of intervention and strategy would work best to arrest corruption within agencies.

Open Public Documents

Corruption thrives when there is information asymmetry. Opening public documents aims to make available to the concerned public critical and frequently requested official documents. All public documents must be accessible to scrutiny by the citizenry. Through the power of information, the concerned public and the vigilant media can successfully expose mischief and help make public officials answerable for their actions.

Through the deft use of information and communication technology, important documents may be readily provided to the public. Those documents include agency annual reports, budget documents, financial statements, public accounts and auditing reports, court decisions, proceedings of public forums, laws, and ordinances.

Lifestyle Check

Lifestyle check is a character test for public officials: are they consistently upright in the way they perform their duties and earn their living? Lavish lifestyles seem irreconcilable with the modest ways in which public office—with its call to higher purposes—is served and conducted, and should invite scrutiny.

This program can check whether government officials' ways of living are compatible with their incomes. Any excessively high earnings might suggest corrupt behavior, such as the use of public office to cut questionable deals. Lifestyle checks would examine the officials' assets declaration and visible determinants of extravagance (such as luxurious properties) against their paychecks for any sign of inconsistencies.

Necessarily, this effort is anchored on freedom of information, and would require reasonable access to important data such as statements of assets and liabilities and income tax returns. To generate a list of public officials whose lifestyles need to be audited, the program would use state-of-the art database construction and maintenance.

Report Card Survey

The report card can tell whether an agency gets a passing mark for good service delivery. More important, it can expose possible corruption across different public services.

Here is how it works: first, the direct users of different public services in a locality are surveyed; second, the service providers are rated, based on aggregation of the survey findings; and third, the findings are made public to generate discussion between the agency and the users of its services. That process can prompt the rated agencies to respond positively to civic calls for improvement in services.

The report card survey can show whether citizens are pleased with the quality of service provided (for example, are health services reliable?) or the quality of problem-solving action by national or local agencies (for example, are complaints resolved quickly?). Report cards also provide estimates of hidden costs incurred by citizens (like bribes for building permits and licenses or for falsifying public documents).

Anticorruption Vanguards

If inert civil servants are the company it keeps, the anticorruption campaign will go the way of Sisyphus—a few steps forward and constant reversals—for it is the ubiquitous presence of active government workers, acting as lookouts, that can make the difference between success and failed attempts at continuous housecleaning.

Within the bureaucracy there are public personnel, whether career executive service officers (CESOs) or rank-and-file employees, who have had direct experience with government operations and transactions. They can be the internal reformers—sentries who patrol the bureaucracy and spot transgressions. They can be credible guardians of public goods and services. They need to become an organized force and to have a strong hand on civil service reforms, such as the promotion of meritocracy and enforcement of ethical standards.

This program is built on the idea of "an autonomous civic constituency that recognizes the value of reform and dedicates itself to monitoring and defending the reform strategy, including its leaders" (World Bank 2000a, p. 41). That constituency can serve as an effective damper on the abuse of power, but it will need training on corruption detection to sensitize and equip it.

High remuneration maintains integrity. High pay would certainly help civil servants resist the temptations of corruption. CESOs and government workers should be compensated appropriately and given such benefits as children's educational allowances, free medical service, and free staff headquarters (for the vanguards).

Public Ethics

There are fundamental values for which government institutions stand. These include ethical values such as integrity, honesty, public service, justice, transparency and accountability, and the rule of law. Those values face enormous challenges because of the spread of corruption. There is an urgent need to discover and understand the practical difficulties in realizing these values seen through the weaknesses of Philippine institutions.

The focus of the public ethics program is on interventions that strengthen the capacity of agencies to adopt the above values. It will identify regimes for their articulation and enforcement as well as incentives that would encourage government officials and employees to embrace these values. There are several ways in which the public ethics program can be carried out: *ethics management, ethics audit,* and *ethics maintenance.*

Ethics management guidance can be offered on the various ways of bringing sound ethical practices into a public agency's management processes and practices. This could involve drawing up the agency's code of conduct—anchored on the Code of Conduct and Ethical Standards for Public Officials and Employees—and connecting it to the agency's mission and organizational culture. The end goal is to institutionalize ethics into the way the agency conducts its business or delivers its services. *Ethics audit* research and inquiry can be conducted to assess whether the agency is "predisposed" to unethical practices. Its policies, rules, and regulations will be examined to uncover their strengths (those that can reinforce ethical regimes) and weaknesses (those that can lead to conflicts of interest and unlawful behavior). The objective of *ethics maintenance* is to make the ethical gains of the agency sustainable. The forms of assistance, which can be offered by anticorruption bodies, civil society organizations, and private firms, can include technical advice on how to sustain best practices and improve on them and monitoring of how effective the public ethics programs are.

Civil Society Watchdogs

A key plank of the people-centered anticorruption strategy is to empower civil society and ensure its participation in the campaign. It is only right for citizens to demand transparency and accountability in the use of public funds. This can be exemplified by NGOs acting as sentinels.

Civil society watchdogs can monitor critical and substantially funded government projects and agencies with frontline transactions. Here, civil society organizations are paired or matched with government agencies that are corruption prone and inefficient. As accredited organizations, civil society watchdogs are expected to expose irregularities, file cases against errant government personnel, and advocate integrity improvement in the agency being watched.

The Philippine Motor Association, for example, can be deputized to check possible irregularities in the Land Transportation Office's operations in the issuance of registrations, licenses, or certificates. Likewise, the Fellowship of Christians in Government can be accredited to sniff out bribery, under-assessments, and other shady practices in the Bureau of Internal Revenue. Procurement Watch Inc. must continue to observe and provide feedback on how honestly the procurement of public goods and services is being carried out in large agencies. It can also broker integrity pacts, which commit government procurement agencies and contractors of goods and services to bribery-free contracting. A credible civil society organization is needed to oversee that the pact is being followed by both parties. Bidders who violate their commitment will be subject to such penalties as disqualification, loss of contract, liability for damages, and forfeiture of bid security. The government agency, in turn, will commit itself to prevent price fixing and the acceptance of bribes by its officials and to follow transparent procurement rules.

Such quick-start programs can supply the impetus for the initial phase. Expansion and intensification of the program is the next phase. This follow-on stage will depend on how much of a headstart was achieved during the initial phase. This stage includes growth and further development of initial projects. An important action would be expansion of the campaign activity-wise and selectively beyond the national government. It must have an eye toward localizing initiatives and replicating the programs in other regions.

A deepening of the program—from reprieve to reform—is also called for at this juncture. Agencies undergoing reform should reap dividends in the form of incentives and rewards where they are due and appropriate. At this point a more refined incentive structure and stiffer sanctions should come into being. Meanwhile, reforms that could lead to pay decompression could be installed. Policy inadequacies should lead to more effective legislation. Nonlegislative actions include supporting capacity-building in such critical areas as forensic audit, case management, and prosecutorial diligence.

The final stage is institutionalizing structural improvements and sustainability programming. This is the hardest part because it means pushing the limits imposed by a fair governance environment. But gains in policy reforms, capability, and culture building, refinement of incentive systems, and localization can be consolidated and enhanced and can lead to a virtuous circle in which the benefits include a better governance structure.

Attaining high levels of efficiency in anticorruption operations is expected in this last phase, suggesting significant reductions in the levels and extent of corruption. Such progress would allow government to reap economic, political, and social dividends. When corruption is kept at a minimum, there would be more efficient and accountable use of public resources. A collateral program on social engineering would ensure public intolerance of corruption, vigilance of civil society, and good corporate governance.

Addressing Wider Governance Issues and Sustaining the Campaign

To sustain the anticorruption campaign means assembling a critical mass of mutually reinforcing reforms, using executive action and legislative sustenance as key planks. Islands of integrity cut off from each other will not work for long as they will be overwhelmed by corruption in other areas. The reforms must represent a mix of prevention and enforcement (but more on prevention), combined with substantial public involvement to strengthen the constituency for reform.

The critical mass will revolve around those policies and programs identified as having medium impact. To raise integrity in public service, good practice reforms in the civil service, financial management, and procurement must continue as should improvements in accounting and auditing. Decentralization would require more progress, especially in strengthening financial accountability at the local levels.

A long-term measure that ought to be adopted is restoring the police force to local government units. Decentralization would make it more responsive to local security and protection needs. A core of strong and independent police professionals would guarantee fair application of the rule of law. Furthermore, a rights-based approach to capacity-building in investigation, apprehension, and community relations would go a long way in restoring its credibility and evenhandedness in dealing with the public.

Complementary measures to build the capacity of the Supreme Court to administer the judiciary must be supported. Such measures include improving case adjudication and access to justice, enhancing the integrity infrastructure of the judiciary, supporting reform outreach activities, and sharing knowledge.

Congress also needs to enhance its capacity to legislate credible anticorruption laws (such as conflict of interest legislation and clear guidelines on campaign financing) and to exercise its oversight function more competently. Congress will be able to help in the government's anticorruption campaign by means of legislation (for example, fast-tracking the passage of the government auditing code, the government accounting act, the civil service code, and the procurement bill), conducting legislative oversight on a regular basis, and demonstrating transparency within congress, particularly in the management of its budget, pork-barrel fund, and campaign funds. Ridding the legislative branch of inappropriate practices would lend credibility to the efforts (World Bank 2000a).

Reforming campaign financing is a worthy but difficult cause. Giving government subsidy to political parties with workable platforms and making campaign contributions transparent by making these contributions tax deductible may do the trick. In recognition of the fact that political parties play a public interest role, public funding may be helpful. Political parties make an essential contribution to political contestability and the decentralized expression of diverse values and interests. Public funding reduces the opportunity for private interests to buy influence and can reinforce limits on spending because of public resistance to excessive public expenditure (World Bank 2000a). Because of the patronage nature of Philippine political culture, however, reforming campaign financing is a tough challenge.

Economic policy reform obviously must go on, especially in the area of deregulation and competitive restructuring of concentrated sectors. In the private sector, to reduce the sources of state capture, reforms that must be pursued include pushing forward stock exchange restructuring, strengthening antibribery actions and anti-money-laundering legislation, providing stiffer penalties for insider trading, and promoting good corporate citizenship. Greater citizen participation could be expected by enhancing public access to information and conducting periodic report card surveys. The development of a broad coalition consisting of professional societies, chambers of commerce, civil society organizations, and church groups to support the anticorruption strategy would be crucial. It is equally important to make civil organizations accountable.

Appendix 3.1. Evaluation of Anticorruption Policies and Programs in the Philippines

Anticorruption pillars of action	Recent efforts in the Philippines	Cost-benefit evaluation	Administrative and technical content	Extent of participation	Sustainability and duration	Overall evaluation of impact
Pillar 1: Developing effective and transparent systems for public service						
A. Public sector management						
1. Integrity in public service						
Public sector wage increases	Implementation of salary standardization	Low	Low	High	Medium	Low
Reduction of wage compression	At discussion level only	Medium	Low	High	Low	Medium
Anticorruption agencies	Reactivation of the Presidential Anti-Graft Commission in 2001; Strengthening of Presidential Committee on Effective Governance	Low	Medium	High	Medium	Medium
Meritocracy in civil service	Proposed revision of the Civil Service Code	Medium	Low	Medium	Medium	Medium
Ethics office	Norms and codes of conduct for public officials and employees; Values orientation workshop	Low	High	Low	Low	Low
2. Accountability and transparency of public service						
Financial accountability	Medium-Term Expenditure Framework; Organizational Performance Indicators Framework; Electronic procurement system; Procurement reform bill	High	Medium	Low	Medium	Medium

Efficient and client-friendly bureaucratic culture	Audit and accounting reforms					
	Reforms in revenue collection agencies					
	Signature reduction project	Medium	Medium	Low	Medium	Medium
	e-Commerce Act of 2000					
Decentralization	Local Government Code of 1991	Medium	Low	Low	High	Medium
	Report card surveys for local government units					
Reduction of public sector size/employment	Privatization of government corporations	Low	High	Low	Low	Low
	Reengineering bill					
	Abolition of ad hoc bodies					

B. Institutional restraints

1. Accountability and transparency in public service through effective legal framework

Rule of law	Anticorruption laws	High	Medium	Medium	Low	Medium
	Action Program for Judicial Reform					
	Reforming police agencies					
Judicial independence	Judicial reform	High	Medium	Low	Medium	Medium
	Supreme Court initiatives to strengthen lower courts and obtain fiscal autonomy					

2. Enhancing institutions for public scrutiny and oversight

Parliamentary oversight	Periodic budget hearings	Medium	Low	Low	Medium	Medium
	Congressional/senate investigation of graft and corruption cases					
Ombudsman	Capacity-building in the Office of the Ombudsman	High	Low	Medium	Low	Medium

(Appendix continues on the following page.)

Appendix 3.1. (continued)

Anticorruption pillars of action	Recent efforts in the Philippines	Cost-benefit evaluation	Administrative and technical content	Extent of participation	Sustainability and duration	Overall evaluation of impact
C. Political accountability						
1. Accountability and transparency in public service						
Transparency in party financing	Reform of COMELEC disclosure rules	High	Low	Low	Low	Low
	Proposals to reform campaign financing					
Political competition	Multiparty system	Medium	Medium	Low	Low	Low
Asset declaration and conflict of interest rules	Mandatory filing of statement of assets and liabilities for public officials	High	Medium	Low	Medium	Medium
	Divestment rules for top government officials					
D. Competitive private sector						
1. Simplification of the regulatory environment						
Economic policy reform	Continuing deregulation	High	Low	Medium	Medium	Medium
Competitive restructuring of monopolies	Restructuring of concentrated sectors	High	Low	High	Low	Medium
Pillar 2: Strengthening antibribery actions and promoting integrity in business operations						
1. Effective prevention, investigation, and prosecution of bribery						
Promotion of integrity in business and banking operations	Anti-Money-Laundering Act of 2001	High	Medium	Medium	Medium	Medium

2. Corporate responsibility and accountability

Corporate gover-nance reforms	Securities Regulation Code of 2000 Stock exchange restructuring Code of ethics	High	Medium	Medium	Medium	Medium	Medium

Pillar 3: Supporting active public involvement

1. Public discussion of corruption

Seminars to raise public awareness of corruption	Seminars and forums on corruption	Low	High	Low	Low	Low	Low
Public opinion surveys	Surveys on perceptions of corruption Report card surveys	Medium	High	Medium	High	High	Medium
Media independence and participation	Jurisprudence favoring free press Exposés by the Philippine Center for Investigative Journalism of alleged corrupt practices	Medium	Medium	Medium	High	High	Medium

2. Access to information

Public access to information	Right to information	Medium	Medium	Low	Medium	Medium

3. Public participation

Citizen participation	Procurement Watch Inc. Institute for Popular Democracy Concerned Citizens of Abra for Good Government Bantay Katarungan Transparency and Accountability Network	Medium	Medium	Low	Medium	Medium

Appendix 3.2. Philippine Government Anticorruption Bodies, as of 2001

Agency	Mandate

Office of the Ombudsman
  Legal Status: Constitutional
  Established: 1986
	Investigates and prosecutes; adjudicates administrative cases and takes criminal cases to court or to Sandiganbayan, depending on the rank of the government official charged).

Sandiganbayan
  Legal Status: Constitutional
  Established: 1986
	As the main antigraft court, adjudicates criminal cases brought to it by the Office of the Ombudsman; deals only with cases of high-ranking officials.

Commission on Audit
  Legal Status: Constitutional
  Established: 1986
	Conducts independent audits of government agencies and refers financial irregularities discovered in audits to the Office of the Ombudsman.

Civil Service Commission
  Legal Status: Constitutional
  Established: 1986
	Plays a preventive role by setting standards and norms for civil service appointments and a punitive role by meting out penalties and punishments for violations; oversees reforms in civil service.

Judiciary (headed by
the Supreme Court)
  Legal Status: Constitutional
  Established: 1901
	Adjudicates law in all areas.

Department of Justice
  Legal Status: Executive Branch
  Established: n.d.
	Serves as the primary criminal prosecuting arm of the government.

Presidential Commission on
Good Government
  Legal Status: Executive Order 1
  Established: February 1986
	Oversees recovery of ill-gotten wealth from the Marcos family.[20]

Securities and Exchange
Commission
  Legal basis: Commonwealth
  Act 83 or Securities Act
  Established: October 1936
	Oversees registration of securities, evaluation of financial condition and operations of applicants for security issue, and supervision of stocks and bonds brokers, as well as stock exchanges.

Commission on Elections
  Legal Status: Constitutional
  Established: 1986
	Promotes effective and efficient implementation of the objectives of ensuring the holding of free, orderly, honest, peaceful, and credible elections.

Department of Budget
and Management
  Legal basis: Executive Order
  292 (has the force of law)
  Established: 1936
	Oversees reforms in public expenditure management, streamlining the bureaucracy.

n.d. No date.

Appendix 3.3. Presidential Antigraft and Investigation Agencies Established since 1950

Agency	President	Period	Duration
Integrity Board	Elpidio Quirino	May 1950–November 1950	Six months
Presidential Complaints and Action Committee	Ramon Magsaysay	December 1955–July 1958	Four years, seven months
Presidential Committee on Administrative Performance and Efficiency	Carlos Garcia	July 1958–December 1961	Two years, five months
Presidential Anti-Graft Committee	Carlos Garcia	February 1960–December 1961	One year, one month
Presidential Anti-Graft Committee	Diosdado Macapagal	January 1962–January 1966	Four years
Presidential Agency on Reforms in Government Office	Ferdinand Marcos	January 1966–September 1966	Eight months
Presidential Complaints and Action Office	Ferdinand Marcos	September 1966–October 1967	One year
Presidential Agency on Reforms and Government Operations	Ferdinand Marcos	October 1967–February 1970	Two years, four months
Complaints and Investigation Office	Ferdinand Marcos	February 1970–February 1986	Sixteen years
Public Ethics and Accountability Task Force	Corazon Aquino	1986–1988	Almost two years
Presidential Commission Against Graft and Corruption	Fidel Ramos	February 1994–April 2001	More than six years
National Anti-Corruption Commission	Joseph Estrada	Created in July 2001	Not activated
Inter-Agency Anti-Graft Coordinating Council	Joseph Estrada	August 1999–present	More than two years
Presidential Anti-Graft Commission	Gloria Macapagal-Arroyo	April 2001–present	More than one year

Notes

1. In Southeast Asia, only the Philippines has a presidential form of government. Malaysia, Singapore, and Thailand have parliamentary systems. Indonesia has a semipresidential form.

2. EDSA I refers to the 1986 People Power revolution that ended the rule of President Ferdinand Marcos. EDSA II refers to the popular revolt in 2001 that ousted President Joseph Estrada.

3. The most notorious corruption case before Marcos's time involved the tobacco tycoon, Harry Stonehill. His bluebook of who received payoffs contained names of cabinet-level officials. He was hastily deported without court proceedings in 1963 as an undesirable alien guilty of economic sabotage.

4. Toward the latter part of Aquino's term there were allegations of the involvement of Aquino and Cojuangco relatives in corrupt deals—hence the label *Kamag-anak* ("relatives"), *Incorporated* (Coronel 1998).

5. From Asian Development Bank Key Indicators of Developing Asian and Pacific Countries, available at www.adb.org.

6. Through the Priority Development Assistance Fund (PDAF), each senator is entitled to PhP 200 million worth of projects every year from various departments and public works funds of the Department of Public Works and Highways. A congressman is entitled to PhP 65 million in PDAF (which was formerly called the Countryside Development Fund (Javellana 2002).

7. Firm ownership profiles also suggest substantial family holdings, which is not surprising because most of the firms in the Philippines started as family businesses and are still under the control of the founders or their offspring. In 1997 nonfinancial corporations owned 71.1 percent of the shares of an average publicly listed nonfinancial company held by the top five shareholders. Nonfinancial corporations also held majority ownership in four out of nine industrial sectors. Most of these nonfinancial corporations are holding companies owned by families (Saldaña 2001).

8. The Best World (BW) scandal rocked the Philippine stock market in 1999. From PhP 2 at the start of 1999, the price of BW stock shares reached a high of PhP 107 on October 11 of the same year. The average value of daily trades reached PhP 3.1 billion in 1999, compared with PhP 2.7 billion in 1996 when emerging markets like the Philippines were at their peak. At the height of the bubble, trading in BW shares accounted for as much as half of total market turnover. Within a week after it peaked the stock lost 60 percent of its value. By February 2000 it had dropped to PhP 3 per share. Investigations by the Philippine Stock Exchange and the Exchange Commission revealed a grand scheme of market manipulation involving several cronies of Estrada led by Dante Tan and a group of influential brokers (Pascual and Lim 2001).

9. The components of the summary rating of this measure of economic freedom are the following: size of government, structure of the economy and use of mar-

kets, monetary policy and price stability, freedom to use alternative currencies, legal structure and property rights, international exchange, and freedom of exchange in financial markets (Gwartney and Lawson 2001).

10. Percent satisfied minus percent dissatisfied.

11. The ADB-OECD Anti-Corruption Action Plan for Asia and the Pacific was prepared by a working party consisting of the Asian Development Bank, Japan, the Kyrgyz Republic, Malaysia, Nepal, the Organisation for Economic Co-operation and Development, the Pacific Economic Council, Pakistan, Papua New Guinea, the Philippines, the Republic of Korea, Singapore, Thailand, Transparency International, and Vietnam. It was adopted in Tokyo on November 30, 2001.

12. The nine key elements recommended by the World Bank for the national anticorruption program are (1) reducing opportunities for corruption through policy reforms and regulations, (2) reforming campaign financing, (3) increasing public oversight, (4) reforming budget processes, (5) improving meritocracy in civil service, (6) targeting selected departments and agencies, (7) enhancing sanctions against corruption, (8) developing partnerships with the private sector, and (9) supporting judicial reform.

13. The National Anti-Corruption Plan prepared by DAP adopted a three-pronged approach to fight corruption: prosecution, prevention, and promotion of intolerance on corruption. The plan features the Ten-Point Jump-start Program that includes (1) key appointments watch, (2) random lifestyle check, (3) fast-tracking of high-profile cases, (4) open public documents, (5) mandatory citizen charters, (6) reengineering of transactions in selected agencies, (7) report card surveys, (8) civil society watchdogs, (9) integrity pacts, and (10) anticorruption legislative agendas.

14. Among the national agencies, DOH is the most decentralized agency since the passage of the Local Government Code in 1991.

15. Based on World Bank 2000c, p. 109.

16. Associated with the Transparency and Accountability in Governance Project are the Social Weather Stations, Philippine Center for Investigative Journalism, Philippine Center for Policy Studies at the University of the Philippines, Makati Business Club, and the Asia Foundation. It is also support by the U.S. Agency for International Development.

17. The Philippines (along with Thailand) tops the list in the PCIJ survey on the public accessibility of government-held records (Chua 2001).

18. The 1987 Constitution restated clearly the right to information on matters of public concern. Article 3, Section 7 of the 1987 Constitution's Bill of Rights reads: "The right of the people to information on matters of public concern shall be recognized. Access to official records, and to documents, and papers pertaining to official acts, transactions, or decisions, as well as to government research data used as basis for policy development, shall be afforded the citizen, subject to limitations as may be provided by law." In addition, the Constitution (Article 2, Section 28) mandates that the State adopt and implement "a policy of full disclosure of all transactions involving public interest."

19. The Office of the Ombudsman has the power to investigate and prosecute on its own initiative or on the basis of complaints of mismanagement and corruption in government.
20. The PCGG is now responsible for a similar recovery effort with regard to Joseph Estrada.

References

The word "processed" describes informally produced works that may not be available commonly through libraries.

Azfar, Omar, Tugrul Gurgur, Satu Kahkonen, Anthony Lanyi, and Patrick Meagher. 2000. "Decentralization and Governance: An Empirical Investigation of Public Service Delivery in the Philippines." University of Maryland Center for Institutional Reform and the Informal Sector, College Park, Md.

Blair, Harry. 1996. "Supporting Democratic Local Governance: Lessons from International Donor Experience—Initial Concepts and Some Preliminary Findings." Paper presented at American Political Science Association Meetings, August 29–September 1, San Francisco.

Chua, Yvonne. 2001. "The Power of an Informed Citizenry." In *The Right to Know: Access to Information in Southeast Asia.* Quezon City, Philippines: Philippine Center for Investigative Journalism.

Claessens, Stijn, Simeon Djankov and Larry H.P. Lang. 1999. "Who Controls East Asian Corporations?" World Bank Working Paper 2054. Washington, D.C.

Coronel, Sheila, ed. 1998. *Pork and Other Perks.* Quezon City, Philippines: Philippine Center for Investigative Journalism.

De Dios, Emmanuel S., and Ricardo D. Ferrer. 2001. "Corruption in the Philippines: Framework and Context." *Public Policy* 5 (1): 1–42.

Djankov, Simeon, Rafael La Porta, Florencio Lopez-de-Silanes, and Andrei Shleifer. 2002. "The Regulation of Entry." *Quarterly Journal of Economics* 117 (1): 1–37.

Elliott, Kimberly Ann. 1997. "Corruption as an International Policy Problem: Overview and Recommendations." In Kimberly Ann Elliott, ed., *Corruption and the Global Economy.* Washington, D.C.: Institute for International Economics.

Gonzalez, Eduardo T. 2001. "The State as Regulator of Political Parties: A Study of Political Incentives and Constraints." Paper prepared for Friedrich Ebert Stiftung, Pasig City, Philippines.

Gonzalez, Eduardo T., and Magdalena L. Mendoza. 2002. "Governance in Southeast Asia: Issues and Options." Paper prepared for the Japan Bank for International Cooperation, Tokyo.

Gwartney, James, and Robert Lawson. 2001. *Economic Freedom of the World 2001 Annual Report.* Vancouver: Fraser Institute.

Hellman, Joel S., Geraint Jones, and Daniel Kaufmann. 2001. "'Seize the State, Seize the Day': State Capture, Corruption and Influence in Transition." World Bank Working Paper 2444. Washington, D.C.

Huther, Jeff, and Anwar Shah. 1998. "Applying a Simple Measure of Good Governance to the Debate on Fiscal Decentralization." World Bank Working Paper 1894. Washington, D.C.

————. 2000. "Anticorruption Policies and Programs: A Framework for Evaluation." World Bank Policy Research Working Paper 2501. Washington, D.C.

Initorio, Francis. 2001. "Policing the Judiciary." *Benchmark* 2 (3).

Javellana, Juliet L. 2002. "P21B of Budget Lost to Graft, Says Solon." *Philippine Daily Inquirer,* May 28. Available at http://www.inq7.net.

Kaufmann, Daniel, Aart Kraay, and Massimo Mastruzzi. 2003. "Governance Matters III: Governance Indicators for 1996–2002." World Bank Policy Research Working Paper 3106. Washington, D.C. Paper and data available at http://www.worldbank.org/wbi/governance/govdata2002/index.html

Mauro, Paolo. 1998. "The Effects of Corruption on Growth, Investment, and Government Expenditure." International Monetary Fund Working Paper 96/98. Washington, D.C.

Mendoza, Amado M., Jr. 2001. "The Industrial Anatomy of Corruption: Government Procurement, Bidding, and Award of Contracts." *Public Policy* 5 (1): 43–71.

Mendoza, Magdalena L. 2001. "The Crisis of Management Culture in the Philippines: Neither East Asian nor Western." Governance and Development Discussion Paper. Development Academy of the Philippines, Pasig City, Philippines.

North, Douglass. 1990. *Institutions, Institutional Change and Economic Performance*. Cambridge, U.K.: Cambridge University Press.

Office of the Ombudsman. 1997. *Annual Report*. Manila, Philippines.

Office of the Ombudsman, Manila. 2001. *Ombudsman's Journal* 6 (1): 14.

Pascual, Clarence, and Joseph Lim. 2001. "Corruption and Weak Markets: The BW Resources Stock Market Scam." *Public Policy* 5 (1): 109–29.

"Philippine Corruption Rating Improves Slightly." 2002. *Philippine Daily Inquirer*, March 10. Available at http://www.inq7.net.

Rocamora, Joel. 1998. "Introduction: Corruption in the Philippines, A Beginner's Guide." In Sheila Coronel, ed., *Pork and Other Perks*. Quezon City, Philippines: Philippine Center for Investigative Journalism.

Rose-Ackerman, Susan. 1999. *Corruption and Government: Causes, Consequences, and Reform*. Cambridge, U.K.: Cambridge University Press.

Saldaña, Cesar. 2001. "The Philippines." In Juzhong Zhuang, David Edwards, and Virginia Capulong, eds., *Corporate Governance and Finance in East Asia*. Manila: Asian Development Bank.

"The Short Arm of the Law." 2002. *The Economist*, March 2. Available at www.economist.com.

SWS (Social Weather Stations). Various years. National Surveys. Quezon City, Philippines.

Talisayon, Serafin. n.d. *Relevance*. Quezon City: University of the Philippines.

Virtucio, Marie Antoinette G., and Melchor P. Lalunio. 2001. "Tender Mercies: Contracts, Concessions and Privatization." *Public Policy* 5 (1): 73–107.

World Bank. 1997. *World Development Report 1997: The State in a Changing World.* Washington, D.C.

———. 2000a. *Anticorruption in Transition: A Contribution to the Policy Debate.* Washington, D.C.

———. 2000b. *Combating Corruption in the Philippines.* Pasig City, Philippines: World Bank Philippine Country Management Unit, East Asia and Pacific Region.

———. 2000c. "Philippines—Growth with Equity: The Remaining Agenda." A World Bank Social and Structural Review. Washington, D.C.

———. 2001. "Philippines: Progress Report on Public Sector Reform." Washington, D.C. Processed.

———. 2002. "Philippines Development Policy Review: An Opportunity for Renewed Poverty Reduction." Report 23629-PH. Poverty Reduction and Economic Management Sector Unit, East Asia and Pacific Regional Office. Washington, D.C.

4

State Capture under Good Governance: The Challenge of the Republic of Korea's Experience

Corruption is a widespread phenomenon that undermines good governance, erodes the rule of law, hampers economic growth and efforts for poverty reduction, and distorts competitive conditions in business transactions. The case of the Republic of Korea is not an exception. Corruption in Korea has remained one of the primary obstacles to socioeconomic development and Koreans want more effective and decisive government measures against corruption than ever before. In response to the people's strong clamor for a clean and transparent society the government began setting up comprehensive anticorruption policies and programs in August 1999.[1] But the story, of course, does not begin there.

Korea achieved the "miracle" on the Han River out of the rubble of war in a short span of 40 years. The authoritarian state planned and managed this condensed development, and in the process it took total control of resource allocation. But there was a tradeoff. The state control of the market led to collusion between those with political power and the economic elite. To make things worse, the past governments—lacking political legitimacy and popular support—relied on illicit funds and docile bureaucrats to stay in power. Rampant state capture and bureaucratic corruption were the inevitable results.

Those circumstances explain why previous anticorruption policies and programs were ineffectual. There were periodic all-out campaigns, especially when the regimes changed hands. Purging of wrongdoers in the government and business was more of a ritual than anything of substance. Although unethical conduct was attributable largely to structural

This case study was contributed by Jhungsoo Park, professor at the University of Seoul and research director of the Seoul Institute for Transparency.

causes within the system, the government tended to focus on individual irregularities, turning a blind eye to the system and mechanisms themselves. A wholesale surgery of the system was in need, which in turn called for a change in circumstances and leadership of the government. The preconditions for such change presented themselves as the growth-oriented, state-managed structure proved incapable of adjusting to the needs of the changing times and collapsed in the face of the globalizing world economy.

In the wake of the 1997 foreign currency crisis, President Kim Dae-jung's government came into office. The new regime perceived the corruption issue not only as a sociopolitical problem but also as a top-priority task that needed completion if the nation were to overcome the impending crisis and to sustain economic progress. Despite the wake-up call from the crisis, however, the state capture problem clearly remains serious in Korea.[2] Some of the newly formed information technology companies, which suffered most from the economic downturn and have since been resurrected, are now found to have been involved in corruption with political powerbrokers. Although significant changes are taking place in Korea, the ascendancy of collusion and illicit networks over technology and productivity has never been stronger (TI 2001).

This case study seeks to explain the current patterns of corruption in the country and their historical origins, and offers an analysis of the governance conditions and anticorruption institutions that are presently in place in the country. It is very interesting as a case study because it exemplifies an advanced industrial country, a member of the Organisation for Economic Co-operation and Development (OECD), that is grappling with issues of state capture that more commonly afflict less developed countries. It underscores the fact that corruption is an acute problem of governance and cuts across all kinds of governance and operating environments. At the same time it presents a different kind of challenge for anticorruption policy, precisely because its governance conditions are different from others.

The Burden of History

For a thorough diagnosis of the conditions of national anticorruption policies and programs in Korea we need to use the lens of Korean culture and history.

Philosophically, Confucianism helped to justify the existence of a centralized, benevolent monarchy as a legitimate form of moral government. Historical and cultural tendencies to centralization were intensified by the homogeneous characteristics of the Korean people. Another explanation for the existence of strong centralization has been the need for economic rationality and administrative efficiency. The need for centralization has also been emphasized because of overriding national security and economic development goals. In fact, the constant threat from the Democratic People's Republic of Korea seemed to many people a reasonable argument for dictatorship.[3]

During the Chosun Dynasty (1392–1910) strong centripetal tendencies were developed and maintained. Among the factors that enabled the dynasty to survive was the relative ethnic, philosophical, linguistic, and cultural homogeneity of the country. Authoritarianism and loyalty to the king were supported philosophically by Confucianism. The *Sonbi spirit*— the idea of disciplining oneself before presuming to govern others—mandated that leaders must set an example of integrity and principles for ordinary people to follow. Collective thinking at the levels of family, business, and nation also prized responsibility and sacrifice. In that regard the Chosun Dynasty depended heavily on the ethics of the individual rather than on its governance of the state.

From 1910 to 1945 the Korean peninsula was colonized by Imperial Japan. In that period the administrative system served primarily to suppress political rights and to combat the independence movement. Thus the political system was even more centralized and authoritarian. After the Allied Powers defeated the Japanese in 1945 Korea was finally liberated. Three years later following a period of U.S. and Soviet rule, the Republic of Korea was founded on August 15, 1948. In 1950, however, ideological conflict caused war to break out between the democracy-oriented south of Korea and the Communist-controlled north of Korea. Relative calm returned only after a ceasefire was arranged in July 1953.

During the first half of the 20th century there was little awareness of the dangers of corruption and correspondingly few efforts to deal with it. But after the founding of the Republic of Korea certain patterns of corruption appeared. The new government had taken over from the Japanese the management of public properties. The government also assumed control of finance and economic matters. Government intervention in the market became extensive, especially in the financial arena. Substantial economic rent was created and allocated by the central government in the course of the country's economic development. It was in this environment that "cozy relations between politics and economics" developed between the government and newly rising business tycoons (Park 2001, p. 31).

The historical and sociocultural legacy brought about by technocratic and economic necessity, and the vested interests of economic, bureaucratic, and political forces, converged to help undermine ethical and trustworthy government. Popular dissatisfaction emerged not only because resources were allocated lopsidedly to industrial regions and privileged groups, but also because citizens were given little voice in the policymaking process. The Park Chung-hee government, which took power in 1972 through a military coup, focused on obtaining political legitimacy. Nevertheless the government was seemingly more aware of the perils of corruption than previous governments had been. Then-President Park declared poverty, corruption, and communism to be the three enemies of the people that must be fought for the sake of national restoration.

The rhetoric, however, did not match reality. The government continued its opaque control of state financial organizations, including interest rates and distribution of loans, budgets, and personnel management. In the process, large-scale corruption in the financial system spread. Close relationships between public officials and business groups underpinned a structure of corruption that became absolute necessities for sustaining political power, commercial success, and illegal profiteering among individuals in the public service.

The long dictatorship of the Park government ended when the president was assassinated in 1979 and a new military figure took over to form the Fifth Republic. But the succeeding government paid secondary attention to corruption and focused primarily on stabilizing its political power. Many questioned whether its "Social Purification Campaign" was truly intended to deal with corruption.

The people's accumulated dissatisfaction may have found its outlet in the Kwangju Uprising of 1980, which was considered a watershed of national disintegration and which caused many Koreans to ask serious questions about the future development of the nation. Since then, "people's power" has obtained broader participation by citizens in the policymaking process, advanced democratization of the political system, and accommodated popular clamor for more transparent administration. An important landmark in this regard came in 1992 when a civilian, Kim Young-sam, was at last elected president and democracy settled in. The approval rating of the new government was more than 90 percent in the early stages. Under the slogan "Creating a New Korea," the government proclaimed three major national tasks: eradicating corruption, activating the economy, and establishing national discipline. In this period the new president's determination to get rid of corruption was clearly strong. After his assumption into office, reforms of laws and institutions were made and sweeping assessment activities were carried out. This period saw the first attempt of the state to carry out comprehensive and systematic efforts to reduce and prevent corruption.

When the opposition party won the presidential election in 1997, it marked a turning point in the country's progress toward becoming a viable democracy. For the first time, a change of presidential power was effected through popular elections. The new government pushed for an integrated election campaign law and passed political funding legislation to ensure fair, transparent, and low-cost elections. It also embarked on the daunting task of overcoming the national economic crisis of 1997. Judging that a fundamental cause of the crisis was widespread corruption in society and collusion among the public officials and the *chaebols* (the so-called giant corporate groups and trusts), the government under President Kim declared a "war on corruption."

As shown in Figure 4.1, Korea was evaluated as a partly free country in 1973 and in the latter half of the 1980s it was categorized in the fourth- to sixth-grade group as a dictatorship and military regime. However, from 1988 Korea was considered already a free country and evaluated as one to two-and-a-half grades and then getting better and better after the 1992 elections. This index by Freedom House measures the degree of democracy, where the lower number means the greater the political freedom. According to Rose-Ackerman (1996), a hallmark of modern democratic society is a formal separation between state and the rest of society. Democracy and the free market are not invariably a cure for corruption. The complex organizational structure of democratic legislatures and the formal separation of powers increase the costs of bribery and may deter all but the most valuable corrupt deals.[4]

According to assessments of governance quality, Korea has been ranked as demonstrating good governance. In one index combining measures of citizen participation, government operation, social development,

Figure 4.1. Trend of Freedom in Korea, Selected Years, 1973–97

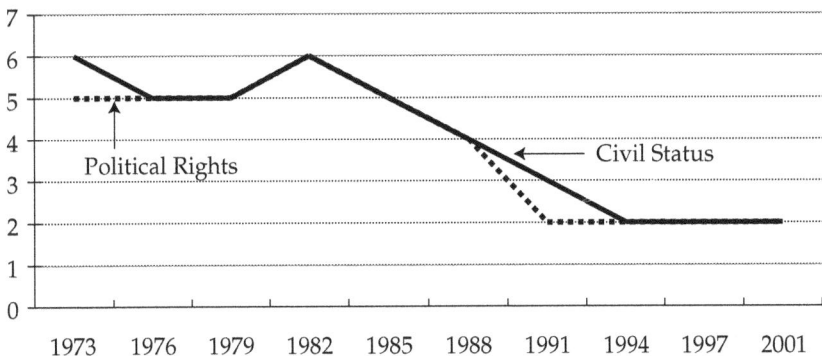

Source: Freedom House 2002.

and economic management, Korea placed 21st among 80 countries in the world and is characterized as having "good" governance (see Huther and Shah 1998). It is a ranking reflective of the relatively strong institutionalization of government practices, but this characterization of "good" governance masked continuing "bad" practices, specifically corruption.

2001: A Year of Corruption Scandals

A series of exposés about corruption was prominent throughout 2001, making front-page headlines practically every day. The government responded with various probes, but its investigations failed to clear clouds of suspicion surrounding the scandals, some of which worsened with close scrutiny. The country's system for investigating and prosecuting allegations of corruption went through tremendous stress.

During the course of the year allegations of complicity of senior prosecutors in the Lee Yong-Ho financial scandal marred the reputation of the prosecution. Public criticism also grew over its failure to fully investigate corruption cases involving intelligence officials. Three senior prosecutors were subsequently relieved of their posts. Another senior prosecutor resigned after remarking that the prosecution was subordinate to the ruling elite, thus casting doubt on the integrity of the prosecutor-general's office. The prosecution's image reached a nadir when Prosecutor-General Shin Seung-nam faced impeachment before parliament for his alleged attempt to cover up the Lee scandal and his refusal to testify before the National Assembly.

Previously the prosecutor-general's office had pledged that whenever it faced a difficult situation it would be a fair and just executor of law and order. But, as many prosecutors realize, the public thinks they have failed to make good on their promises. Many believe that establishing an independent counsel office on a permanent basis may be unavoidable if the prosecution's neutrality is not ensured through fair and independent personnel management. A series of precedents in this regard were already being established. Independent counsels were appointed as early as 1999 to look into two separate scandals—the so-called fur-gate or dress-for-lobbying scandal involving the wives of high-ranking government officials and a jailed business tycoon, and the labor strike–rigging scandal at a state-run minting corporation.

To the prosecution's further disappointment, the ruling party accepted the opposition's demand that the National Assembly appoint an independent counsel to reopen the probe of jailed businessman Lee Yong-ho. The National Assembly set a fixed term for the investigation, and that limited time was the biggest obstacle to the probe on "Lee Yong-ho Gate."

The team of investigators led by special prosecutor Cha Jong-il wrapped up its 105-day inquiry with the announcement of its findings. According to Jong-il's report, Kim Sung-hwan, a close friend of Kim Hong-up (the second son of President Kim Dae-jung) received 9 billion won (US$6.9 million) from some businessmen via six bank accounts established under borrowed names. Kim Sung-hwan is suspected of having acted as a lobbyist for Lee Yong-ho, the jailed head of G&G Group. Some of the money was also found to have been funneled to the Kim Dae-jung Peace Foundation, at which the junior Kim is the number-two official.

But Cha's team couldn't delve further into the allegations because its mandate ran out. It handed over the voluminous records of its probe to the prosecutor, who had previously labeled the scandal a simple financial crime by a failed businessman. Despite skepticism in the early stages, the 47-member team has gained prominence for its accomplishments during the relatively short period. Only a month after launching the probe, the investigation team arrested Shin Seung-hwan, younger brother of former Prosecutor-General Shin Seung-nam, for receiving 66 million won (US$50,000) from Lee Yong-ho. Earlier, the younger Shin was exonerated by the Supreme Public Prosecutor's Office, but that event, which led to the dishonorable resignation of the chief prosecutor, was a precursor of a whirlwind of arrests. Cha's team prosecuted Lee Hyong-taek (a nephew-in-law of President Kim), Kim Bong-ho (an ex–ruling party lawmaker who was in charge of the party's fundraising), and Lee Su-dong. It indicted 12 people in connection with the wide web of lobbying activities by Lee Yong-ho (Lee Chi-dong 2002). In addition, prosecutors have started investigations into three senior former or incumbent government officials who are accused of corruption by the newly founded presidential anti-corruption panel. The Korean Independent Commission Against Corruption (KICAC) filed complaints against one current minister-level official, one former prosecutor-general, and one vice minister–level prosecutor with the Supreme Public Prosecutor's Office, on charges of offering or receiving bribes.

The latest work of the KICAC is seen as heralding an era of active whistleblowing that reaches the higher echelons of government. In particular the commission has the power to formally refer senior officials at or above the vice ministerial level directly to the prosecutors for investigation. One thousand cases were reported between January 25 and April 30, 2002 (KICAC 2002). However, the commission's referral to the prosecutor is not necessarily a simple matter because there are internal difficulties within the prosecutor's office itself. Internal corruption is a problem and has been hard to purge because it means that officials have to conduct investigations in their own ranks.

Corruption Conditions in Korea

In March 2002 Moody's Investor Service raised Korea's sovereign rating by two notches and acknowledged that the Korean economy had at long last climbed out of its abyss and was now nearing pre–Asian crisis levels. For many, the nation's economy certainly deserved a better appraisal than the previous level of Baa2, a rating that indicated potential difficulty in meeting its debt obligations in the long term despite its ability to service debt in the short term. The ratings upgrade reflects the resilience of the nation's economy and the comeback it has made in a short period. The nation had indeed made a remarkable recovery, with its foreign exchange reserves kept well above the US$100 billion mark—a complete change from the days when its coffers were nearly depleted at the outset of the 1997–98 foreign currency crisis.

With 2002's growth well over 6 percent, the Korean economy has come a long way under President Kim's leadership. But his administration has much to do to help the nation recover the Standard and Poor's A1 rating it enjoyed before the currency crisis. The administration recognizes the need to fortify the financial system continuously and to restrain *chaebols* from reverting to their past habits of borrowing and spending for expansion and collusion with political power groups.[5]

Several surveys have been conducted to shed light on the problem of corruption in Korea. A recent series of polls focused on the perceptions and experiences of corruption among citizens and government officials. The Office of the Prime Minister commissioned these polls as part of a research project on anticorruption evaluation and strategy, with funding from the World Bank. Again in November 2001 there was a general survey about the corruption led by the Presidential Commission on Anticorruption.

Among the findings of these surveys were the following:[6]

- Politicians were seen as more corrupt than bureaucrats, as 43 percent of respondents concurred with a statement to that effect and only 20 percent agreed with an opposite statement.
- Most Koreans perceived that the level of corruption in Korea is seriously high. Thirty-seven percent of respondents perceived the problem of corruption to be very serious and 34.6 percent saw it as serious. In sum, 71.6 percent of the public worried about the corruption in Korean society.
- There was relatively little public awareness about anticorruption initiatives. Only 34 percent registered awareness; 66 percent did not. Among public officials, 59 percent said they knew about anticorruption efforts, 18 percent said they did not, 15 percent replied that they were not sure, and 8 percent said they had no idea.

- Citizens ranked corruption in the public sector as the fourth most serious national problem, just below economic stability, north-south relations, and regional nepotism.[7]
- The results also showed that 62 percent said the government's reforms of areas prone to corruption had helped to get rid of the problem, whereas 33 percent replied they were not much help, and 5 percent had no opinion.
- With regard to prioritizing and sequencing of policies, the respondents considered the following three policy areas to be most important: nationwide anticorruption movement (30 percent), monitoring by citizens and enlargement of participation (24 percent), and severe punishment and strengthening of investigation activity of prosecutors and police (16 percent).
- The public sector was perceived to be more corrupt (74.2 percent) than the private sector (25.8 percent).
- Eighty percent of the officials surveyed thought there had been some improvement in the fight against corruption; only 2 percent replied that there had been no improvement. In addition, 81 percent of polled officials positively evaluated their organizational head's commitment to prevent corruption; only 3 percent gave negative evaluations.

Since the inception of President Kim Dae-jung's administration, the number of reported irregularities committed by public officials has actually increased as a result of high-intensity surveillance and investigations. But the fact that the number of corrupt officials has been decreasing since 1999 could be evidence that a cleaner atmosphere is gradually emerging at government offices. As shown in figure 4.2, the number of officials punished for corruption stood at 7,420 in 1998, but that number decreased to 7,086 in 1999 and to 5,091 in 2000. Of course that statistic may be misleading. The drop in conviction rates may not mean lesser corruption but poorer prosecution. However, the number of complaints also dropped sharply to 1,185 in 1998, to 1,030 in 1999, and then to 682 cases in 2000 (Office of the Prime Minister 2001, p. 5).

In terms of international perceptions of corruption as identified by Transparency International (TI), the conditions in Korea in 2001 remained relatively problematic (see figure 4.3). Using TI's Corruption Perceptions Index (a number from 0 to 10 where the score of 0 indicates most corrupt and 10 indicates least corrupt), Korea's score has been stagnant in recent years. From 5.02 in 1996, it dropped to 3.8 in 1999. In 2001 it rose to 4.2, a slight increase that put the country 42nd among 91 countries included in the TI survey (TI 2002, p. 5).[8]

In recent years TI has also developed a Bribe Payers Index (BPI) to highlight the bribe-giving side of the corruption coin. In the 2002 BPI (see

Figure 4.2. Trend in Corruption Convictions in Korea, 1997–2000

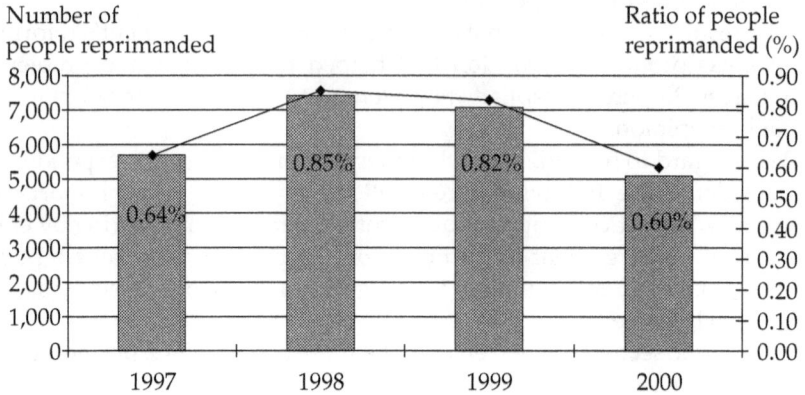

Source: Office of the Prime Minister 2001.

Figure 4.3. Transparency International Corruption Perceptions Index, Korea Scores, Selected Years, 1980–2002

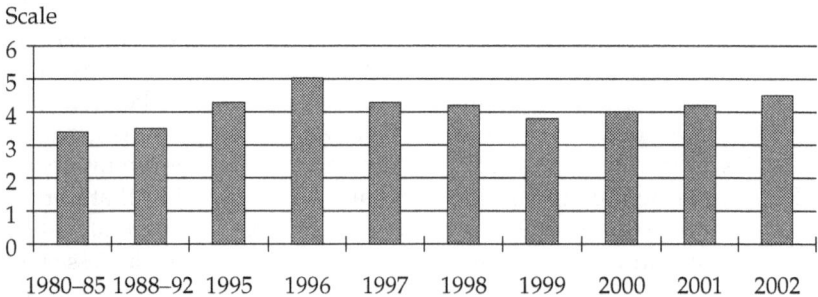

Source: Transparency International, available at www.transparency.org.

table 4.1), Korea placed 18th among 21 countries surveyed. Although the set of countries surveyed was selective, the low ranking of Korea relative to the other countries was telling. It reflected the "too-close-for-comfort" government–business relationships and the customary practices that treat graft and bribery as a necessary means to getting things done.[9]

Another perspective on the conditions of corruption in the country was given by the aggregate assessments of governance indicators developed by Daniel Kaufman, Aart Kraay, and Pablo Zoido-Lobatón (2002).

Table 4.1. Transparency International Bribe Payers Index, 2002

Rank	Economy	Score	Rank	Economy	Score
1	Australia	8.5	12	France	5.5
2	Sweden	8.4	13	Japan	5.3
2	Switzerland	8.4	13	United States	5.3
4	Austria	8.2	15	Hong Kong, China	4.3
5	Canada	8.1	15	Malaysia	4.3
6	Belgium	7.8	17	Italy	4.1
6	Netherlands	7.8	18	**Korea, Rep. of**	**3.9**
8	United Kingdom	6.9	19	Taiwan, China	3.8
9	Germany	6.3	20	China	3.5
9	Singapore	6.3	21	Russia	3.2
11	Spain	5.8			

Source: Transparency International, available at www.transparency.org.

Using six dimensions of governance for 175 countries, they defined governance as the traditions and institutions by which authority in a country is exercised. Among the six aggregate indicators was control of corruption.[10] In their ranking Korea placed 17th among 19 countries surveyed (using the same set of countries as the BPI used) (see table 4.2) and 49th when all 175 countries were taken into consideration. Considering that governance indicators were oriented so that higher values corresponded to better outcomes, on a scale from –2.5 to 2.5, the estimated point of 0.37 implied a low ranking of Korea relative to the other countries. It is reflective of the presence of corruption in terms of both the frequency of additional payments to get things done and the effects of corruption on the business environment and grand corruption in the political arena.

Explaining Corruption in Korea

Corruption occurs because the people involved in the transaction calculate that the benefits to corrupt behavior outweigh the risks. Some scholars have actually tried to explain this calculation more specifically—that is, that corruption may be considered a function of four factors, namely, the number of opportunities for corruption, the size of the benefits from corruption, the magnitude of the penalties involved, and the risks of the penalty being applied (see Huther and Shah 2000). In short, corruption persists because it often rewards and rarely punishes the corrupt.

In this regard, if corruption is a matter of costs and benefits among the parties involved, then it stands to reason that controlling it requires dealing with the sources of those costs and benefits. Thus it could be argued

Table 4.2. Estimates of Governance (Control of Corruption), FY 2000/01

Rank	Economy	Score	Rank	Economy	Score
1	Sweden	2.21	11	Germany	1.38
2	Singapore	2.13	12	Japan	1.20
3	Netherlands	2.09	13	France	1.15
4	Canada	2.05	14	Belgium	1.05
5	Switzerland	1.91	15	Italy	0.63
6	United Kingdom	1.86	16	Taiwan, China	0.53
7	Australia	1.75	17	**Korea, Rep. of**	**0.37**
8	Austria	1.56	18	Malaysia	0.13
9	Spain	1.45	19	China	–0.30
9	United States	1.45			

Source: Kaufmann, Kraay, and Zoido-Lobatón 2002.

that counter-corruption measures should try to lower the number of opportunities for corruption, reduce the possible benefits from corruptible transactions, and increase the penalties and the risks of actually being penalized (see Bhargava and Bolongaita 2001).

A major part of the reason that corruption pervaded Korea was the explosive growth of its economy steered by the state in conjunction with big business groups that had vested interests. The economy had grown very rapidly during the 40 years preceding the recent East Asia financial crisis. From 1962 to 1996 Korea's economy grew at an average annual rate of about 8 percent in real terms (SaKong 1993, p. 1). Few countries in the world can match this record. Explaining the spread of corruption by economic growth goes against some of the established facts in the economics of corruption, such as those cited in Mauro (1997). As explained below, however, it is more the result of certain aspects of the development (regulations and protectionism) that encourage rent-seeking behavior and corruption.

In the process of pursuing government-led economic development policies in the past, corruption began to mount as a result of excessive regulation governing the issuance of permits, licenses, and the like. Political corruption became an accepted practice as politicians solicited political campaign funds from large conglomerates in exchange for offers of privileged business opportunities. A variety of sociocultural factors also contributed to the spread of corruption throughout society, including authoritarianism, factionalism, and favoritism stemming from personal connections or various personal ties.

That rapid economic growth was made possible by an economic system of regulated capitalism under which the government either directly participates in or indirectly renders guidance to industries and enterprises. Its intervention in the market, especially in the financial arena, was extensive. Consequently, the regulatory environment became fertile ground for corruption where shady opportunities abounded, illicit benefits grew, and risks were low. A business sector prone to corruption, therefore, may be seen as the product of the coalition between the state and the *chaebols*. Thus the role of *chaebols* in the Korean economy has a double-faced image. Positively, they devoted themselves to the rapid rise of the economy by driving exports. Negatively, they contributed to making the economy extremely centralized and highly dependent on bureaucratic decisions, which detered the stability and fair distribution of benefits (Park 1992).

To be sure, the state of corruption in the country has not been static. It may be said to have improved and worsened at certain periods. Part of the explanation for the improvement may be the increase in the country's economic freedom, which in theory would reduce the opportunities for corruption. James Gwartney and Robert Lawson (2001) defined "economic freedom" in terms of size of government, structure of economy and use of markets, monetary policy and price stability, freedom to use alternative currencies, legal structure and property rights, international exchange, and freedom of exchange in financial markets.[11] They argued that greater economic freedom correlates with, if not causes, lower levels of corruption. In that regard it might be pointed out that Korea's ratings of economic freedom (where 1 is least freedom and 10 is most) rose from 5.8 in 1985 to 7.1 in 1999, as shown in figure 4.4.

Figure 4.4. Summary Ratings of Economic Freedom, Korea Scores, Selected Years, 1970–99

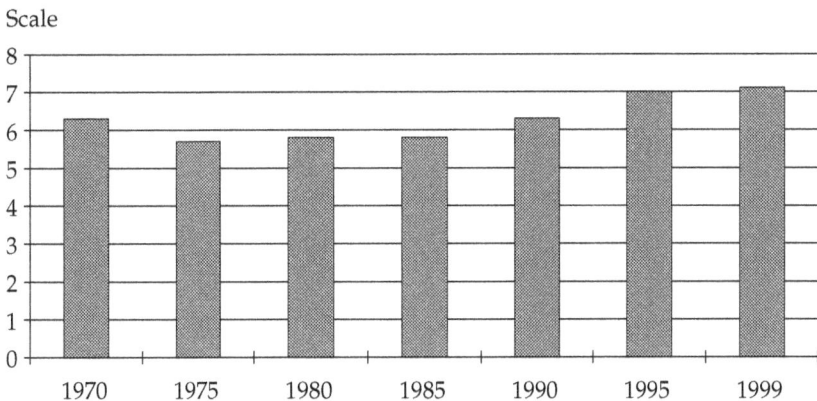

Source: Gwartney and Lawson 2001, available at www.fraserinstitute.ca/publications/books/efw_2001.

In sum, the causes of corruption in Korea could be summarized as a result of dilapidated systems with insufficient risks and abundant gains for corruption, opaque administrative process, sociocultural customs, and unclear ethical determination. Collusion among businesspeople, politicians, and bureaucrats is routinely an accepted practice. The government-led economic development has created too many unrealistic rules and unnecessary regulations, and their administrative procedures contain numerous ambiguous standards. And the mindset of public officials often overlooks the code of ethics amid a blurring of official and personal distinctions.

Anticorruption Policies and Programs

In recent years there has been an increase in the rules and regulations to fight corruption. A system to register and publicly disclose property held by government officials and the enactment of the law to return illegally gained profits were established in 1993 to prevent public officials from accumulating property through illegal means. A real-name financial system, which makes pseudonyms on bank accounts illegal, was set up in 1994 to help expose irregular political funds, bribery, and other secret funds related to parliament and political parties.

The Administrative Procedures Act, the Act on Disclosure of Information by Public Agencies, and the Framework Act on Administrative Regulations also guarantee access to information. These laws aim to block corruption by institutionalizing transparent and open administration through proper procedures and by abolishing unnecessary administrative regulations.

In addition, the Residents' Request for Inspection System was adopted in 1999 for monitoring and participation by civil society in local government. The Online Procedures Enhancement for Civil Applications (OPEN) system has also been created as a major anticorruption initiative in the administrative, public service, and local government sectors. Under the OPEN system the whole process of civil affairs administration, from acceptance to the final processing, is made public on the Internet using information technology. OPEN has attracted considerable attention at home and abroad since its introduction in April 1999. Actually, two-thirds of citizens who participated in the survey performed in 2001 expressed the belief that the OPEN system was beneficial to the citizenry as well as to the government (see Park, Kim, and Lee 2001).

Integrity Pacts have also been formed as a corruption-prevention device in public procurement. The Integrity Pact of Seoul Metropolitan Government is an agreement between the administrative body and companies submitting bids that bribes will neither be offered nor accepted in relation to bids for any public contracts. A sanction of up to a two-year ban in public bidding will apply if there is any violation of the pact. Although the Integrity Pact system, promoted by TI, is viewed with great skepticism by most other experts, the case of Seoul shows some positive effects (see TI 2000a and Holzer and Kim 2002).

Furthermore, research on various corruption indicators has provided standards for government anticorruption strategy and campaigns by evaluating corruption and its countermeasures. Finally, the country's participation in the OECD Bribery Prevention Agreement and enactment of related laws, the Money-Laundering Prevention Act, and the introduction of the special prosecutor system were also undertaken to fight corruption.

In 1999 a large number of specialists from universities and citizen groups participated in a series of in-depth discussions to develop ways to eradicate corruption. Various opinions and suggested approaches emerged from the process. On the basis of a consensus, a set of first-phase comprehensive measures was developed by the prime minister's office, with support from the World Bank, and was adopted to fight corruption. Some of those measures called for improving detection systems, reforming administrative units that were prone to corruption (such as tax administration, police, housing, construction, and environment and sanitation), and establishing a nationwide public service campaign against corruption.[12]

In 2000 the Korean government, with continuing support from the World Bank, adopted a set of second-phase comprehensive measures.[13] Those steps aimed to address corruption-prone areas that had not been tackled previously, namely schools, procurement procedures, government expenditures, and information access.

Perhaps partly as a result of the increased attention to the problem and the series of reform initiatives undertaken by national and local governments, perceptions about the level of corruption have been improved recently. According to a citizens' survey conducted by Hyundai Research, the number of people who see corruption as a serious problem has declined: in 1999, 91 percent of respondents considered corruption to be a serious issue, but in 2000 that figure fell to 75 percent (Office of the Prime Minister 2001). Several international organizations, including the World Bank and the OECD, have also remarked on the relative success of the Korean Government's corruption-fighting efforts (Kang 2001, Shelton-Colby 2001).

Korea's anticorruption strategy could thus be described as composed of four elements, namely, building an anticorruption infrastructure, implementing administrative and institutional reform, promoting public awareness against corruption, and strengthening detection and punishment. In addition, since 2000 the second-phase measures have been

implemented and they now include new transparent procurement procedures, a clean education system, reform of local governments, government expenditure reviews, new social welfare facilities, improvement in
small and medium-size industries that receive government subsidies,
and expansion of the public's access to information (see table 4.3).[14]

According to the Anti-Corruption Action Plan for Asia and the Pacific
developed by the Asian Development Bank and the OECD and endorsed
by 17 countries in the region, three pillars of action have been recommended.[15] The plan acknowledged that fighting corruption is a complex
undertaking and requires the involvement of all elements of society—
government, the business sector, and civil society need to develop "core
competence" in promoting integrity and fighting against corruption.

Analyzing the three pillars in the plan in the Korean context, we find
that reforms in public sector programs are already in place. Public discussions of corruption and public participation have accelerated the

Table 4.3. The Second Phase of Anticorruption Measures in the Republic of Korea

Measure	Major contents
Digital administration	Invigorate e-commerce, expand e-bidding, encourage use of credit cards in the procurement process, and use of research stipends and social welfare subsidies
Expansion of information access	Expand the scope of information access through the Internet, promote open and transparent school man-agement, and impose standards and goals for government subsidies
Transparency in procedures and standards	Preset the maximum number and amount of discre-tionary projects, and launch one-stop service in pro-viding government funds to small and medium-size industries
Improved governance structure	Strengthen school operations committees, introduce outside board members to welfare facilities, and strengthen coordinating functions among govern-ment agencies
Expanded monitoring by citizens	Relax rules concerning citizens' requests for audits of school administration and unlawful budget execu-tion
Strengthened follow-ups	Establish an Internet audit system, and introduce outside board members to social welfare organiza-tions

Source: Office of the Prime Minister 2001.

process. Integrity initiatives in public service, and accountability and transparency programs are also under way. To be sure, although Korea has already begun to establish a comprehensive infrastructure of anticorruption policies, such as disclosure of personal assets and liabilities and protection of whistleblowers, it remains to be seen whether the costs of regulation and enforcement will pay off and be sustained.

With regard to the corporate sector, strengthening of antibribery actions and promoting integrity in business operations are seen as relatively less solid means of combating corruption in Korea.[16] For all the measures adopted at the initiation of the government after the 1997 financial crisis, the rule-bending business culture is persistent and the implementation of corporate governance measures is not evenly achieved. Surely there has been substantial reform in corporate governance practices, and a number of initiatives to promote good practices (such as the accounting reform initiative in business ethics) have been implemented. There is some international recognition of this progress by such organizations as the International Monetary Fund and the World Bank. As is the case in the public sector, changes cannot be implemented overnight, although the regulatory reforms are in place in both sectors.

Concerning the role of nongovernmental organizations (NGOs), active public involvement has grown and been quite effective. Among the major NGOs are the People's Solidarity for Participatory Democracy (PSPD), TI-Korea, the Citizens' Coalition for Economic Justice (CCEJ), and the Citizens United for Better Society, all of which have worked to promote better governance. During the 1990s Korean citizens' movements sprouted and contributed greatly to the development of civil society and the democratic order by expanding citizens' participation in the public sector. Through their advocacy of alternatives, they are shaping the popular consensus to meet the needs of the times, constructively monitoring and criticizing the existing social systems, and applying pressure for the sound development of all areas of Korean society, especially its anticorruption movement (Citizens' Coalition for Economic Justice 2002).

Coalition-Building against Corruption

The brunt of the burden for fighting corruption lies with the country's anticorruption institutions. There are seven major state actors involved in controlling corruption. These are:

1. The President's Secretary
2. The Office of the Prime Minister
3. The Board of Audit and Inspection (BAI)
4. The Public Prosecutor's Office

5. The Korean Independent Commission Against Corruption
6. The Inspector General of each ministry
7. The Ombudsman.

Of those seven, the Public Prosecutor's Office, the BAI, and the KICAC are at the forefront.

Under Article 246 of the Criminal Procedure Law, the Public Prosecutor's Office has full authority and duties to deal with various crimes, from investigation to prosecution. It directs the police and other investigative agencies, submits to the court petitions for the appropriate application of laws and regulations, and supervises the execution of criminal convictions. It is also involved in managing civil and administrative litigation in which the government is a party or intervener. A major part of the job is the prosecutorial function in criminal proceedings.

The BAI was established on the basis of constitutional law and the BAI Act. It is the supreme audit and inspection organization among governmental units for preventing corruption in Korea. It is organized under the office of the president, but it assumes independence in performing its duties. The responsibilities of BAI include audits of all public expenditures and inspections of government operations and the performance of the duties of civil servants.

To strengthen governmental capacity, nationwide anticorruption offices and anticorruption investigation departments were established in the national prosecutor's office. New professionals and additional resources were put into those departments to form a strong lineup for investigating structural and chronic corruption in corruption-prone areas. Some prosecutors have launched a crackdown on corruption of high-ranking as well as mid- and lower-level public officials. The national prosecutor's office has also traced the assets of public officials accused of corruption for the purpose of confiscation and forfeiture of illicit proceeds.

The Office of the Prosecutor-General organizes meetings of senior prosecutors in charge of special investigations at least once a year and holds seminars several times annually. The meetings and seminars provide opportunities for developing and disseminating investigative techniques and promoting close working relationships among local prosecutors' offices. In February 2000 the Supreme Prosecutor's Office and the Seoul District Prosecutor's Office established computer crime investigation departments and teams aimed at assisting investigations of new forms of corruption that employ modern computer techniques.

In 1993 President Kim Young-sam established the Commission for Prevention of Corruption as an advisory body composed mostly of private citizens to help the chair of BAI. The commission's functions include analyzing the causes of misconduct and corruption; developing ways to

correct defects in laws, decrees, and institutions that tend to foster irregularities; and providing recommendations on how to improve the activities
of the BAI. President Kim Young-sam also established the Public Official
Ethics Committee to prevent public officials from gaining unlawful property, to ensure fairness in the implementation of public services, and to
establish a code of ethics of public officials as servants of the people.

For his part, President Kim Dae-jung decided to create the Presidential
Commission on Anticorruption (PCAC) to serve as a presidential advisory group.[17] Effective January 25, 2002, in accordance with the Anti-
Corruption Act of Korea enacted in July 2001, the PCAC was transformed
into the Korean Independent Commission Against Corruption or KICAC
(see box 4.1).

Box 4.1. The Korean Independent Commission Against Corruption

The main functions of KICAC are providing anticorruption policies and
institutional improvement measures for the public sector, surveying and
evaluating anticorruption policy and enforcement progress, educating
about and campaigning against corruption, supporting nongovernmental
organizations' efforts to prevent corruption, and promoting international
cooperation among anticorruption organizations. It also responds to corruption complaints, protects complainants, and carries out other various
activities related to combating corruption.

Responses to corruption complaints against high-ranking public officials
are managed in seven steps.[1] When the complainant files the complaint,
KICAC receives it and starts its fact-finding operations. All fact-finding
should be completed within 30 days of receipt of the complaint. When
enough material has been gathered and verified, KICAC forwards the case
to the Public Prosecutor's Office (PPO). PPO starts its investigation and
then notifies KICAC of the results. KICAC applies for adjudication with the
High Court. Finally, KICAC notifies the complainant of the outcome.

To encourage whistleblowing about the corrupt activities of public officials, KICAC is well-equipped with legal and institutional measures to
protect corruption complainants from any reprisals. The Anti-Corruption
Act stipulates that any complainant shall not be subject to any harm to his
or her position or suffer any discrimination in his or her working conditions. The complainant may also request KICAC for reinstatement (in the
event of summary dismissal), transfer, or other forms of relief. The commission can ask the relevant public agency to take disciplinary actions
and impose a fine of up to 10 million won against a person who acts
against a complainant.

(Box continues on the following page.)

Box 4.1 (continued)

No investigative agency may disclose or suggest the identity of the person who reported the issue without his or her consent. The agency should also take additional serious steps to protect his or her identity. KICAC can also request an investigation into any disclosure and take disciplinary action against the offenders. The commission can refer the issue to another investigative agency with the complainant's identity protected if he or she does not want to disclose his or her identity. If necessary KICAC will ask the head of a competent police station to provide physical protection for the complainant.

In cases where the corruption report brings material benefits to a related public institution or prevents a possible loss, the complainant may be rewarded up to 200 million won. Upon receipt of a request for reward payment, the KICAC Compensation Deliberative Board meets to determine the amount of the reward. After deliberation KICAC pays the appropriate amount of reward according to legal procedures.

When it comes to handling corruption complaints, KICAC is closely related to existing investigative agencies, such as the PPO and BAI. KICAC necessarily plays its role in collaboration with other investigative agencies. As a newly institutionalized body, KICAC faces both the internal difficulties of making KICAC's 160 staff cohere within the new organization and the external difficulties produced by the sensitivities of investigative and prosecutorial agencies.[2]

Notes

1. High-ranking public officials are administrative officials with the rank of vice minister or higher, mayors or governors of metropolitan cities, police officers with the rank of superintendent general or higher, judges or public prosecutors, military officers with the rank of general, and members of the National Assembly.

2. From an interview with Chul-Kyu Kang, KICAC chair, conducted by Emil Bolongaita, May 2002.

An anticorruption body, KICAC seeks to improve the system of anticorruption laws and policies. Its establishment recognizes that eradicating corruption is one of the most urgent tasks that must be accomplished if Korea wants to become a globally competitive nation and join the ranks of leading countries in the world. In terms of direction, KICAC shifts attention away from detecting and punishing corruption to removing its cultural, social, and institutional breeding grounds.

Business associations such as the Federation of Korean Industries (FKI) have started to adopt their own codes of business ethics and are encouraging their members to comply with them. The FKI announced its Chapter of Business Ethics in 1999 and established the Committee on Business Ethics to promote the awareness and adoption of such ethics among its member firms. In 2000 the FKI published its *Manual for Business Ethics Practice.*

In the mid-1990s leading Korean businesses, such as POSCO, LG, Samsung, and Hyundai, began to prepare codes of business ethics, but most of those codes were too abstract for practical application. In 2000 a few large companies, such as Korean Air and Shinsegae, started to reinforce their business ethics codes and to introduce guidelines for business conduct. They have also established bureaus for business ethics as the driving engine for business ethics management. In general, however, businesses' efforts to promote ethics management are still in their infancy (Rhee 2000). TI-Korea did a survey on the "Actual Condition of Businesses with a Code of Ethics," and found that only 14 of the 28 local firms that responded had codes of ethics for their employees (TI-Korea 2001).[18]

Recent Anticorruption Initiatives from Civil Society

Even as the government works to pursue reforms to curb corruption, citizen involvement has also been growing because of the work of such NGOs as the CCEJ, the PSPD, and TI-Korea. A majority of the public wants credibility in the government's anticorruption efforts. According to public opinion surveys, about 80 percent want anticorruption investigations to begin focusing on powerful government organizations (Kwon 2000).

Before CCEJ came into being in 1989 there was no organization that pointed out the structural corruption problems in the Korean economy and that engaged citizens in a movement for governance reform. There was, however, a base of critical consciousness developed through the people's resistance to three decades of military dictatorship, and it was that awareness, brought to a focus in the nationwide demonstrations of June 1987, that turned the nation to civilian political rule. Thus CCEJ was founded as a movement that would be defined by the following features: it would (a) be led by ordinary citizens; (b) use legal and nonviolent methods; (c) seek workable alternatives; (d) speak for the interests of all people, regardless of economic standing; and (e) work to overcome greed and egoism in order to build a sharing society.

Since its establishment in 1994, PSPD has been serving as a watchdog against abuse of power and has been providing alternatives to a government-monopolized policy process. The organization has developed various activities to bring justice and democracy to many areas in Korean society: PSPD evokes public awareness through campaigns, watches and

questions social and political activities, files administrative and public lit-
igations, and petitions legislators.

The Civil Actions for 2000 General Election and the Minority
Shareholders' Campaign might be said to be the most successful activities.
As corruption and irregularities threaten public life and degrade national
prestige, the need for eliminating corruption has increased in Korea. Thus
PSPD established the Transparent Society Campaign Center on January 9,
1996, with the objective of attaining a better and cleaner society. In 1996
the center, led by attorney Kim Chang-kuk, focused on the campaign to
enact an anticorruption law and organized a public hearing, a lawmakers'
signature-collecting drive, and a legislative petition for the law.

On December 8, 2000, after a campaign that began five years earlier, the
proposed anti-corruption law was presented to the Legislation and
Judiciary Committee of the Korean Parliament and was passed on June 28,
2001. Some people criticized it for lacking certain powers, such as a special prosecutor system, but many hailed the enactment of the law as significant because it allows every citizen to participate in activities to control
corruption—a role that was previously conducted mainly by law enforcement authorities, such as prosecutors, police, and the BAI. The enactment
of the law was led by the civil society rather than by a political group.

Leadership and Management of Anticorruption Efforts

Without leadership, any attempt to achieve major reforms in an environment of systemic corruption is bound to fail. Leadership is vital and leaders must "walk the talk" rather than mouth platitudes (TI 2000a). This is
especially true in Korea where authority relationships are quite vertical
or heavily concentrated at the top. In this context the role of leadership in
anticorruption is even more important.

Without the factor of leadership in the cases of Mayor Goh Kun of
Seoul and President Kim Dae-jung, it would be difficult to explain the
implementation of anticorruption measures in their respective jurisdictions.[19] Mayor Goh was particularly effective in implementing the OPEN
system in a relatively short period of time by combining information and
communication technology with strategic and systematic approaches to
eliminating corruption.

Although President Kim inaugurated his presidency with a call to
crush corruption, his leadership has recently been tarnished by charges of
corruption brought against his two sons. The situation has actually
become reminiscent of the last days of his predecessor, Kim Young-sam.
To some observers it was clear that certain political-opposition forces
would like the current presidency to suffer the same fate as the earlier
Kim, whose presidency had collapsed at its final stage when his son was

sent to prison for taking bribes. Nevertheless, it might be said that the arrests of President Kim Dae-jung's sons signify that anticorruption efforts are continuing to move forward (TI 2000b). In other countries it would be impossible, if not unthinkable, for anticorruption agencies to pursue an incumbent's family.

Nevertheless, these cases against the president's sons demonstrate that a country that has received relatively good marks for governance can still suffer from state capture. Korea clearly needs to promote corporate responsibility and accountability, especially targeting its *chaebols* and other enterprises that continue to have the propensity to bribe. In this regard an active civil society and a competent and professional bureaucracy are twin pillars of a constructive relationship between state and society. They are essential to a strategy of increasing the risks of corruption and reducing its opportunities and rewards.

Despite gains achieved thus far, 75 percent of the Korean public in 2000 viewed corruption as a serious problem (Office of the Prime Minister 2000, p. 1). Although that is a 16 percent decline from the year before, it remains a very high number. Moreover, the decline in conviction rates does not necessarily mean that corruption has become less frequent; it could mean that the prosecution has become less effective.

Thus there is surely no such thing as a quick fix for corruption. There may be areas in which quick wins can be gained, such as streamlining procedures in public procurement, tax administration, and customs administration, but there is no easy solution to dealing with state capture issues.

Corruption Monitoring and Reporting Mechanisms

The present set of anticorruption policies and programs in Korea may be more comprehensive than in other countries, but achieving actual effects is as important as creating the system itself. Experience shows that unless processes are established for continuous monitoring, forces of anticorruption sooner or later find a way to embed themselves and eradicating them would require yet another extraordinary effort. It is not enough to remove corrupt officials without also removing opportunities and ensuring that honest officials are being appointed to positions of trust (TI 2000a). In Korea the law provides for the Office of the Prime Minister to manage the monitoring procedure. With the 1990s' eruption of citizens' movements for monitoring administrative processes and information, the prospects for a fairer monitoring of the system have improved. This is exemplified, for example, by groups such as the Korean Institute of Certified Public Accountants (see box 4.2).

Although it would be difficult to conclusively evaluate the performance of the country's existing initiatives against corruption because

---

Box 4.2. The Role of the Korean Institute of Certified Public Accountants

The November 1997 Asian financial crisis and its aftermath underscored the need for auditing standards and practices. The role of the Korean Institute of Certified Public Accountants (KICPA), strengthened with support from the World Bank, is to improve the skills and knowledge of 3,000 active practitioners in the proper application of international auditing standards adopted in 1999 and to help enhance their understanding of the roles and responsibilities of audit committees, effective internal audit, and external auditors. KICPA's mandate is (a) to develop practical interpretations for the Korean Auditing Standards and translate international technical pronouncements about auditing into the Korean language; (b) to develop educational material for continuing professional education for practitioners; and (c) to hold workshops and seminars to promote best practices in auditing and to enhance practitioners' understanding of the functions of audit committees, of effective internal audit, and of external audit best practices and their interrelationships.

---

they are relatively new, it is possible to identify several notable characteristics among the reforms:

1. The government is pursuing a comprehensive and systematic anticorruption plan. The previous integrity systems were fragmented and scattered. Various laws and systems were formulated, but they were enacted without effective planning and execution.
2. Objective and scientific approaches are being applied to build a corruption-prevention infrastructure and to reform the system, such as those embodied in the Anti-Corruption Act and the Money-Laundering Prevention Act.
3. The government is concentrating on preventing as well as punishing corruption. To make this possible, the government is maximizing the measures by strictly punishing any case of corruption regardless of rank of the offender and by giving equal levels of punishment to suppliers as well as recipients of the corrupt transactions.
4. Enforcement and evaluation actions are being carried out to ensure that anticorruption measures are actually implemented. The government is checking the effects and conditions of the measures by evaluating them in detail through responsible organizations and local self-governing bodies.

5. Strong participation from the NGOs has strengthened the independence of KICAC and has helped pass new legislation that includes the protection of whistleblowers. NGOs have also campaigned against political candidates and carried out a movement to protect minority shareholders' rights that has led to the restructuring of corporate governance and reform of past questionable accounting practices. One cannot assimilate the role of shareholder activism into corporate governance—the role is positive, of course, but not the driving force behind the reforms in Korea or elsewhere. Corporate sector reforms have contributed to reforms in corporate governance and the development of codes of ethics.

6. Korea is leveraging its well-developed information technology environment for administrative reforms. There is measurement expertise that, if applied to corruption, can help depoliticize issues. Such measurement can help establish priorities by identifying activities and agencies where corruption is concentrated, and could be useful in establishing standards against which the successes and failures of reform can be assessed (Kaufmann, Pradhan, and Ryterman 1998).

Even though Korea's anticorruption initiatives have made significant progress, it is crucial that the next steps squarely address the continuing issues of state capture and the state's capability to resist capture and execute reforms. In that regard, enforcement and implementation can be enhanced by promoting competitive pressures from outside and from within the institutions, and by strengthening formal checks and balances anchored around core institutions. Promoting good corporate governance is necessarily critical and the next steps should advance codes of conduct, the establishment of channels for communication, the protection of employees who report corruption, the enhancement of transparency of firms, and staff training.[20] (For a cursory overview and assessment of the relevance of anticorruption instruments as recommended in the ADB-OECD Anticorruption Action Plan for South Korea, please see the appendix to this chapter.)

Conclusion

Korea's problems of corruption are clearly complex and require long-term solutions. It is crucial that reforms be carefully planned and executed. There are many possible solutions but realistically not all can be tried and tested. It is crucial to choose the policies that are appropriate to the country and to prioritize and sequence them according to their expected effects in controlling corruption.

This case study has shown that, despite its relatively strong marks in governance, Korea remains seriously afflicted by corruption at the highest levels. State institutions maintain opaque relationships with big-business groups that prevent a more efficient allocation of resources and that weaken mechanisms for accountability. However, although Korea's problems of state capture may seem similar to problems of state capture in less developed countries, the challenge of addressing the problem is much different. In many ways Korea is in a better position to fight state capture because of its relatively strong governance institutions.

During the presidency of Kim Dae-jung, a series of comprehensive anticorruption measures was undertaken, with strong support from civil society groups. The first set involved improving detection systems, reforming administrative units that were corruption prone, and establishing a nationwide public service campaign against corruption. The second set tackled remaining corruption-prone areas, such as schools, procurement procedures, government expenditures, and means of access to information. For the first time a full-blown war against corruption was pursued. It should be noted that Korea's advanced state in information technology infrastructure has helped enhance the management and monitoring of policies and programs—something that less developed economies cannot easily employ.

The comprehensive measures pursued by the country are made possible in many ways by the relatively good governance conditions of the country. Anticorruption agencies have achieved notable gains, including the prosecution of high-level personalities such as the two sons of President Kim Dae-jung. These events signal the country's commitment to controlling corruption. It is surely serving notice to all that the risks of corruption will continue to increase and that these will outweigh whatever rewards might be gained. Moreover, Korea's continuing economic openness, despite the setback of the Asian financial crisis, means that its *chaebols* will continue to face the cleansing power of competition. What must not be neglected, however, is the need to strengthen the country's prosecutorial, legal, and judicial institutions. Ultimately, those are the institutions that will ensure that corruption does not pay.

Coalition-building with active civil society, strategic use of information and communication technology, and voluntary compliance with the pressure from international organizations, including the World Bank and the International Monetary Fund, have significantly supported the anticorruption battle. Korea, well known for its very centralized governance, has achieved some progress in administrative transparency, decentralization, and the safeguarding of integrity through systemic approaches. For overcoming the problem of state capture, however, it should pursue vigorously its comprehensive policy through public education and by engaging citizens in cultural change. Although much progress has been made in implementing the anticorruption programs and policies in

Korea, many arduous battles still lie ahead. Many corruption problems are deeply rooted in the country's political and institutional power structure. It will take years before the governance reforms become sustainable.

I would like to conclude this chapter with the famous recommendation of the World Bank (2000): "The focus on countries with relatively low levels of administrative corruption and relatively high level of state capture should be to expand political and economic competition to unblock potential for further structural reforms" (p. 6).

Appendix: Anticorruption Instruments: Analysis of Likely Effectiveness

Instrument	Likely contribution in combating corruption				Key assumptions/comments
	Reduce opportunity	Reduce gains/ motivation	Increase risk of punishment	Increase severity of penalty	
Pillar 1: Developing effective and transparent systems for public service					
Integrity in public service					
Adequate compensation	Medium	High	Medium	Medium	Recent increases in compensation
Transparent hiring and promotion	Medium	Medium	Medium	Medium	Strong merit system
Discretionary decision oversight	Medium	Medium	Medium	Medium	Strong BAI
Regular and timely rotation of assignments	Medium/low	Medium/low	Medium/low	Medium/low	Regular rotation practice
Conflict of interest prohibition	Medium	Medium	Medium	Medium	Public–private mix of culture
Disclosure of personal assets	High	High	Medium	Medium	Inadequate monitoring and liabilities
Contacts between government officials and business services users	High	High	Medium	Medium	Information technology, e-government
Promotion of codes of conduct	Medium	Medium	Medium	Medium	Aligned with Confucianism
Protection of whistleblowers	Medium	Medium	Medium	Medium	Anti-Corruption Act
Accountability and transparency					
Fiscal transparency	Medium	Medium	High	Medium	Accounting principle reform
Regulation and supervision of financial institutions	Medium	Medium	High	Medium	Strengthened after financial crisis

Auditing procedures, public reporting	High	Medium	High	Medium	BAI strengthened
Public procurement transparency	High	Medium	High	Medium	E-procurement
Public scrutiny and oversight	High	Medium	High	Medium	Public Prosecutor's Office strengthened
Information availability about political financing/application processing procedures	Medium/low	Medium/low	Medium/low	Medium/low	State capture
Simplification of the regulatory environment	High	High	Medium	Medium	Rapid change after the crisis
Pillar 2: Strengthening antibribery actions and promoting integrity in business					
Effective prevention, investigation, and prosecution					
Antibribery legislation	Medium	Medium	Medium	Medium	Anti-Corruption Act
Anti-money-laundering legislation	Medium	Medium	Medium	Medium	Two anti-money-laundering acts
Bribery offense enforcement	High	High	High	High	Public Prosecutor's Office strengthened
Strengthening of investigative and prosecutorial capacities	Medium	Medium	Medium	Medium	Recent reform and scandals
Cooperation in investigations and other legal proceedings	Medium	Medium	High	Medium	Public Prosecutor's Office/police

(Appendix continues on the following page.)

Appendix (continued)

Instrument	Likely contribution in combating corruption				Key assumptions/comments
	Reduce opportunity	Reduce gains/ motivation	Increase risk of punishment	Increase severity of penalty	
Corporate responsibility and accountability					
Promotion of good corporate governance	High	High	Medium	Medium	Rapid change after the crisis
Enforcement of legislation to eliminate direct support of bribery	Medium	Medium	Medium	Medium	Tax law/antibribery law
Transparent company accounts	Medium	Medium	Medium	Medium	After the crisis, strengthened
Public licenses, procurement contract	High	High	High	Medium	E-procurement
Pillar 3: Supporting active public involvement					
Public discussion of corruption					
Initiation of public awareness campaigns	High	High	High	Medium	Active NGOs' program
Support of NGOs	High	High	High	Medium	Active NGOs' program
Anticorruption cultural education program	High	Medium	High	Medium	Active NGOs' education program
Access to information					
Public reporting requirements for justice	Medium	Medium	Medium	Medium	e-government public reporting

Public right of access to appropriate information	High	High	High	Medium	Information Disclosure Act
Public participation					
Cooperative relationships with civil society groups	High	High	High	Medium	Active NGOs' coalition
Protection of whistleblowers	Medium	Medium	High	High	Anti-Corruption Act
Involvement of NGOs in monitoring of public sector programs	High	High	High	Medium	PSPD, TI-Korea, CCEJ, and others

Notes

1. It is important to note that government reform has also been supplemented by initiatives from the civil society and the private sector. That fact could be what makes the present anticorruption drive different from government-led drives.

2. State capture is synonymous with grand corruption, when the highest levels of government are corrupted and "captured" by external actors. According to Hellman, Jones, and Kaufmann (2000), in a decade of transition, fear of a leviathan state is giving way to increased focus on oligarchs who "capture the state." In the capture economy, the policy and legal environment is shaped to the captor firm's huge advantage, at the expense of the rest of the enterprise sector.

3. The cultural background is not only influencing the governmental organization but also shaping the business relationships. For instance, in Chinese culture it is associated with the Guanxi (network-based business).

4. For further reference on the relationship between democracy and state capture, see Rose-Ackerman 1996.

5. The focus above has been about grand corruption and the private–public connection, rather than about how corruption has been diffused at the lower level of government and in everyday life. Compared with other Asian countries, the level of bureaucratic corruption has been reduced significantly during the past decade.

6. Both surveys' sample sizes were 500 and the margin of error was plus or minus 4.3 percent.

7. "North-south relations" mean the issue of reunification and national security, and "regional nepotism"means the personal ties with the same territorial origin. This uniqueness of Korean factionalism and favoritism has been criticized by the people.

8. We have to admit that it is very difficult, if not impossible, to interpret the time evolution of the TI Index for a given country.

9. This can be misleading because it is about Korean practice abroad and not about what is happening inside Korea. Also, the interpretation of the BPI is problematic because of a size bias.

10. They used the available governance data, including 194 different measures drawn from 17 different sources of subjective governance data constructed by 15 different organizations. These sources include international organizations, political and business risk-rating agencies, think tanks, and NGOs. They summarized the data into six clusters corresponding to six basic aspects of governance: (1) voice and accountability, (2) political stability, (3) government effectiveness, (4) regulatory quality, (5) rule of law, and (6) control of corruption. They used an unobserved-components model that expresses the observed data in each cluster as a linear function of the unobserved common component of governance, plus a

disturbance term capturing perception errors and/or sampling variation in each indicator. Their choice of units for governance ensured that the estimates of governance had a mean of zero, a standard deviation of one, and range from around –2.5 to around 2.5. The aggregate indicators were oriented such that higher values corresponded to better outcomes.

11. Gwartney and Lawson defined "economic freedom" in terms of size of government, structure of economy and use of markets, monetary policy and price stability, freedom to use alternative currencies, legal structure and property rights, international exchange, and freedom of exchange in financial markets.

12. Further information about each vulnerable fields' measures can be found in the Office of the Prime Minister's reports (2000, 2001).

13. Details of these measures are available at www.korea.net/learnabout korea/library/corruption/html.

14. Details of these measures are available at www.korea.net/learnboutkorea/ library/corruption.html.

15. See www1.oecd.org/daf/ASIAcom/ActionPlan.htm.

16. According to the 2002 BPI, that still put Korean companies among the worse offenders. And according to Office of the Prime Minister surveys (1999, 2000), the seriousness of corporate corruption had not improved.

17. See www.kicac.go.kr.

18. Korean efforts must be considered as really serious, with an interesting system of collective monitoring. One must remember that the implementation of a compliance system is quite a recent trend worldwide outside the United States. Although TI globally contributed enormously to the spread and the establishment of standards, the country-by-country relationship between the corporate sector and the TI chapter varies enormously. In Korea TI might not have the trust of the corporate sector to carry out some of the evaluation. In addition, 7 of the 14 firms either have an inadequate set of ethical principles or are reluctant to share them with the public, which is a worldwide phenomenon.

19. For further information see Park, Kim, and Lee (2001).

20. ADB-OECD Anti-Corruption Action Plan for Asia-Pacific, 2001.

References

Bhargava, V. K., and E. P. Bolongaita, Jr. 2001. "Making National Anti-Corruption Policies and Programs More Effective: An Analytical Framework." Paper prepared for the World Bank's Global Distance Learning Program on Combating Corruption in the Asia-Pacific Region. June 18.

Citizens' Coalition for Economic Justice. 2002. *Annual Report*. Seoul.

Freedom House. 2002. *Freedom in the World Countries Ratings.* Washington, D.C.

Gwartney, James, and Robert Lawson. 2001. *Economic Freedom of the World 2001 Annual Report.* Vancouver, B.C.: Fraser Institute.

Hellman, Joel S., Geraint Jones, and Daniel Kaufmann. 2000. "Seize the State, Seize the Day: State Capture, Corruption, and Influence in Transition." World Bank Working Paper 2444. Washington, D.C.

Holzer, Marc, and Byong-Joon Kim. 2002. *Building Good Governance: Reforms in Seoul.* Seoul: SDI.

Huther, Jeff, and Anwar Shah. 1998. "Applying a Simple Measure of Good Governance to the Debate on Fiscal Decentralization." World Bank Policy Research Working Paper 1894. Washington, D.C.

————. 2000. "Anticorruption Policies and Programs: A Framework for Evaluation." World Bank Policy Research Working Paper 2501. Washington, D.C.

Kang, Hong Bin. 2001. "Cleaning up the City Government of Seoul: A Systematic Approach." Paper presented at the Seoul Anticorruption Symposium, "The Role of Online Procedures in Promoting Good Governance." August 30–31. Seoul.

Kaufmann, Daniel, Aart Kraay, and Pablo Zoido-Lobatón. 2002. "Governance Matters II." World Bank Policy Research Working Paper 2772. Washington, D.C.

Kaufmann, Daniel, Sanjay Pradhan, and Randi Ryterman, with James Anderson. 1998. "Diagnosing and Combating Corruption: A Framework with Application to Transition Economies." Washington, D.C.: World Bank Economic Development Institute.

KICAC (Korean Independent Commission Against Corruption). 2002. *Newsletter,* 4.

Kwon, Yule-jung. 2000. "Anti-corruption Campaign." *Korea Herald,* November 25, p. 5.

Lee Chi-dong. 2002. "Independent Counsel Ends Probe of Corruption Scandal." *Korea Times,* March 26, p. 4.

Mauro, Paolo. 1997. "The Effects of Corruption on Growth, Investment, and Government Expenditure: A Cross-Country Analysis." In Kimberly Ann Elliot, ed., *Corruption and the Global Economy.* Washington D.C.: Institute for International Economics.

Office of the Prime Minister. 1999. *Diagnosis of Korean Corruption and Determinants Study.* Seoul.

————. 2000. *Evaluation and Management of Anti-corruption Policy.* Seoul.

————. 2001. *Combating Corruption in Korea.* Seoul.

Park, Jhungsoo. 1992. "Can Decentralization Policy Constrain the Leviathan?" Ph.D. dissertation, University of Pittsburgh.

————. 2001. "Democracy and Integrity in Korea." Paper presented to the Global Forum II, May 28–31. The Hague, Netherlands.

Park, Jhungsoo, Y. Kim, and G. Lee. 2001. "A Study on the Effectiveness of Anti-Corruption Policy in Seoul Metropolitan Government: The Case of the OPEN System." Seoul: Seoul Institute for Transparency.

Rhee, Zusun. 2000. "Efforts to Create an Anti-Corruption Corporate Culture in Korea." In Asian Development Bank, ed., *Progress in the Fight against Corruption in Asia and the Pacific.* Manila.

Rose-Ackerman, Susan. 1996. "Democracy and Grand Corruption." *International Social Science Journal* 149: 365–80.

SaKong, Il. 1993. *Korea in the World Economy.* Washington, D.C.: Institute for International Economics.

Shelton-Colby, Sally. 2001. "Anticorruption and ICT for Good Governance." Paper presented at the Seoul Anticorruption Symposium, "The Role of Online Procedures in Promoting Good Governance." August 30–31. Seoul.

TI (Transparency International). 2000a. *Confronting Corruption: The Elements of a National Integrity System: TI Source Book.* Berlin.

————. 2000b. *Korea's National Integrity System.* Berlin.

————. 2001. *Global Corruption Report 2001.* Berlin.

TI-Korea. 2001. *Effectiveness of Business Ethics Code in Korea.* Seoul.

World Bank. 2000. *Helping Countries Combat Corruption.* Washington, D.C.

5

Controlling Corruption in Thailand: Transforming the Problems and Paradoxes

Corruption has been a serious challenge in Thailand for many years. It has been widespread, deeply rooted, well-organized, and tolerated. The 1997 Asian economic crisis revealed Thailand's three most important problems: mismanagement of macroeconomic policies, weak structure of real sectors, and widespread corruption. During the past five years, however, attempts to combat corruption have increased considerably. This chapter (a) examines the nature of Thailand's country governance, (b) discusses changes in its environments through the political reforms to fight corruption, and (c) analyzes the effectiveness of the new regime.

Country Governance

If corruption is a disease, then many see Thailand as quite infected and difficult to cure. "No money, no service" is a common perception of what it takes to deal with government agencies. Although Thailand has received a reputation of having competent and committed officials, many are also seen as more focused on their own interests and neglectful in serving the public.

For some observers, part of the problem appears rooted in Thai culture. Wealthy people are valued regardless of the source of their fortune. In a sense there are weak cultural controls against abuses of power for private gain. In fact, many people see corruption as a shortcut to prosperity and to wider acceptance in society. As one writer noted, "in Thailand, being rich is considered a virtue, and being rich is practically godly" ("In the Clear" 2001, p. 14).

This case study was contributed by Nualnoi Treerat, assistant professor of economics, Chulalongkorn University, Bangkok.

Like many other countries, corruption in Thailand has become diverse and complex both in size and form. The acts involve small to large sums of money, from petty to grand corruption. The transactions implicate junior to high-ranking government officials, both bureaucrats and politicians. It is a scourge that spans both the public and private sectors.

Perhaps the most excessive examples of corruption involving large sums of money, and a complicated cast of players that includes politicians, bureaucrats, and private parties, can be found in government procurement. As one study pointed out, "corruption in government procurement normally involves a network consisting of a politician who supervises the department, high-ranking bureaucrats in the department, as well as lower-ranking officials in charge of the project" (Poapongsakorn, Nikomborirak, and Tulyawasinphong 2000, p. ii).

The problem manifests itself in convoluted ways. It includes bribery, extortion, embezzlement, graft, collusion, abuse of power, and conflicts of interest, all surrounded by a lack of transparency and accountability in government operations. For a long time these patterns of public action for private gain were relatively undisturbed. But several changes in Thai society since the 1980s have begun to reshape public perceptions. The first was the expansion of civil society fostered by years of strong economic growth, which produced a larger middle class. The second related factor was the increasing democratization of the country, which favored increasing reliance on electoral legitimacy for government as opposed to its long history of military-led administrations.

Contemporary Patterns of Corruption

Several surveys have been conducted to better define the nature of corruption in Thailand. One series of surveys in particular—focusing on the perceptions and experiences of corruption among Thai households (Phongpaichit and others 2000), businesspeople (Thairungroj and others 2000) and civil servants (Yaowaprapas 2000)—was conducted as part of a Civil Service Commission research project on strategies for combating corruption, funded by the World Bank and the Asia Foundation.

The survey of households yielded the following results:

- Household heads ranked corruption in the public sector as the third most serious national problem, after the poor economy and high cost of living. They viewed politicians as more corrupt than bureaucrats. They believed corruption was getting worse, especially among politicians.
- The vast majority of people did not have to pay "squeeze money" at government offices, public utilities, and similar places; and generally

they were satisfied with the services they received. The bribe-taking from households was concentrated in a small number of offices, but the amounts were truly large. The offices were those with influence over significant monetary transactions, namely, the land department, the revenue and customs offices, the transportation department (which controls vehicle licensing), and the police department. Those five offices accounted for 95 percent of perceived total corruption income.

- In comparison, corruption in government offices providing households with utilities and services was relatively small in scale and extent. In general, people were confident that bribes paid to government offices would ensure a better service or result.
- Almost one-third of households were offered money to buy their votes during the last general election in 1996. And one-tenth of households were solicited for bribes by some public office. The average amount asked from each solicited household was around 10,000 baht (US$250) a year (Phongpaichit and others 2000).

The survey of enterprises yielded the following results:

- Business enterprises experienced inefficiencies related to bureaucratic red tape. On average, senior managers spent 14 percent of their management time dealing with laws and regulations. To avoid bureaucratic inefficiency, business firms gave irregular "additional payments" to get things done. Approximately 79 percent of the interviewed firms said that it was "always, mostly and frequently" common to pay some extra money. About 74 percent admitted that they "always, mostly and frequently" knew in advance about how much this extra money was to be, and that after the payment was made the service was delivered as agreed.
- The public officials who most frequently requested extra payments after contact was established were government procurement agents (57 percent), politicians influencing policies affecting enterprises (44 percent), and traffic and other police officers (39 percent). When considering average annual amounts of extra payments, firms paid the highest amounts to the customs authority, followed by government procurement offices, politicians influencing firms, and finally the tax agency.
- In the bidding process to get government contracts, firms said unofficial payment was one of the major problems. About 18 percent of responding firms paid as much as 5 percent of the contract value in extra money; around 11 percent said they paid up to 10 percent; about 8 percent paid up to 20 percent; and around 2 percent paid more than 20 percent (Thairungroj and others 2000).

The survey of public officials yielded the following results:

- Most respondents thought corruption was part of life in Thai society. Bribery was seen as normal and customary.
- "Position buying" in government sectors was said to be the root of corruption. Approximately 43 percent admitted that there was "position buying" in their own departments.
- "Position buying" was done using money and nonmoney approaches over a long period of time. The process involved politicians and their representatives (Yaowaprapas 2000).

The research project that undertook those surveys also looked at government procurement. The findings showed that the procurement process was characterized by a high number of barriers to entry, enabling corrupt officials and crooked businessmen to extract large amounts of economic rent. Many artificial barriers were created to limit the number of potential bidders, from the specification of the products to be procured to the qualification of the contractors eligible to bid. There were even outright dirty tactics such as physically hauling away competitors who happened to show up. And when the bidding succeeded in including all possible competitors, the bidders often colluded (Poapongsakorn, Nikomborirak, and Tulyawasinphong 2000).

The study also pointed out that bribes occur at every step in the procurement process, beginning at the stage of departmental budget preparation where politicians and businessmen, with the cooperation of civil servants, initiate "pork-barrel" projects (Poapongsakorn, Nikomborirak, and Tulyawasinphong 2000). Although the collusion among businessmen, bureaucrats, and politicians in office is the common pattern of corruption in Thailand, there are some exceptions. For example, in the construction sectors, the owners of construction companies or their relatives would enter politics directly to ensure they would get the government contracts.

In sum, most of the corruption in Thailand involves business deals. The parties involved are businesspeople and the bureaucrats and political officeholders who are in the position to influence business profits. There is also some gatekeeping and racketeering among the police. But the big issue and the big money are about the interface between business and government.

Money Politics

Money politics has been argued to be the main root of corruption in Thailand. It refers to the large sums of money that flow in Thai politics, beginning with election campaigns and continuing through maintaining the stability of the government. Party leaders have to offer cash to attract good electoral candidates. Parliamentary candidates, in turn, invest huge sums to get elected. Some observers noted that the schedule of payoffs follows defined formulas:

> Recently, we have had so-called fertiliser formulas, like 5-10-10-20, which indicate the sums (in millions of baht) a candidate will receive when he expresses interest (5 million); when he signs up to join the party (10 million); when he succeeds in getting elected (10 million); and so on. (Phongpaichit and Baker 2002)

And leaders have to pay retainers to keep their parties together. Money is also paid for votes on parliament motions. Of course these expenditure are seen as investments that have to be recouped. With position-buying in bureaucracy common, it is not surprising that the politicians and bureaucrats would collude for their own benefit when large sums of money are involved. A recent study suggested that the large amounts of money invested in money politics probably originate in business, involving both legal (business with government contacts) and illegal activities (Phongpaichit, Piriyarangsan, and Treerat 1999). That rent-seeking behavior shows the connections and networks of illegal businesses whose operations need protection by people who have political and bureaucratic power.

Although it is understood that vote-buying will result in unscrupulous politicians gaining seats in the assembly and the cabinet, other issues surrounding vote-buying are less understood. It is a complex problem because it is tied to rural poverty, the patronage system, and feudal attitudes. In a sense vote-buying is at the heart of a so-called political paradox in Thailand. The issue of the political paradox is that the country's democratic system allows the rural majority to choose the government, whereas the minority middle class, which has less influence on the composition of the parliament and cabinet, has the power to form an alliance to oust the elected government. In other words, those who put the government into power and those who end its life are not the same people.

Moreover, those groups hold incompatible views of democracy (Laothamatas 1996). For rural people democracy is a means to bring greater benefits and official attention to themselves and their villages. Voting in rural areas is not guided by political principles, policy issues, or what is perceived as the national interests. Besides, voting decisions in rural Thailand have been conditioned initially by the relationships between patrons and clients. But for the educated middle class, democracy is a form of legitimate rule to recruit honest and capable people, a view more oriented to the Western concept of democracy (Laothamatas 1996).

The political dilemma is, indeed, the mirror of the economic dilemma in Thai society. Although the middle class has always called for more freedom and more democracy, they have done less to actually solve the real problem of the political paradox. It is very hard for democracy to get rid of corruption as long as there is the huge socioeconomic gap between urban and rural areas, or between rich and poor populations.

In conclusion, the bulk of corruption in Thailand seems to be occurring mainly at the intersection of business and politics. Businesspeople buy opportunities (both legal and illegal businesses) and favors. Officeholders sell opportunities (both legal and illegal businesses) and favors. For legal business, rent-generating advantages in the forms of policies, law, and regulations are sold by public officials and politicians. Because Thailand has a rather weak rule of law and a relatively primitive form of capitalism, illegal or semilegal business activities are significant channels in the process of capital accumulation. Such businesses have special needs for the kinds of opportunities and favors that politics can provide (particularly protection, status, and immunity). Hence, rent accumulation from both sources contributes significantly to the political investments that drive money politics in the country.

Rent Seeking and Corruption

Those holding political and administrative power have the ability to create rents, particularly in the form of abnormally high levels of business profits. They can do that in many ways: by creating a monopoly, by providing protection against foreign competition, by sheltering an illegal business, and so on.

The impact of these rents on the economy depends on how large they are and, more important, how they are distributed. Some economists believe that rent may not be all bad for economic growth if the rents are structured in such a way that the rent-seeking entrepreneur invests a large part of the rent income and invests it in the right things (such as in innovation, in adapting new technology and knowledge, in good management, and the like). In such a situation the result will be growth.

But the rent-seeking entrepreneur may not innovate. Instead he may decide to buy himself luxury goods. The politician may grab a large share of the rent and decide to spend it for consumption, or the rents may be distributed to petty bureaucrats who consume but do not invest. In all of those cases the rents will not contribute to economic growth.

A study by Mushtaq Khan (2000) compared models of corrupt and rent-seeking behavior in three countries: Bangladesh, the Republic of Korea, and Thailand. He concluded that Korea's economy grew very fast because the political leaders allowed the entrepreneurs to make high rents but also forced them to reinvest those rents in productive ways. Furthermore, rents were not dissipated by redistribution to groups outside the business sector. By contrast, the Bangladesh economy has gone nowhere because rents are spent on luxury consumption or dissipated among petty bureaucrats and those outside the business groups, and little is left for investment.

Thailand in the 1970s and 1980s was in the middle of the above dichotomy. The government created quite high rents but was totally ineffectual at telling the rent-seeking entrepreneurs how to use them. Thailand's political system, however, was not a dictatorship but a sort of competitive oligarchy, with power spread among different bureaucratic and political factions who competed for the rent-seeking opportunities. The successful competitors then allocated these opportunities to their group of business friends. This oligarchic competition at the political level was then reproduced within the ranks of business groups. The favored entrepreneurs were motivated to invest a high proportion of the rents to stay ahead of their competitors and thus remain in the market for capturing more rents in the future. The system has been described as "competitive clientelism" (Doner and Ramsay 2000). In the end, more of the rent was dissipated than was the case in Korea, but enough of it was invested to deliver higher economic growth than in Bangladesh.

To make this phenomenon much more distinctive, Phongpaichit and Baker (2002)[1] put forth the following formula to explain the pattern of corruption:

$$V = A + B - K$$

where V is the total rent or final net corruption revenue, which is made up of two sorts of income, A and B, less the costs incurred, K. Of the income, A is the kind of "corruption tax" that politicians and bureaucrats collect by taking commission fees, padding expenditure budgets, and so on. This is simple theft and is very familiar. The second type, B, is more complex. This is the corruption or rent that politicians and their friends earn from businesses that are able to charge high prices. Some of these businesses are illegal, such as oil-smuggling; others are businesses that have been granted a monopoly. K represents the costs. Under a democratic system of government with a well-functioning judicial system, corruption has two kinds of costs. First there are the costs of getting caught. Corrupt politicians might be caught, tried, fined, and jailed. They could be barred from politics for a certain number of years. The second cost is the possible loss of office and the resulting social derision. They might fail at the next polls and may thus lose the benefits of the "externalities" attached to political office.

Net corruption income therefore equals commission fees plus monopoly profits less costs. Once in power, political parties will try to maximize their corruption revenue by increasing the amount of A and B. They will also do several things to ensure that K is minimized. They will try to control the judiciary and to suppress sources of opposition such as the media, opposition parties, and activist elements in civil society.

Rating and Ranking Thailand's Corruption

"Corruption takes many forms and is a universal cancer," explains Peter Eigen, chair of Transparency International (TI), a leading anticorruption nongovernmental organization (NGO). TI is well known for its Corruption Perceptions Index (CPI), which ranks countries around the world using various polls conducted by different organizations.[2] If we view Thailand's CPI scores from a longer perspective, it can be noted that the country experienced an improvement from a score of 1.85 during the period 1988–92 to a score of 3.33 in 1996 (see figure 5.1).[3]

It is interesting that the improvement partly coincides with an increase in the summary ratings of economic freedom for the country, as measured by the *Economic Freedom of the World Report*, where Thailand scored 6.0 in 1985, 6.6 in 1990, and 7.3 in 1995 (see Gwartney and Lawson 2001).[4] That may be seen as evidence of the finding of researchers that there is a significant correlation between greater economic freedom and lower levels of corruption (Gwartney and Lawson 2001). Such an association has parallels with the experience of the Philippines where a period of improving perceptions of corruption, as expressed in the country's CPI ratings, coincided approximately with a period of increasing economic freedom (see chapter 3 of this volume).

Figure 5.1. Transparency International Corruption Perceptions Index, Thailand Scores, Selected Years, 1980–98

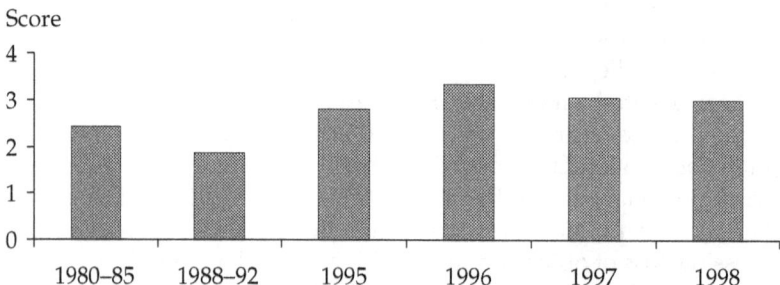

Source: Transparency International, available at www.transparency.org.

Notice, however, that the index for Thailand slipped after 1996, from 3.33 to 3.00 in 1998.[5] That decline occurred during the period of the Asian financial crisis when problems of governance were seen as partly to blame. The index for Thailand, however, remained stable at 3.2 during the period 1999–2002. In that regard, although progress has been made in combating corruption in Thailand, much remains to be done. As Eigen remarked

> ...the fight against corruption dare not be relaxed. We all yearn for improvement, but positive change only comes slowly when the enemy is endemic corruption. Perception of levels of corruption does not change greatly from one year to the next. Positive results are only going to emerge from tireless and consistent multi-year efforts. (Transparency International 2000, p. 2)

From a broader perspective, corruption in Thailand may be understood in relation to its "quality of governance." An index in that regard, developed by Jeff Huther and Anwar Shah, combines measurements of citizen participation, government orientation, social development, and economic management (see Huther and Shah 1998). In the Huther and Shah ranking of governance quality, Thailand placed 43rd among 80 countries in the world and was characterized as having "fair" governance.

That index of governance quality, of course, presented only a snapshot of Thailand and could not capture the full range of issues. Such a snapshot of a country, however, does provide a glimpse at its governance and operating environment. To be sure, that ranking of Thailand is not static and should shift, depending on changes in its environment.

Another perspective of the quality of governance in Thailand was estimated by Kaufman, Kraay, and Mastruzzi (2003). Their study covered six dimensions of governance for 175 countries: control of corruption, rule of law, regulatory framework, government effectiveness, political stability/lack of violence, and voice and accountability. On a scale from –2.5 to 2.5, in which the higher values corresponded to better outcomes, Thailand received scores of –0.15, 0.30, 0.34, 0.10, 0.28, and 0.20 for control of corruption, rule of law, regulatory quality, government effectiveness, political stability, and voice and accountability, respectively, in 2002. When compared with the indicators in 1996, the 2002 indicators for control of corruption, political stability, and voice and accountability received higher scores but the rest received lower scores. In general, however, the indicators still point out that Thailand has relatively fair governance.

Furthermore, freedom of the press is an important indicator of the level of corruption because media are major mechanisms in fighting corruption. The 2002 Annual Survey of Press Freedom published by

Freedom House (Sussman and Karlikar 2002) showed significant improvement for Thailand, from a score of 54 in 1994 to a score of 31 in 1996 (see figure 5.2). That result implied that the Thailand press was partly free. The score increased slightly to 34 in 1997—a pattern that coincided with the CPI score. From 1998 to 2002, however, the index remained at around 29 to 31, pointing out that Thailand has relative liberty for the media.

The Changing Constitutional Environment

One of the most significant changes in Thailand in recent years has been the growth and influence of NGOs. That development can partly be traced to groups working on rural development and environmental issues in the 1980s. NGOs since that time have generally gained enhanced status and helped propel the movement for a stronger civil society. A common goal has been to empower people and communities through approaches favoring greater decentralization and participation in political and policy processes. The growing strength of civil society was most

Figure 5.2. Freedom House Annual Survey of Press Freedom, Thailand Scores, 1994–2002

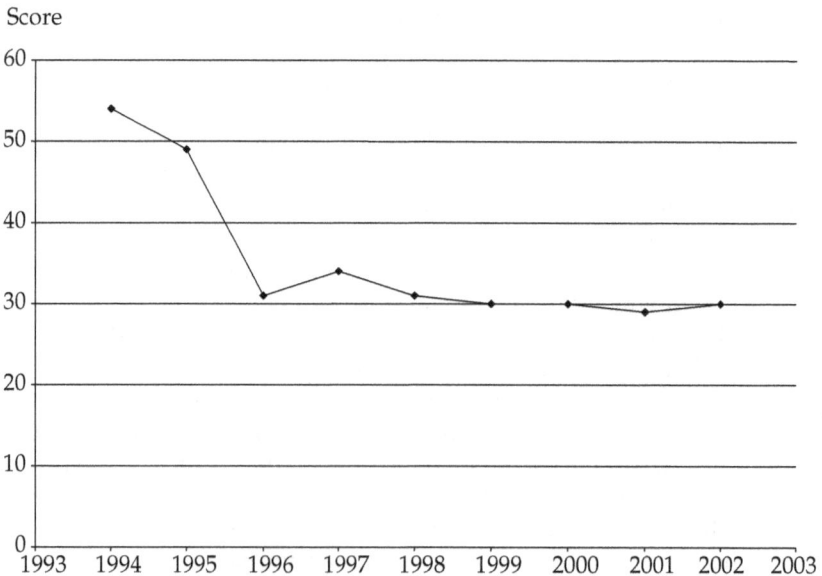

Source: Sussman and Karlikar 2002.

felt during the constitutional reform process that began around 1991–92, highlighted by a long protest against the unelected prime minister that subsequently led to the May 1992 military crackdown. The hard work of civil society finally paid off in 1997 when the country promulgated a new constitution, aptly called the "People's Constitution."

The process leading to creation of the 1997 constitution resonated with calls for more transparency and accountability in government. As a result the charter has a section on rights and freedoms and establishes greater checks and balances against undemocratic government. It also seeks to improve the political structure for greater stability and efficiency.

Under the 1997 constitution, the democratization of the country's political institutions has been advanced in various ways. The members of the Senate, not only the House of Representatives, now must go through the electoral process. That amendment changes what had previously been an appointive body. As Anand Panyarachun, former prime minister and head of the Constitutional Drafting Assembly, said,

> We have converted the Senate from a rather ineffective law-making body into a monitoring institution. Senators will not have the power to initiate legislation…but they will have much more power to monitor the performance of the government and the performance of the elected members of the House of Representatives." (Laird 2000, p. 166)

To deepen democratic politics, the constitution also has effected changes in electoral rules and introduced a "combination system" of elections. The new rules added a party-list system for one-fifth of the seats in the lower house (100 seats), and maintained the traditional single-member constituency elections for the rest of the House (400 seats).[6] The expressed reasons for that amendment were threefold: (1) the party system would be strengthened because people would cast their votes directly for parties instead of for individual candidates; (2) the parties effectively would have the whole country as their national constituency and that would make vote-buying more prohibitive; and (3) representatives from party lists would be encouraged to adopt a national vision because they would be appealing to voters nationwide.

The constitution also has barred multiple candidacies; that is, it is not possible to be a candidate on both the party list and in constituency elections. Moreover, unlike in the past, if a representative elected on a constituency basis is appointed as minister, he or she must resign his or her seat in parliament within 30 days of being appointed. To avoid "nuisance parties" there is a minimum threshold: a party must receive at least 5 percent of the total votes for its candidates to be eligible; anything less means the party does not count.

As clamored for by civil society, the changes in the rules of the political process were expressly intended to require greater accountability of elected officials. To quote Anand Panyarachun further,

> In the past, politicians could sin, commit wrong-doings, and they would go scot-free. We introduced a system of monitoring, a system of impeachment. We strengthened all the existing institutions and we created new ones, to make them more independent—not subservient to the government, but responsible to the Parliament." (Laird 2000, p. 166)

The constitution, thus, has introduced a system of monitoring and a system of removal from office as a means to check the behavior and performance of politicians and high bureaucrats. The Senate especially has been converted from a passive lawmaking body into a more active monitoring institution.

In addition to the provisions described above, the constitution ensures civil rights and civil liberties by allowing people to participate directly in state decisionmaking. Those measures include

- *The right to know*—The people are entitled to access to information concerning the records of government agencies except when disclosure of such information would jeopardize national security, public safety, or individuals' interests as protected by law. This right is defined in detail by the Information Act. Under section 59, individuals are entitled to receive information, explanations, and reasons from government agencies, state enterprises, or local administrative organizations before approving or carrying out projects or any activity that could affect the environment, health, quality of life, or benefits of individuals and their communities (Constitution, Articles 58–59).
- *Freedom of the press*—The government may not impose a ban on printing, newspaper publishing, or radio or television broadcasting, except when it is imposed by a court judge corresponding to law or when the country is in a state of war or armed conflict. The constitution decrees that an independent state agency will be set up by the Senate to distribute radio frequencies and supervise radio and television broadcasting. Officials or employees of media organizations, including those of state-owned organizations, shall enjoy the liberty to present news and express their opinions under the constitutional restrictions without the mandate of any government agency, state agency, state enterprises, or the owner of such businesses, providing that it is not contrary to their professional ethics (Constitution, Articles 39–41).

- *Administrative decentralization*—Under Article 78 the state shall decentralize powers to localities for the purpose of independence and self-determination of local affairs and to develop local economies, public utilities, systems, and information infrastructure thoroughly and equally throughout the country. During the political reform, decentralization was also requested as the way to receive real democratization, reduce vote buying and money politics, and fight corruption. To be sure, although local governments have greater autonomy for their governance, administration, personnel administration, and finance, the state still has regulatory responsibility (Constitution, Articles 78, 282–290). But the policies on administrative decentralization became inexorable as many local governments were created. (Currently, Thailand has 7,950 local governments.)
- *Fiscal decentralization*—In the past, all local spending coursed through the national budget. Local stakeholders had no channels to monitor spending decisions made at that level. Constituency members of parliament (MPs) competed to gain access to the national budget. Local influential people acted as canvassers for these MPs at election time. Voters who were poor had to rely on local influential people in times of need (for loans, jobs, and so forth) and they sold their votes to these canvassers both for direct gain and because they owed debts of obligation. Hence, vote buying and selling persisted. Decentralization was intended to attack this problem in several ways. First, it transferred spending decisions from the national budget process to local bodies. Second, it empowered local people to monitor and oversee local budget spending. Third, local spending was seen as contributing to the reduction of poverty. The law determined that the total local budget must account for at least 20 percent of the national budget in the fiscal year 2001 and that proportion increases to 35 percent in fiscal year 2006. This provision ensures that the central government must transfer budget, personnel, and projects to local governments. The development of local governments in Thailand is in the first stage, however, and there are still many problems, such as corruption in local procurement,[7] inefficiency in administration, low levels of public participation, local influence-peddling, and vote-buying.

To summarize, the march toward political reform through constitutional change has increased not only the degree of democratization in the country, but also the degrees of decentralization and public participation. It is hoped that this will give rise to a more equitable distribution of political as well as economic power among the people.

New Actors, New Rules in the Battle against Corruption

Independent institutions created by the 1997 constitution to combat corruption and wrongdoing include the National Counter-Corruption Commission (NCCC), the Election Commission of Thailand, the Constitutional Court, the Ombudsman, the Administrative Court, and the State Audit Commission. These organizations are independent in that their structure and operations are beyond the formal control or influence of politicians and political parties. Moreover, the nominations of members to these bodies are made by qualified selection committees and appropriate state and nonstate bodies; reviewed by independent, expert selection committees; and finally approved by the Senate.

A review of the functions and powers of these post-1997 constitutional agencies shows an extensive institutional network devoted to controlling corruption:

- *The National Counter-Corruption Commission:* This commission replaced the former Counter-Corruption Commission and has assumed more powers and broader duties. With its commissioners appointed by the Senate, the organization is independent from any government agency (unlike its predecessor that was founded in 1976 and operated under the prime minister's office). Its mandate is to investigate allegations of corruption involving members of the House of Representatives, the Senate, the cabinet, and other high-ranking government officials. By its own authority, the commission can cause the dismissal of politicians who are found guilty. To help ensure that the commissioners themselves are people of integrity, they are required to declare their assets and liabilities and those of their spouses and dependent children within 30 days of assuming office and within 30 days of leaving office.
- *The Election Commission:* This commission is charged with controlling, managing, and organizing elections for members of both houses of parliament and for members of local administrations and assemblies. The commission aims to ensure fair and clean public referenda. It is empowered to order recounts of votes, validate election results, and call for new elections. Its role is considered crucial to counter the country's notorious "money politics." The constitution aims to combat vote-buying through stronger monitoring and through the newly instituted powers of the Election Commission.
- *The Constitutional Court:* This court's work focuses on complaints involving laws or state actions that are alleged to contradict provisions of the constitution. It also responds to disputes regarding the power or duties of state organizations under the constitution. It is the final arbiter with regard to legal questions about cases of corruption.

- *The Ombudsman:* Like its counterparts in the Philippines and other countries, the Ombudsman is empowered to investigate and prosecute, on the bases of people's complaints, officials and employees of government agencies, state enterprises, and local administrations.[8]
- *The Administrative Court:* This court has jurisdiction over cases arising from disputes among government agencies, local administrations, and officials involving their performance of duties, such as abuses of power or failure to perform their functions. It is the venue for citizens' right to sue government agencies.
- *The Audit Commissioners and Office of the Auditor General:* This office replaced the Office of Auditor that was previously under the supervision of the prime minister's office. Its operational independence is enhanced by the fact that the Senate, not the prime minister, appoints the commissioners. It is in charge of monitoring the management of state revenues and fostering improvements in the efficiency and effectiveness of the state's resources.

Apart from measures to increase competition in parliamentary elections, enhance electoral accountability in the Senate, and foster independent checking institutions, the 1997 constitution also aimed at fortifying the country's legal backbone to combat corruption in other areas via the following provisions (Sopchokchai, Suwanraks, and Binsri 2000):

- *Reducing the potential conflicts of interest of public officials:* Cabinet members cannot hold partnerships or own shares of more than 5 percent in business companies, and cannot take part in commercial transactions with state agencies. Political parties also have to declare the size and source of donations received to the Election Commission for public disclosure.
- *Monitoring the wealth of public officials:* The new rules require that top politicians and senior civil servants declare their assets and liabilities to the NCCC before and after gaining their positions. The commissioners can verify whether the declared assets and liabilities are correct. In the event of faults and flaws in the disclosure, the commission is empowered to investigate and prosecute.
- *Increasing investigation of abuses of public office:* The constitution mandates that the National Counter-Corruption Commission will investigate complaints of corrupt practices and will prosecute officials and propose penalties for violators, including removal from office. Public officials and private businesses involved in corruption in state transactions, as well as public officials who are aware of corrupt practices but who fail to act against them, are subject to severe sanctions.
- *Developing new channels to report and complain about corrupt practices:* There are now more channels for the public to complain against the

abuse of power and corruption of public officials. People can file a case at the Administrative Court or report to the Ombudsman. After gathering no less than 50,000 signatures, they also may petition the Senate to compel investigation of the highest officials of government.

Building on the momentum of constitutional reforms, Parliament enacted the Official Information Act to enhance transparency by enhancing the public's access to information regarding government operations. The law was passed just a month ahead of the ratification of the 1997 constitution, ushering in the opening of what has historically been largely restricted from public view. The act seeks to also encourage popular participation in monitoring government activities, both at the national and local levels, because the public, armed with information, can analyze and decide for themselves. In effect, by providing greater information access, the law expands the public's rights relative to the state.

During this period of constitutional reform several attempts were made to reform the bureaucracy itself, aiming to increase its performance and probity. Those efforts started as early as 1996 when the Civil Service Commission initiated an action plan for bureaucratic reform. Several seminars were organized on issues of good governance and bureaucratic reform. In May 1997 the Chavalit Government unveiled a master plan for bureaucratic reform that would result in reducing the number of government officials. After the People's Constitution was completed, the Civil Service Commission approved measures to change the roles and responsibilities of government agencies to comply with the new charter, focusing on citizens' rights to efficient and cost-effective public services. In the aftermath of the Asian financial crisis, the government also agreed with the International Monetary Fund on a rescue plan that targeted the bureaucracy as one of the areas needing structural reform. The measures included reducing the size of the public sector work force, continuing privatization, and pushing for greater efficiency and effectiveness of government agencies. In October 2002 new bureaucratic reforms were initiated, focusing on two main changes: structures were reformed to become less complex and more focused on core responsibilities, and a performance budgeting process was adopted to ensure greater financial accountability among government agencies.

To summarize, the rapid development of Thailand's economy contributed to the expansion of its civil society, whose growing clamor for good governance in the 1990s resulted in major institutional reforms, as exemplified in the 1997 People's Constitution. Thus, the political and legal environments in Thailand have been given a stronger foundation for the promotion of good governance. By increasing people's awareness of their rights and encouraging their participation in the new institutions, many people are hopeful that a "virtuous cycle" will ensue and that the prospects of controlling corruption will be better than before.

The Challenge for Civil Society: Building a Coalition against Corruption

For some time, observers of anticorruption efforts have been cautious about the capacity of Thailand's civil society to shift its involvement from advocacy to impact. As one commentator put it,

> Yet while civil society is gaining strength, it is not sufficiently advanced to bring about broad political reforms on its own. The public sector must build stronger links among its members and also with the overseeing bodies mandated by the Constitution in order to achieve broad political reforms. Then one can move from awareness to action. (Phongpaichit and others 2000)

Although the 1997 constitution lays down infrastructure for fighting corruption, law enforcement in Thailand is still weak. Civil society and social movements play an important role in pressuring the government to enforce the law. The 1997 constitution itself is a good example of the success of social movements. More specifically, recent events surrounding the Ministry of Public Health's drug procurement scandal underscore the potency of social movements (see the details in box 5.1).

When news of corruption in medicine and medical supplies procurement in the Ministry of Public Health surfaced in 1998 there was a public outcry. The news was notable because an NGO blew the whistle loudly. To come out against corruption by public officials is not new in Thai society, but it is rare. This particular case differed from others, however, because the movement against corruption covered a long period, had continuity, and eventually extended to other areas. It was in many ways a strange, new phenomenon for Thai society.

The 1997 economic crisis had resulted in considerable reduction of budget allocation for procurement of equipment, construction, and investment. That restriction forced government administrators accustomed to personal gain from such allocation to look for other sources. However, the budget for medicine and medical supplies procurement could hardly be reduced. Instead, it was increased especially because the crisis reduced the number of patients attending private hospitals and correspondingly increased the numbers being seen in public hospitals. With increasing unemployment and declining income, more people had to rely on public sector service at the time when the state had to tighten its belt. These factors affected the budgets of community hospitals and forced

Box 5.1. A Social Movement against Corruption in the Public Health Ministry

It all started on June 15, 1998. The president of the Rural Doctor Society (RDS), Yongyos Thammawut, sent a letter to society members warning them about procurement anomalies in the Public Health Ministry's budget allocation for welfare services for low-income people. He contended that some doctors were told to buy drugs, medical equipment, and supplies from companies named by a senior person in the ministry. The prices turned out to be two or three times higher than market prices.

To gather data about the anomaly the RDS distributed questionnaires on the issue to its members in district hospitals. Doctors in more than 100 district hospitals confirmed in the questionnaires that they had been ordered by politicians and senior health officials to buy the overpriced products (*The Nation*, September 2, 1998). Because of the extensive problem, Yongyos took his concerns public and gave interviews to several newspapers, alleging that the additional budget allocated to district hospitals was being abused (*Matichon*, August 12, 1998; *The Nation*, August 15, 1998. As one newspaper reported, "for example, medical masks, which usually sell at no more than Bt 20 each, were purchased for Bt 120 each, while a disposable cap, normally selling at Bt 5, rises to Bt 150" (*The Nation*, September 3, 1998.)

The RDS urged that irregular purchasing documents be submitted for investigation to the Counter-Corruption Commission and to the Office of the Auditor-General. The public health minister, Rakkiat Sukthana, insisted, however, that there were no irregularities and refused to set up a committee to investigate the case, as demanded by the RDS. In response, Yongyos explained to the press: "We have substantial documents to prove that corruption did take place, so stop telling a lie by denying that it was not true....We cannot rely on the Health Ministry, because some of the executives may also have participated in the corruption" (*The Nation*, August 15, 1998).

Yongyos' actions were uncharacteristic in Thailand, where it was unusual for a civil servant to challenge orders of higher officials, particularly politicians. Doing so could result in harassment, in transfer to remote areas, or in receipt of an inactive post. Asked about his motives, Yongyos said he decided to take action against corruption because it was a clear case of scarce government resources being stolen at a time when the country was facing economic difficulties. He also added that he did not want new graduate doctors to perceive corruption as the social norm (*The Nation*, December 26, 1998).

Subsequently the RDS' complaints got the attention of a group of Thammasat University lecturers. Sixty-seven faculty members signed an open letter calling for an independent investigation into the drugs and medical supplies scandal. This fueled more media attention, with newspapers, radio stations, and television networks reporting continuously on the pro-curement scandal. Information and views from people in the ministry con-firmed the corruption and urged the public health community to take action. Some people mentioned that orders came from two politicians and three senior officers. There were calls to establish an investigating committee.

Finally, an independent fact-finding committee led by a retired senior public health official, Dr. Banlu Siripanit, was appointed in September 1998 to investigate the estimated Bt 1.4 billion scandal. At that time, the permanent secretary of the public health ministry, Dr. Prakom Vuthipongse, had remarked that the RDS was motivated to pursue the issue by its loss of a 10 percent commission from drugs and equipment purchases. This remark prompted protest by RDS members and public health officials. Eventually, the permanent secretary had to apologize for the remarks to the members of the RDS.

The public pressure was enhanced by a group of 30 NGOs led by Rosana Tositrakul. The group called for the resignation of the ministers and permanent secretary, and announced it would gather the 50,000 sig-natures necessary to request a Senate dismissal of the ministers and senior officials. The NGOs also called on the government to protect the doctors and pharmacists who had been forced to buy at inflated prices and to spare them as witnesses. The public health minister and his deputy finally resigned from their posts in September.

In late September the fact-finding committee concluded that certain politicians had collaborated with senior officials to force state hospitals to abuse the Bt 1.4 billion budget for purchasing medicines and medical sup-plies. The report was sent to the prime minister, who forwarded it to the Counter-Corruption Commission (renamed the National Counter-Corruption Commission in 1999). At the same time a disciplinary commit-tee was appointed to investigate implicated officials. The permanent sec-retary was permanently transferred out of the ministry.

In two months the NGO network collected over 50,000 signatures, with the aid of public donations and various volunteers. Confounding skeptics who believed it could not be done, the signature campaign became the first case of a public petition addressed to the Senate under the terms of the 1997 constitution. Since then, there have been several attempts at simi-lar public mobilizations. NGOs and media have also made use of the Information Act to request the government to prevent cover-ups of offi-cials and politicians involved in corruption.

By late 1998, the extensive corruption scandal in the procurement of drugs and medical supplies in the public health ministry revealed that social activation was a critical factor to push anticorruption efforts. For Ms. Tositrakul and the other members of the NGO network, their involve-ment became a pioneering example of a strong civil society developing as a check against official misconduct. This was crucial because transparency,

(Box continues on the following page.)

Box 5.1 (continued)

as the NGO leaders realized, has little meaning if no one outside the state can demand a meaningful accounting that is backed up by credible threats of political or legal sanctions.

Despite the mounting protests over the corruption scandal, however, resistance from the public health ministry persisted. The permanent secretary's libel suit against Rosana demonstrated that the resistance was serious. Together with other NGO leaders, Rosana realized that the momentum of the coalition could be slowed down and might even lose steam as a result of counterattacks by top health officials.

Nevertheless, this episode offers a number of lessons. First, Thailand's legal and regulatory frameworks can be applied to increase the punitive risks for corrupt officials. Second, the constitutional rights of access to information and press freedom are powerful tools in the fight against corruption. Third, the effectiveness of the executive branch to detect and prosecute cases of alleged corruption is limited in an environment where governance is only fair. In such an environment, the participation of civil society is a potent and effective means of combating corruption and putting pressure for action on the executive branch.

---

staff, especially hospital administrators, to solve problems of resource shortage in their respective hospitals. At the same time, those seeking their own interest, who in the past hardly interfered with such budgets, got more involved in medicine and medical supplies procurement.

More expensive prices of medicine immediately affected patients because they had to pay real prices without any subsidies from the government, except for people who were defined as poor. With deteriorating economic conditions among the public, this problem put a great deal of pressure on community hospitals.

The strength and shape of these changes in Thailand became evident following the 1997 Asian financial crisis triggered by the collapse of the Thai baht. For many people it was a rude awakening of the destructive consequences of the corrupt behavior of public officials. Across Thai society there was growing demand for fundamental institutional reforms through constitutional changes. The need for good governance was brought to the fore because the crisis was seen as an opportunity for reform.

In short, the anticorruption movement started by the Rural Doctor Society (RDS) became widely supported by society, not just among NGOs in the public health field. The RDS movement seemed to emerge at the right time when Thai people had a new constitution on their side that provided new mechanisms to monitor and pursue wrongdoers. Although it was unable to reach culpable high-level politicians and administrators, Thai society had been exposed to new constitutional mechanisms for scrutinizing and holding the state accountable. However, the movement was only the beginning of a learning process that would lead toward a more transparent society.

Success of the movement sprang from an accumulation of and a growing clamor for political reform, going back as far as October 14, 1973, when the ideology of service to society had spread extensively to medical students. The ideology took concrete form when those students became rural doctors and established the Rural Doctor Federation, which later became the Rural Doctor Society. When the RDS stepped into a new role of scrutinizing the performance of the Public Health Ministry, it had been more than 20 years since the society had been involved with social development and rural public health systems. RDS began moving against corruption on a continuing basis, thus avoiding loss of budget and punishing some culprits, albeit only partially. The success of the movement cannot be separated from the social movement calling for more political reform, although the evolution of the RDS constituted an important internal factor.

Although the reform movement was started by the RDS, the hard work of the coalition—comprising the NGO network, a group of retired public health officials, and the media, with support from the public—contributed significantly to making the case against corruption. The movement created reaction and public participation through the process of the new constitution. It resulted in the resignations of 2 ministers, the transfer of the permanent secretary, dismissal of 3 high-level officials, the sacking of 5 high-level officials, and the reprimanding of 22 other officials. In addition, the consultant to the health minister was sentenced to jail for six years by the Criminal Court for Politicians in Positions. (That was also the first case tried before such a court founded under the 1997 constitution.)

To penalize the wrongdoers the NGO network called the NCCC to proceed with legal action against politicians as well as other high-level officials who escaped from the first-round investigation, which many believed did not go deep enough. Finally, in November 2002 the NCCC found the ex-minister of public health guilty of dishonesty on duty. There was evidence that he received 5 million baht from the pharmaceutical company. Previously, NCCC had accused him of acquiring unusual wealth.

The Criminal Court for Politicians in Positions was to have read its verdict on the charge of dishonesty on September 19, 2003. But Mr. Rakkiat Sukthana failed to show up. The judge then issued a warrant for his arrest and set a new date to read the verdict on October 28, 2003. If found guilty, he would be jailed. For the unusual wealth charge, the court found him guilty and ordered the seizure of 233.88 million baht (approximately 5.8 million in U.S. dollars) on September 30, 2003. In addition, the Constitutional Court found Mr. Rakkiat Sukthana guilty of concealing his assets. He was banned from political positions for five years.

Assessing the Impact of Anticorruption Institutions

With new institutions and rules in Thailand to fight corruption, a critical challenge for anticorruption actors is to assess those institutions and rules so that they can be made more effective. At the basic level, if the goal is to make corruption a high-risk and low-reward activity, the institutions and rules may be subjected to the following four criteria focused on curbing opportunities and incentives for corruption (see Huther and Shah, 2000):[9]

1. Do they lessen the number of transactions and opportunities for corruption?
2. Do they reduce expected gains or benefits from corrupt transactions?
3. Do they increase the likelihood or probability that corrupt officials will be detected or exposed, prosecuted, and punished?
4. Do they add to the magnitude of penalties for corrupt acts?[10]

If the answer is yes to one or more of those questions, then the institutions and rules contain anticorruption power. In addition to assessing policies and programs from this perspective, it is also crucial to evaluate them in relationship to a country's "quality of governance." The importance of appreciating a country's governance and operating environment in designing policies and programs to deal with problems of corruption is critical. Bhargava and Bolongaita (2001) explained that the

> ...effectiveness of a particular set of anti-corruption instruments will vary depending upon the quality of a country's governance environment. Certain anti-corruption instruments would likely have maximum positive impact in some countries, but will have minimal, even negative, effects in others. (p. 13)

For example, they point out that certain policies, such as reducing state involvement in the economy and allowing more competition in the private sector, have anticorruption effects, especially in a poor governance environment, because they would reduce the scope of corruption and curb the number of opportunities. In contrast, an anticorruption agency introduced in a poor-governance country where corruption is endemic may have little effect because it is embedded in a context where sanctions are not effectively enforced, corruption opportunities are rampant, and state accountability institutions are weak.

Following the passage of Thailand's constitutional reforms, many observers were concerned about the available financial and human resources to support the new institutions. Such resource constraints would naturally limit the ability of these organizations. Reports of attempts by some politicians to place their people in these new offices only served to fan public fears. To many people, the disclosure of major cases of corruption had been too few and far between. The cases thus far suggest that generally only lower-ranking officials are punished.

Other observers have found fault with the stringent requirements of certain constitutional provisions. Of particular issue was the number of signatures needed for popular petitions to force Senate investigations of high-level corruption. As Duenden Nikomborirak, an economics research specialist at the Thailand Development and Research Foundation, explained,

> This is surely a most powerful tool set up with the best intention, but in practice, it is very difficult to use. The founder of such a petition would first have to identify himself to the Senate and authenticate each of the 50,000 signatures, at the risk of going to jail if some signatures are found to be falsified. It puts the people and organizations willing to fight corruption into the spotlight, which can be very dangerous. This is a conspiracy to undermine the use of law. (quoted in the *Bangkok Post* November 8, 2000)

That implies that the constitution's anticorruption provisions present obstacles for people to participate in monitoring the use of power. If the transaction cost of public participation is too high, the level of public participation will be low. The problem of high transaction costs is compounded by the fear of backlash. The witness protection mechanism in Thailand is quite weak, especially in cases against influential people. To strengthen the role of public participation, legislation for whistleblower protection as well as mechanisms to reduce transaction costs are needed.

For other observers, the issue of effective anticorruption was related to the lack of "social capital." As one scholar observed,

> While institutional reforms enhancing transparency and accountability in state and economic institutions are indispensable parts of any anticorruption strategy, they also need a *long-term social foundation*, particularly where corruption is systemic. Social empowerment—expanding and protecting the range of political and economic resources and alternatives open to ordinary citizens—is one

way to address this task. Social empowerment entails strengthening civil society in order to enhance its political and economic vitality, providing more orderly paths of access and rules of interaction between state and society, and balancing economic and political opportunities. (Johnston 1998, p. 85)

In many ways it was the stirrings of social empowerment that made the Thai ground fertile for major changes in its basic political charter and other institutions. The expansion and assertion of civil society combined with the work of reformist officials to effect sweeping shifts in governance. But the challenge of making this change in Thailand a "long-term" proposition remains.

In that regard some people argue that aspects of Thailand's hierarchical and deferential culture may need to be shaken because the culture helps sustain a patronage system that perpetrates corruption in political and economic spheres. But attempting to change culture and values of Thai society undoubtedly will require enormous effort from the public and private sectors as well as civil society. Past efforts along such lines have been generally ineffective—a result that hardly seems surprising because previous attempts to change values were not combined with efforts to reduce the opportunities for corruption and increase the risks of being convicted for corruption.

Evaluating Institutional Performance

There are a number of anticorruption instruments that may be considered to tackle corruption in Thailand (see appendix to this chapter). The question, of course, is to what extent the institutions and rules fostered by the 1997 constitution are making an impact in the fight against corruption. Over the last two years the NCCC has produced some significant results. It tackled several cases of false statements of assets and liabilities submitted by high-ranking politicians. These include the cases involving Thaksin Shinawatra, the prime minister, and Sanan Kachornprasart, the former minister of interior and secretary-general of the Democrat party. Kachornprasart resigned from his cabinet post before the Constitutional Court could issue its verdict. The court eventually found him guilty. He immediately resigned as a member of the House and was banned from public office for five years. The commission also found Shinawatra guilty of concealing his assets and the case was referred on appeal to the Constitutional Court for final adjudication. In early August 2001, by a close and controversial vote of 8 to 7, the Court acquitted him of the charges. However, on the same day, another member of parliament from the Thai Rak Thai Party, Prayuth Hahakitsiri was found guilty of concealing his wealth by a clear 12 to 1 majority and was banned from entering politics for five years.

By October 2002, the Constitutional Court had ruled on 18 cases in which the NCCC indicted officials under the 1997 constitution for providing false or incomplete information in their statement of assets and liabilities (6 cases) or for failing to submit such a statement (12 cases). The court has concurred with the NCCC in 17 of those cases (the exception being the case involving the prime minister, Thaksin Shinawatra) (Klein 2002).

Sanan Kachornprasart, a politician who had earlier been disqualified in a similar case, collected 50,000 signatures to impeach four Constitutional Court judges over the Thaksin verdict. The case was filed for investigation at the NCCC. The four judges filed a writ with the Administrative Court seeking an injunction to prevent the NCCC from conducting an investigation of them. However, the Administrative Court dismissed the case and refused to issue an injunction. At the same time, the house speaker and 50 Thai Rak Thai Party MPs submitted a petition to the Constitutional Court seeking to block the NCCC's investigation. In a 7 to 4 decision the Constitutional Court refused to accept the petition (Klein 2002). The case is now under investigation.

Regarding the workload of the NCCC, it appears that it can barely keep up with the increasing number of cases. There were approximately 1,646 corruption cases filed in 2000; this increased to 2,179 cases in 2001. Most of those cases involved government bureaucrats; only 30 cases involved elected politicians accused of dishonesty or corruption and 45 investigated for unusual wealth.

For its part, the Election Commission of Thailand appears even more burdened. In the general election in 2001 there were more than 1,000 allegations of fraud, but only eight candidates were disqualified. There are also reports of attempts to influence the work of the commission, and there are questions now about the extent of the commission's neutrality and independence (Klein 2002).

Strengthening the Freedom of the Press

Freedom of the press is a critical mechanism in the fight against corruption. Media can help expose and investigate corruption. In Thailand the number of investigative journalists has increased considerably. For example, several of the cases filed before the NCCC were investigated and reported in the newpaper *Prachachart Turakij*. The media's involvement was also crucial in the corruption case regarding drugs and medical supplies procurement. Because of media attention, the public outcry increased pressure on the government to respond. The media helps keep people's attention and helps protect witnesses and the people who expose corruption.

Under the 1997 constitution a person shall enjoy the liberty to express his or her opinion, make speeches, write, print, and publicize. But this has been easier to say than to do. Public officials who have been criticized by growing media freedoms have tried to defend themselves or use measures, both legal and illegal, to protect themselves. Some journalists have been slapped with libel cases, others were threatened or killed (Reporters Without Borders 2002). In the past the government has intervened to influence the electronic media directly because the state owns most of the country's television and radio stations. But the way the 1997 constitution has promoted press freedom led to a change from intervention using state mechanisms to intervention using business power, that is, use of commercial advertising to curry political support in the press. This has been done through the advertising budgets of state agencies and enterprises owned by businesses with ties to politicians. The present government has actually been accused of applying both political and economic pressure on the media to silence critical voices. (See the details in box 5.2.)

Although Thailand's record, as indicated in the Freedom House index, showed signs of improvement in terms of press freedom, problems

---

Box 5.2. The Cases of Freedom of the Press

In February 2001, one day before the lower house of Parliament confirmed Thaksin Shinawatra as the new prime minister, 23 journalists and news anchors at ITV were laid off by the new managing director appointed by the Shin Corporation (founded by Thaksin Shinawatra). At the television station, some of the fired journalists were involved in creating a union to defend an independent editorial policy.

On March 6, 2002, several newspapers reported that the Anti-Money-Laundering Office (AMLO) had launched an investigation into the assets of several journalists. The AMLO had sent official letters, dated February 25, to 17 banks, asking them to provide financial information on five newspapers and 14 people. Most of the targets were prominent journalists who had criticized the government. At the same time, some journalists' radio and television news programs were cancelled by state agencies. The Shin Corporation and state enterprises withdrew advertising contracts with newspapers apparently after those newspapers reported news critical of the government.

Top AMLO officials and the prime minister (who by law must chair the Anti-Money-Laundering Committee) initially denied any knowledge of the investigation. The investigated journalists filed a petition with the Administrative Court against the AMLO and its three top officials, including the prime minister as the board chair. In court the AMLO officials said they launched the investigation after receiving an anonymous letter alleging that the journalists had participated in extortion and blackmail activities with a secret society or criminal organization.

In response the Thai Journalists' Association submitted to the Senate an open letter signed by 1,195 media professionals calling for an inquiry into the government's alleged intimidation of the media. In addition, a petition was submitted to the National Human Rights Commission. A few days later almost 500 academics signed another open letter calling for freedom of the press.

In response to the public outrage, the government appointed a fact-finding committee to investigate the case. This incident led to public debates on several issues regarding the anti-money-laundering law (AMLA), the AMLO, and its enforcement procedures. The Thai Bankers' Association, for example, suggested that the Bank of Thailand serve as an intermediary in screening information requested by law enforcement agencies to create public confidence in the financial system. The bankers also agreed with the committee's suggestion to have a new AMLO framework for handling future information requests. However, no official proposal regarding the AMLA and AMLO has been submitted to the government.

The fact-finding committee determined that the AMLO did order commercial banks to report on the accounts of the journalists, but that there was no evidence that it had been ordered to do so. It also found that the AMLO order for bank records was not properly justified under the AMLA, and that the investigation was highly inappropriate and violated the freedom and privacy guaranteed by the constitution. It said that the AMLO needed to exercise more discretion in balancing respect for privacy with its investigative procedures. But the committee did not draw any conclusion on whether the AMLO committed any criminal or civil violation.

The committee found that the AMLO secretary-general and the director of the Information Technology and Analysis Center failed to carry out their statutory duties in accordance with the law. It recommended the implementation of several reforms at the AMLO, including vesting its operational committee (rather than the secretary-general alone) with the responsibility of making such investigation decisions under a ministerial regulation, establishing a code of conduct or ethics for AMLO staff, and disallowing the secretary-general to delegate his duties.

Some analysts have suggested that, to avoid political influence, the AMLO be reconstituted as an independent agency, similar to the National Counter-Corruption Commission. And some have called for amending the AMLA to reduce the AMLO's power. However, because the secretary-general is selected by the Parliament for a term of four years, some believe that reconstituting AMLO as an independent body can provide a guarantee of AMLO's neutrality and independence. Finally, the AMLO withdrew the order to investigate such cases following the Administrative Court's verdict.

remain. Strengthening and enhancing press freedom is a necessary task to ensure the effectiveness of anticorruption mechanisms.

Conclusion

The governance environment in Thailand has undergone some significant changes as a result of constitutional and legal revisions introduced since the East Asian financial crisis in 1997. These changes in the governance environment are particularly reflected in new, independent accountability institutions and in the stronger legal basis for the public's right to know. These changes, in turn, have provided a conducive environment for potentially powerful anticorruption coalitions. As recent events show, vested interests have reacted and attempted to subvert these new and positive developments on the anticorruption front.

Using the analytical framework presented at the beginning of this book, the priorities for devoting resources and leadership to anticorruption policies and programs are the following:

- Strengthen independent accountability institutions
- Support civil society participation in anticorruption work
- Disseminate through the media factual information on trends in the incidence of corruption and on the performance of public sector accountability mechanisms
- Pursue economic and regulatory reforms that reduce opportunities for corruption.

To summarize, the 1997 constitutional reforms prompted by anticorruption coalitions and social movements have increased the potential for combating corruption. Those first efforts, although a necessary beginning, are insufficient. How the case history on outcomes of cases of alleged corruption evolves over the next few years will tell whether the fight against corruption is being won or lost. The roles played by civil society organizations and the media will make the crucial difference.

Appendix: Overview Assessment of the Effectiveness of Anticorruption Policies and Programs in Thailand

Program	Likelihood of reduced opportunities	Likelihood of reduced gains	Likelihood of increased risk of punishment	Likelihood of increased severity of penalty	Remarks on efforts	Recommendation
Public sector management						
Reforming bureaucracy	Medium	Low	Low	Low	A new bureaucratic system was adopted October 1, 2002, in which the size and scope of ministries tended to decrease but the number of ministries increased. The most progressive step has been the change to performance budgeting. Transparency and accountability, however, remain an important issue in the next steps.	Strengthen the bureaucracy by improving procedures to evaluate officials on the basis of their performance; improve the budgeting system by developing evaluation and feedback processes.
Raising awareness of public officials through seminars on good governance and ethics	Medium	Medium	Low	Low	Seminars, forums, and workshops on transparency and accountability by government, civil society organizations, academia, and international organizations are continuing.	Need to ensure that programs are suitable and appropriate to Thai society.
Establishing officials' code of ethics	Low	Low	Low	Low	The Civil Service Commission has proposed norms and codes of conduct for government employees.	Raise the awareness of public officials and inform the public about the code of ethics.

(Appendix continues on the following page.)

Program	Likelihood of reduced opportunities	Likelihood of reduced gains	Likelihood of increased risk of punishment	Likelihood of increased severity of penalty	Remarks on efforts	Recommendation
Raising public sector wages	Low	Low	Low	Low	The government introduced the bonus system, but the salary schedule is still relatively low compared with the private sector.	Ensure that the bonus system and increases in salary are based on performance; it is crucial to have a good performance evaluation program.
Enforcing financial accountability	Medium	Medium	Low	Low	A new budgeting system has been adopted, e-procurement has been introduced, and customs reforms are in process.	All three broad reforms are important and need to be strengthened using performance feedback from users and stakeholders.
Reducing public employment	Medium	Medium	Medium	Medium	There are efforts to control public employment using means such as an early retirement program.	
Decentralizing government	Medium	Medium	Low	Low	Several attempts have been made to strengthen local government. At least 20 percent of the national budget was allocated to local governments. Education and public health are in the process of reform in line with decentralization. Local organizations are still weak, however,	It is important to strengthen local governments by training officials, raising public awareness about participating in local government, and encouraging local officials to collect taxes more efficiently.

and public participation in local government is at low levels.

(*Appendix continues on the following page.*)

Competition and the private sector

Reforming economic policy	Low	Low	Low	Low	Such reform is potentially powerful, but the privatization schedule is slower than planned, and deregulation and procompetition policies are weak.	Policies must ensure an increase in competition.
Raising private sector awareness of corruption through seminars	Low	Low	Low	Low	Seminars and discussion on corporate governance are conducted by both private and public organizations. Codes of conduct are being pushed for private sector.	

Civil society participation

Raising public awareness of corruption through seminars	Low	Low	Low	Low	Seminars and discussion on corruption by civil society organizations, universities, independent institutions, and international agencies are being conducted.	Continue *and* increase in-depth knowledge of corruption and mechanisms for monitoring and reporting it.
Establishing freedom of the press	Medium	Medium	Medium	Medium	Media are ranked third among tools for curbing corruption. Over the last five years, media have played an important role in providing information on corruption—but there are attempts to influence the media.	Raise public awareness of the important role played by the media and of the value of press freedom. Create programs to train investigative journalists.

Appendix (continued)

Program	Likelihood of reduced opportunities	Likelihood of reduced gains	Likelihood of increased risk of punishment	Likelihood of increased severity of penalty	Remarks on efforts	Recommendation
Encouraging citizen participation	Medium	Medium	Medium	Medium	Although citizen participation was promoted in the 1997 constitution, it is still difficult for the public to participate, especially in policymaking.	Create an awareness of the importance of public participation, adjust mechanisms to lower transaction costs of participation, create a whistleblower program, and find ways to decrease costs for access to government information.
Institutional restraints						
Enforcing rule of law	Low	Low	Low	Low	This is crucial to good governance, but a recent survey shows corruption in the judiciary and the police are high.	Judicial and police reforms are critical.
Establishing anticorruption agencies	Medium	Medium	Medium	Medium	Strengthen various accountability organizations, especially the NCCC and the Administrative Court. Because of limited resources and weak governance environment their performance has been slower than expected.	Increase resources of these organizations; provide training programs, especially in NCCC; and recruit skilled staff.
Establishing parliamentary oversight	Medium	Medium	Medium	Medium	The Senate has played an important role in monitoring government.	

Creating ombudsman position	Low	Low	Low	Low	
Setting up anti-money-laundering office	Medium	Medium	Medium	Medium	There is limited cooperation between the AMLO and NCCC in curbing corruption.	Pursue prospects for cooperation, especially because of the powerful potential synergy of such cooperation.
Political accountability					
Requiring declarations of assets	Medium	Medium	Medium	Medium	There have been a number of successful cases of dismissal from office for violating asset declaration rules.	Continue and improve the mechanism to verify declarations.
Enforcing rules on conflict of interest	Low	Low	Low	Low	Although the rule determines that cabinet members cannot hold shares of more than 5 percent in corporations, politicians avoid this by transferring shares to members of their immediate families.	It is important to modify mechanisms to counter circumventions of the rule.
Requiring transparency in financing of political parties	Low	Low	Low	Low	Political parties must declare their sources of donation, but it is widely known that many are not forthcoming.	Declarations of both revenue and expenditures should be open to the public.
Encouraging political competition	Low	Low	Low	Low	Under the 1997 constitution, the number of political parties declined. Currently there are mainly two large political parties.	More political competition is needed to promote accountability and transparency.

Notes

1. Phongpaichit and Baker adapted the formula from Johnson (1975).

2. The CPI score ranges from 0 to 10: the minimum score of 0 indicates that the country is perceived to be totally corrupt and the maximum score of 10 means that it is perceived to be totally clean. The 1988–92 ranking is a retrospective effort, based on surveys extant during that time.

3. From 1999 to 2001 Thailand's CPI was stable at 3.2.

4. Gwartney and Lawson's (2001) summary rating of economic freedom consists of the following factors: size of government, structure of economy and use of markets, monetary policy and price stability, freedom to use alternative currencies, legal structure and property rights, international exchange, and freedom of exchange in financial markets.

5. The CPI ranking for Thailand has been steady at 3.2 from 2000 to 2002, with a slight uptick to 3.3 in 2003.

6. This amendment is similar to the constitutional change in the Philippines, where the 1987 constitution mandates that one-fifth of the lower house, the House of Representatives, be elected through a party-list system.

7. In many cases the corruption at the local level links with the national level.

8. For an assessment of the performance of the Philippines' Ombudsman as an anticorruption instrument see Bolongaita (2002).

9. For an expanded treatment see Bhargava and Bolongaita 2001.

10. Huther and Shah (2000) noted that research findings suggest that the probability of paying penalties is more likely to have an impact than is the magnitude of the penalty.

References

Bhargava, Vinay K., and Emil P. Bolongaita, Jr. 2001. "Making National Anti-Corruption Policies and Programs More Effective: An Analytical Framework." Paper prepared for the World Bank's Global Distance Learning Program on Combating Corruption in the Asia-Pacific Region. Available at www.fas.nus.edu.sg/ppp/wp/wp08.pdf.

Bolongaita, Emil. 2002. "Improving Governance and Competitiveness of the Philippines: Exploring Approaches to Make the Ombudsman More Effective." Assessment Report prepared for the U.S. Agency for International Development, Manila.

Doner, Rick, and Anil Ramsay. 2000. "Rent-seeking and Economic Development in Thailand." In Mushtaq H. Khan and K. S. Jomo, eds.,

Rents, Rent-Seeking and Economic Development: Theory and Evidence in Asia. Cambridge, U.K.: Cambridge University Press.

Gwartney, James, and Robert Lawson. 2001. *Economic Freedom of the World 2001 Annual Report.* Vancouver, B.C.: Fraser Institute.

Huther, Jeff, and Anwar Shah.1998. "Applying a Simple Measure of Good Governance to the Debate on Fiscal Decentralization." World Bank Working Paper 1894, Washington, D.C.

———. 2000. "Anti-Corruption Policies and Programs: A Framework for Evaluation." World Bank Working Paper 2501. Washington, D.C.

"In the Clear." 2001. *Time,* August 13, p. 14.

Johnson, Omotunde. E. G. 1975. "An Economic Analysis of Corrupt Government, with Special Application to Less Developed Countries." *Kyklos* 28(1): 47–61.

Johnston, Michael. 1998. "Fighting Systemic Corruption: Social Foundations for Institutional Reform." In M. Robinson, ed., *Corruption and Development.* London: Frank Cass.

Kaufmann, Daniel, Aart Kraay, and Massimo Mastruzzi. 2003. "Governance Matters III: Governance Indicators 1996–2002." World Bank Policy Research Working Paper 3106. Washington, D.C.

Khan, Mushtaq H. 2000. "Rent-seeking as Process." In Mushtaq H. Khan and K. S. Jomo, eds., *Rents, Rent-Seeking, and Economic Development: Theory and Evidence in Asia.* Cambridge, U.K.: Cambridge University Press.

Klein, James R. 2002. "The Battle for Rule of Law in Thailand: The Constitutional Court of Thailand." Paper presented at King Prajadhipok's Institute Congress IV: Five Years of Political Reform Under the New Constitution, November 8–10, Bangkok.

Laird, John. 2000. *Money Politics, Globalization, and Crisis: The Case of Thailand.* Singapore: Graham Brash.

Laothamatas, Anek. 1996. "A Tale of Two Democracies: Conflicting Perceptions of Elections and Democracy in Thailand." In R. H. Taylor, ed., *The Politics of Election in Southeast Asia*. New York: Cambridge University Press.

Phongpaichit, Pasuk, and Chris Baker. 2002. "Good Governance, Money Politics, and Honest Mistakes." Paper presented at the Distinguished Alumni Award 2001, May 2, at Monash Asia Institute, Monash University, Melbourne.

Phongpaichit, Pasuk, Sungsidh Piriyarangsan, and Nualnoi Treerat. 1999. *Guns, Girls, Gambling and Ganja: Thailand's Illegal Economy and Public Policy*. Chiangmai, Thailand: Silkworm Book.

Phongpaichit, Pasuk, Nualnoi Treerat, Yongyuth Chaiyapong, and Chris Baker. 2000. "Corruption in the Public Sector in Thailand: Perceptions and Experience of Households." Research Project on Anti-Corruption Strategy in Thailand in the Year 2000. Bangkok: Office of the Civil Service Commission of Thailand.

Poapongsakorn, Nipon, Deunden Nikomborirak, and Suwanna Tulyawasinphong. 2000. "Corruption in the Thai Public Sector: Case Study and Anti-Corruption Strategy from an Economic Perspective." Paper presented at the Conference on Transparent and Clean Public Service Society, November 18-19. Chonburi, Thailand.

Reporters Without Borders. 2002. "Thailand Annual Report 2002." Available at www.rsf.org/.

Sopchokchai, Orapin, Ryratana Suwanraks, and Panniya Binsri. 2000. "The Thai Constitution and New Mechanisms for Transparent and Anti-Corruption Society." Paper presented at the Conference on Transparent and Clean Public Service Society, November 18–19. Chonburi, Thailand.

Sussman, Leonard R., and Karin Deutsch Karlikar. 2002. *The Annual Survey of Press Freedom 2002*. New York: Freedom House.

Thairungroj, Sauwanee, Pornpong Sumanan, Thanavath Pholvichai, Rungroj Benjamasutin, and Nithitah Benjamasutin. 2000. "Thailand: Business Environment and Governance Survey." Research Project on Anti-Corruption Strategy in Thailand in the Year 2000. Bangkok: Office of the Civil Service Commission of Thailand.

Transparency International. 2000. Press release on Corruption Perceptions Index 2000. Available at www.transparency.org/cpi/2000/cpi2000.html.

Yaowaprapas, Supachai. 2000. "Corruption in the Public Sector: Perceptions of the Civil Servants and Anti-Corruption Action Plan." Research Project on Anti-Corruption Strategy in Thailand in the Year 2000. Bangkok: Office of the Civil Service Commission of Thailand.

6

The State of Corruption: Indonesia

The Present Impasse

Indonesia has the unwanted reputation of being one of the most corrupt countries in the world, although fighting corruption has been high on the policy agenda (at least notionally) since the fall of Suharto[1] in May 1998. Corruption, however, simply defined as "the use of public office for private gain in ways that contravene declared rules," remains endemic (Hamilton-Hart 2001, p. 66).[2] In fact, Transparency International listed Indonesia as the third most corrupt country in the world in its 2001 survey (along with Uganda) and fourth most corrupt in 2002 (in company with Kenya) (see the Internet Centre for Corruption Research). Indonesia has scored poorly in recent surveys. In 2000 the Hong Kong (China)–based Political and Economic Risk Consultancy released results that showed expatriates working in Asia viewed Indonesia as the most corrupt of the Asian countries (*Kompas*, March 23, 2000).

Indeed corruption, or what Indonesians generically call KKN (the Indonesian-language acronym for corruption, collusion, and nepotism), remains a debilitating disease that infects institutions in all branches of the Indonesian state apparatus and for which there does not seem to be an immediate cure. Reflecting a real sense of popular disappointment with the outcomes of *reformasi* (reform) in this area, the head of Indonesia Corruption Watch (ICW), a vocal independent watchdog organization, concluded that there has been little concrete progress in eradicating corruption since the fall of Suharto (*Kompas*, April 1, 2002), in spite of early

This case study was contributed by Vedi R. Hadiz, assistant professor, Department of Sociology, National University of Singapore. He would like to thank Kurniawan and Budi Murdono for their research assistance; Luky Djuniardi Djani and Natasha Hamilton-Hart for useful information and discussion; and Emil Bolongaita and two anonymous referees for their comments on previous versions of this chapter.

promises. In its Country Assistance Strategy for Indonesia, the World Bank (2001) observed that "corruption is still rampant and infects the very institutions (the police and judiciary) that are supposed to tackle it" (p. 1).

Vividly illustrating the problem, the short tenure of Suharto's successors in the presidency were tainted by implication in corruption scandals relating to the illicit mobilization of political funds. Furthermore, many other powerful people, past and present, have been implicated in high-profile corruption scandals, including top officials of the former ruling party, Golkar, and members of parliament.[3]

In spite of the slow rate of progress in combating corruption, there has been a significant change in its essential patterns and dynamics. During the long Suharto era, a highly centralized, authoritarian government meant that there was a certain degree of predictability about the corruption that fed into a greatly personalized, patrimonial system of rule centered on the presidency. With the unraveling of Suharto's New Order, power has become much more diffused and decentralized, and I suggest that the patterns and dynamics of corruption have done likewise. Previous efforts to eradicate corruption, however well intentioned, clearly have not had much impact and much tougher and more consistent measures are required.

Corruption has a long history in Indonesia. It has plagued governments since early independence (which was declared in 1945 and internationally recognized in 1949), although it arguably reached the greatest heights—in terms of sheer scale, sophistication, and damage—when the New Order began in 1966. In the period of parliamentary liberal democracy (1950–59) and during the Sukarno-dominated Guided Democracy (1959–65), corruption and abuse of power had already commonly taken the form of alliances among political patrons and business clients (Robison 1986) who were regularly given special privileges in the shape of licenses and other nontransparent business opportunities. This was to be a pattern replicated during the New Order. The big difference was that the economic cake was to grow so much larger—as was the scale of the resources that could be misappropriated.

Furthermore, predatory behavior became much more systematic (and rapacious) than ever before as the power of the state bureaucracy and its officials became paramount in relation to society-based actors. Coalitions of politico-bureaucratic and business interests consolidated and became entrenched, arguably appropriating state power and policy. The influx of foreign investment and aid at the beginning of the New Order, the oil booms of the 1970s, and even the economic deregulation and (selective) privatization of the 1980s and 1990s provided powerful alliances of business and politico-bureaucrats with ample opportunities to use and abuse economic policy and public resources (Robison and Rosser 2000). Thus the opening of Indonesia's economy did not eradicate corruption; on the contrary, it may have further fueled it in numerous areas (perhaps most prominently in banking).

The essential problem was that the process of economic liberalization was driven by the same interests that had already been incubated by the powerful, authoritarian New Order state during the preceding, more protectionist oil boom period. So economic liberalization further encouraged the fusion of business and bureaucratic interests in a powerful coalition that effectively ran the agenda of a highly centralized, authoritarian state (Robison and Hadiz 2002). In Thailand, by contrast, economic liberalization was accompanied by political liberalization and the emergence of new business groups that challenged the hegemony of old banking and industrial conglomerates. But even in Thailand the demands of electoral politics, nationally and locally, "where success depended on access to enormous quantities of money, saw business and elected officials establishing relationships" similar to those that existed prior to economic liberalization (Hewison 2001, p. 89).

It is tempting to suggest that corruption is something innately acceptable to Indonesian culture and that it thrives simply because it does not go against the cultural values of the majority of the Indonesian people. How else should one explain its persistence? Such a position was strongly implied 30 years ago by the influential scholar of Indonesia, Benedict Anderson. Discussing the dominant Javanese culture, in particular, he wrote that there was nothing ethically problematic in the Javanese worldview about powerholders enjoying great wealth: wealth was more or less naturally supposed to flow to those who possessed power—a notion that Anderson suggested is the opposite of the Western view in which wealth begets power (Anderson 1972).

Despite the long history and pervasiveness of corruption, however, there is demonstrably also a great deal of public resentment toward it. That fact is best shown by the very real anger displayed in many sectors of society at the depredations of Suharto's rule, which was seen as allowing for the illicit generation of enormous amounts of wealth for his family members and cronies. A sense of injustice clearly arises in public discussions today when this wealth is contrasted to the poverty that still prevails, especially given the contradiction with the frequently egalitarian rhetoric of the New Order and given the hardships imposed on many by the economic crisis. In fact the ICW has suggested that KKN was responsible for the gravity of the Indonesian manifestation of the recent Asian economic crisis and that the eradication of that corruption would help Indonesia's recovery. A recent survey produced results that showed 70 percent of respondents (totaling 2,300) view corruption as a serious social problem, which was likened to a "disease to combat." The household respondents to the survey (that also included public officials and businesses) ranked corruption as a more serious problem than unemployment or the poor state of the economy (Partnership for Governance Reform in Indonesia 2001, p. 30).

Indeed, cultural determinist explanations for corruption are simply too neat and they run the risk of unintentionally condoning corruption on the basis of a misplaced cultural sensitivity. Moreover, they do not explain why corruption has also been endemic in many other societies—past and present—with cultures that differ markedly from Indonesia's.

Added focus should be placed on a more tangible problem: presently existing institutional frameworks have not allowed public resentment of corruption to be translated into practices that penalize the abuse of power by officials for the sake of generating private wealth. Indeed, the frameworks have more or less ensured that corruption remains an attractive option to those presently in office who have control over or access to state institutions and resources. It remains largely in the interest of these officeholders, nationally—and, increasingly, locally—that effective anticorruption mechanisms are relatively absent. In other words, there is an abiding interest on the part of office holders in ensuring that the institutions that are supposed to check predatory behavior remain weak and generally ineffective. Thus corruption carries little risk, and the benefits associated with it are high. From that standpoint, institutions are understood not simply as collective arrangements that can facilitate efficiency and governance but also as mechanisms for the allocation and distribution of power and the furtherance of embedded interests.

It is significant, however, that Indonesia's new democracy has resulted in greater public scrutiny over the behavior of officeholders. That scrutiny is partly the result of the considerable press freedoms now enjoyed in Indonesia, which allow public pressure to be expressed through revelations and discussion of corrupt practices. The World Bank, in its recent Country Assistance Strategy document (World Bank 2001), reported that "there is now much more open debate in Indonesia over key development issues such as debt, corruption and the participation of civil society in public policy formulation....A free press keeps a watchful eye on the political process and on the courts" (p. i). The unraveling of Suharto's authoritarian system of rule has also meant that there is now a greater level of public expectation of accountability on the part of officeholders. The result is that a host of organizations are now involved in the fight against corruption. It is significant that these include governmental as well as nongovernmental organizations (NGOs).

Nevertheless, there are well-founded fears that even such an elevated level of scrutiny will not be enough to deter the rapacity of powerful elites. Such developments as greater local autonomy over governance and finance could lead to the further decentralization of corrupt behavior and the rise of new, more diffuse systems of patronage than existed during the Suharto era. That possibility goes against the conventional wisdom that decentralization will result in less corruption as officials become more directly accountable to the public. Indeed, some struggles over local offices—such as those of *bupati* (regent) and mayor—have already been particularly ugly and involved widespread reports of money politics and violence as local forms of bossism begin to emerge.[4]

A notable side effect of Indonesia's democracy is that both local and national officeholders cannot be certain how long they will roam the corridors of power. They realize that they could lose an election or in some other way be ousted abruptly from officialdom. Thus it is possible that individuals in office would take every opportunity to accumulate as much wealth as possible within a relatively short period. In popular Indonesian parlance, this is known as the attitude of *aji mumpung* (literally, opportunism), which can lead to ever-increasing levels of greed on the part of officials. Again the basic problem here is that the institutions of Indonesia's democracy have been harnessed by many of the same interests, nationally and locally, that were nurtured by the predatory New Order.

Governance

From the foregoing observations one can see that good governance—including ensuring the rule of law, improving the efficiency and accountability of the public sector, and tackling corruption[5]—evidently remains a distant dream in Indonesia. The political, economic, and social institutions inherited from the Suharto era have been so highly corrupted that various reforms have thus far yielded only limited results. Given the vested interests entrenched in these institutions, this legacy of the New Order will likely remain with Indonesia for a long time to come. In relation to corruption I will present a brief discussion of such key institutions as the courts, the police force, and, given their new position of importance in governance, political parties and parliaments.

The Courts

The Indonesian judiciary is widely thought to be corrupt. The selling and buying of court decisions is reported to be a pervasive problem (*Jakarta Post*, April 1, 2002).[6] In 2001 there were 104 public complaints filed in relation to Indonesia's courts, including the Supreme Court. Those complaints were filed with the short-lived Joint Investigation Team for the Eradication of Corruption (Indonesian-language acronym, TGPTPK), which was tasked with receiving public complaints about and investigating corrupt practices by state officials (Awaluddin n.d.).

Because the Indonesian court system is regarded as corrupt it has been of little use in the fight against corruption. For example, although much hope was placed initially in the country's newly established commercial courts, the courts' performance in deterring corruption has been disappointing—the government has lost almost every case of bad debts it has pursued (Hamilton-Hart 2001). That experience has led the public to hold the courts in even lower esteem. It is hard to convince the general public that the court system will deliver impartial justice in cases of alleged corruption by ex-president Suharto, his family, and other high-ranking officials.[7]

Judges are relatively underpaid for the power they wield. For example, a newly appointed judge would earn only about Rp 2,150,000 a month (US$210). Furthermore, from the beginning of his or her career a judge would have a great incentive to engage in corrupt practices, at the very least to offset the initial investment involved in embarking on that career choice. According to various accounts, to pass a test necessary for a judicial appointment a prospective judge would have to hand out relatively large sums in bribes. To further complicate matters, recruiting prosecutors (a profession also tarnished badly by allegations of corruption) reportedly involves the same practices (*Jakarta Post*, April 23 and 24, 2002).[8] Indeed, the esteem in which judges are held is so low that there was even public discussion recently of importing foreign judges on an as-needed basis. (The preference was for Dutch judges because the roots of the Indonesian legal system are in Dutch law.)

Various reforms have been pursued recently to repair the justice system. There have been attempts particularly to reform the Supreme Court and the courts in Jakarta by mass reassignments. Unlike in the Suharto period, parliament now has a big say in the appointment of Supreme Court judges. That seems to have politicized the Supreme Court, however, because members of parliament nominate political allies. Former President Wahid was embroiled in a long standoff with parliament because of his displeasure with the legislative body's nominees for chief and deputy chief justice. There also have been calls for a complete overhaul of the Supreme Court through the replacement of career judges by legal professionals untainted by allegations of corruption.[9] Indeed, about half of the parliamentary nominees to the Supreme Court in 2000 were not career judges.

A rare example of the Court system's efforts to cleanse itself took place in April 2002 when the Central Jakarta District Court found a Jakarta high court judge guilty of receiving Rp 550 million in bribes while he headed the appeals division of the Supreme Court in 2000. The guilty judge was given a suspended sentence of one year in jail (*Jakarta Post*, April 24, 2002).

The Police Force

Indonesia's national police force used to be part of the armed forces. But the police force has been independent of the armed forces since 2000 in order to underline its nonmilitary nature and functions. Military-like ranks, such as general or colonel, have been replaced with such ranks as police inspector and police commissioner. Like the courts, the police force also suffers from a very low level of public esteem. Petty corruption involving provision of driving licenses, traffic violations, and crimes like robbery and theft is reported to be prevalent among police officers, and members of the public frequently choose not to report crime because they fear extortion by the police.

Part of the problem is, again, that of chronically low salaries, especially in contrast with ever-conspicuous middle- and upper-class consumption. But even in recognition of this, it is clear that another aspect is that police officers can get away with these practices. In other words, nobody effectively polices the police. Thus, like the judiciary, the police force so far has not been an effective tool in the fight against corruption. Indeed, police officers are alleged to break the law with impunity. For example, some policemen themselves recently reported that police personnel receive protection money to turn a blind eye to the lucrative illegal gambling industry.[10]

It is useful to note that the illegal gambling industry is not present only in Jakarta, but also in other large cities such as Surabaya and Medan where gangsters with links to powerful local bureaucrats or to police and military personnel freely practice their trade. A systematic investigation of the problem probably would implicate a considerable number of police officers. In Yogyakarta, for example, a provincial parliamentarian expressed his belief that police were complicit with gangs of youths who raid entertainment spots and gambling dens in the Yogyakarta and Central Java areas, ostensibly for reasons of morality. According to this parliamentarian, these establishments simply open again once they have paid off these youths, who in turn, pay off the local police.[11] Again, the perceived susceptibility of police force members to bribery and collusion does not help the institution eradicate corruption. In a further blow to the standing of the police force, a former Jakarta chief of police was implicated in a case involving the illegal importation of luxury automobiles (*Tempo*, May 27 to June 2, 2002).[12]

Political Parties and Parliaments

Political parties are conventionally understood to be vehicles through which the aspirations and interests of the general public are aggregated and articulated. During the Suharto era, political party life was highly constrained, with only three parties allowed to exist and Golkar dominating heavily controlled elections. The fall of Suharto was followed by the quick relaxation of those laws and there was high public expectation about the role of political parties in the advance of a democratic system with greater transparency, rule of law, and accountability.

Major political parties, however, have mostly functioned as vehicles through which disparate coalitions, with little in common in terms of policy agenda, have sought to gain control over the institutions of the state and their resources. The major parties are inhabited notably by large numbers of people whose careers were nurtured within the New Order system of patronage—former bureaucrats, ex-Golkar officials, retired military and police officers, as well as political and business entrepreneurs. Major political parties are widely believed to be uniformly involved in the pervasive practice of money politics, down to the local level.[13] Though existing political laws govern the process of receiving contributions, they have been very poorly enforced, and the required campaign auditing results have not been made public.

The Indonesia Corruption Watch, as well as press reports, has alleged that national parliamentarians of all parties regularly receive bribes from government bodies and the private sector for voting a particular way on various bills.[14] Moreover, certain parliamentary commissions are widely regarded as being particularly lucrative or "wet"—for example, those that deal with finance and development.

Less discussed, however, are emerging patterns of money politics and corruption at the local level. These patterns are increasingly regarded as a problem because central state authority has now diminished—a situation that has been more or less codified by the promulgation of local autonomy laws, although these laws remain contested.[15]

As is true in the national parliament, certain commissions in local parliaments are considered to be more lucrative than others. In the election of the mayor of the city of Medan, North Sumatra, some parliamentarians admitted to being bribed to cast their votes for the eventual winning candidate (*Kompas*, March 22, 2000).[16] In the new province of North Maluku, the election of a former Suharto aide as governor was rescinded because of allegations of money politics and the minister of the interior called for new elections while the allegations were investigated (*Jakarta Post*, April 22, 2002).[17]

It is likely that the incidence of corruption at the local level will need to be the focus of more attention by government and nongovernmental accountability institutions. Unfortunately, most of the better-equipped accountability institutions are based in Jakarta, whereas it will be especially important to monitor developments in economically significant regions such as industrial centers and resource-rich provinces like East

Kalimantan and Riau where much is at stake in the jostling for control over state institutions and access to state resources.

Corruption Conditions

It is difficult to determine precisely whether corruption has improved or worsened in Indonesia. During the Suharto era the late doyen of Indonesia's economists, Sumitro Djojohadikusumo, suggested that as much as 30 percent of the national budget "evaporated" through corruption (*Jakarta Post*, January 27, 2003). Jeffrey Winters, a U.S.-based Indonesia specialist, even suggested in 1997 that 30 percent of World Bank aid to Indonesia had been misappropriated over the years (*Suara Pembaruan*, August 1, 1997). International NGO Forum on Indonesian Development (INFID), a consortium of NGOs, supported this allegation but it was denied by the World Bank representative in Jakarta. Transparency International's Corruption Perceptions Index for Indonesia has shown scores that rise and fall over time (figure 6.1). (Scores on the index range from 1 to 10, with a higher number indicating a lower perception of corruption.) Nevertheless, it is important to note that polls on which the index is based merely record "perceptions," and in no way capture the "actual" levels of corruption from year to year. In fact, perceptions and reality may not correlate at all.[18]

The impression from anecdotal sources is that corruption has worsened in recent years, but one must take into account the current levels of public scrutiny and open discussion, and the unpredictability that can result when powers are decentralized. For example, a foreign investor with no experience dealing with Indonesia might now be especially perplexed: there is little consensus about whether local autonomy laws

Figure 6.1. Transparency International Corruption Perceptions Index, Indonesia Scores, Selected Years, 1980–2001

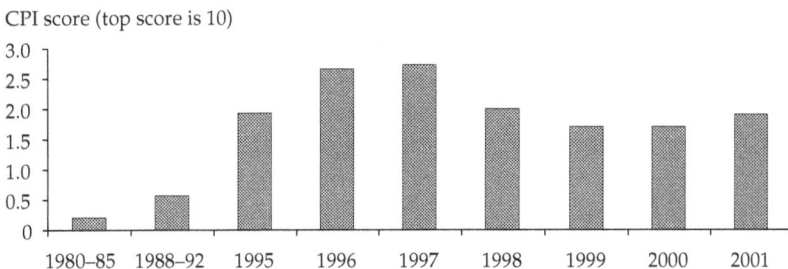

CPI score (top score is 10)

Source: Transparency International, available at www.transparency.org.

require the investor to seek permission to invest from Jakarta, from the governor, or from the local regent.[19] In practical terms this probably means that the investor has to provide kickbacks to various people at different levels of Indonesia's notoriously cumbersome bureaucracy, with relatively little guarantee that the bribes are reaching the right people.

Some observers cite data that might suggest an improved situation. In one account (Hamilton-Hart 2001) it is argued that if the reported abuse of central bank funds were not counted, corruption or mismanagement cost the Indonesian government only Rp 4.7 trillion during the fiscal year up to March 2000, compared with Rp 18.2 trillion reported in the previous fiscal year. The same account asserts that Pertamina, long considered by many to be a corrupt source of informal funds for political projects, reportedly suffered a loss of only Rp 1 trillion as a result of irregularities, compared with Rp 4.7 billion from 1996 to 1998.[20]

However, state audit agencies have subsequently revealed that they uncovered Rp 10.3 trillion worth of irregularities in the administration of government, involving 9,656 cases for the budget year 2000 and the first half of 2001. It is not surprising that the largest "contributors" to these irregularities were again the traditional "cash cows" of Bulog (*Kompas*, September 26, 2001), which enjoyed a monopoly in the distribution of food and some basic necessities, and Pertamina, the state oil company.

Indeed, the degree of state capture by corrupt interests remains at very high levels. The Indonesian Bank Restructuring Agency (IBRA), for example, has been considered a coveted prize. Set up in the last months of the Suharto era, it controlled taken-over private assets worth about Rp 600 trillion and was targeted to raise some Rp 18.9 trillion in cash in the 2000 budget year. By 2002 IBRA had six chairs in only four years (*Jakarta Post*, April 20, 2002). A former head of IBRA has also been the subject of scrutiny, with the Attorney General's Office pressed to investigate the sale of the government's stake in the PT Indomobil Sukses Internasional, a prized taken-over asset of the Salim Group.[21]

Other key economic institutions are also facing allegations of corruption. The Bank of Indonesia, the country's central bank, has been alleged to be involved in the misappropriation of allocated liquidity funds designed to help ailing banks during the height of the economic crisis. The Financial Audit Body (Indonesian-language acronym, BPK) found that Rp 84 trillion of the Rp 144.5 trillion allocated until January 1999 were misused by recipients (*Kompas*, August 5, 2000). Most observers believe that such a state of affairs is unlikely to have transpired without the connivance of some officials from the Bank of Indonesia (*Jakarta Post*, June 26, 2000).

In the wake of these incidents several bankers have been prosecuted, but so far that has not yielded many results. One banker accused of misusing Bank of Indonesia liquidity funds was tried in absentia while he fought extradition from Australia (*Kompas*, March 13, 2002), and another facing the same charges has been in Singapore claiming illness and has so far refused to reappear in Indonesia (*Tempo*, May 20–26, 2002). A former IBRA chief was also alleged to have been protecting this tycoon's interests (*Tempo*, March 4–10, 2002). Still another banker escaped punishment for allegedly breaching regulations on lending to his other businesses, a fairly common practice since Indonesia's banking sector was liberalized in the late 1980s. That case was dismissed in court on a legal technicality (*Kompas*, April 27, 2002).

Anticorruption Policies and Institutions

As I mentioned earlier, fighting corruption is officially high on the government's agenda. Indeed, MPR (People's Consultative Assembly) Decree No. 11/1998 (produced during the first post-Suharto session) calls for a "State administration that is clean and free of corruption, collusion and nepotism." It also affirms that no past or present state official, or members of their families, will be above the law.

The government has sought to pursue a number of anticorruption measures to improve governance in the judiciary, civil service, corporate sector, and executive branch. In November 2001 it signed on to the Asian Development Bank (ADB)-Organisation for Economic Co-operation and Development (OECD) Anti-Corruption Action Plan for Asia and the Pacific.

Some of the pillars of the ADB-OECD plan are already present in Indonesia, at least to some extent. For example, new systems are now in place to promote transparency through disclosure and monitoring of personal assets. But other pillars of the plan are absent—for example, some elements of Pillar 1 dealing with the integrity of the public service. That lack was demonstrated in the earlier discussion of some of the institutions of governance. It has been pointed out that judges and police personnel, for example, are not properly compensated for their work, as they should be according to the plan.[22] It was also shown, for example, that bribery remains an important means of attaining a position, whether as bureaucrat or elected official. Moreover, bribery rather than transparent criteria is seen to be an important part in promotions and placement in lucrative positions for many individual civil servants.[23]

Also relatively absent are many elements of Pillar 2 dealing with anti-bribery actions and promoting integrity in business operations. Bribing officials is widely perceived as crucial to ensuring the successful operations of a business. However, the decentralization of powers has created some confusion in the business community: a major problem for foreign as well as domestic investors is figuring out the "correct" individuals and offices to bribe. That element of predictability and certainty of the Suharto era is gone, and businesspeople are more anxious.[24]

On the positive side, in accordance with Pillar 2 there is a new body that monitors the conditions under which businesses operate in Indonesia. However, it too is not free from controversy. The alleged links between officials of key state financial institutions and business tycoons, and the importance of business contributions to political parties, suggest that politico-bureaucratic-business alliances still remain a feature of Indonesian life. Moreover, leading members of the local business community may have very little credibility as reformists, given their history of complicity with corrupt practices.[25]

Perhaps most obviously present in the discussion that follows is the growing prominence of public involvement in combating corruption— Pillar 3 of the ADB-OECD plan—at least as represented by independent, civil society–based accountability institutions. Public involvement is surely much assisted by the current existence of a free press. Although there are limits to what the accountability institutions can achieve in their current condition and in the wider context, they have been instrumental in widening access to information and placing public pressure.

Anticorruption Government Bodies

A number of government bodies are tasked with dealing with corruption in Indonesia. What follows are profiles of the most important of these bodies. (In addition to these bodies, on November 29, 2002, the Indonesian parliament endorsed a bill to set up an Anti-Corruption Commission (www.detik.com). It is not yet possible to assess this institution because it has not been established and its prospective composition remains unclear.)

- *Badan Pemeriksa Keuangan* (Financial Audit Body):[26] The BPK's legal standing is on par with that of parliament and the presidency. In theory it is free of the influence of those bodies, although that certainly was not the case during the Suharto era. The BPK was established to fulfill the constitutional requirement for the existence of a body responsible for auditing state finances and was organized according to a 1973 law. The body is mostly concerned with examining expenditure of the national budget and it audits the books of government ministries and other institutions. Its findings are conveyed to the parliament. The BPK also advises the government should there be findings that involve criminal acts or that impose costs on state finances. The BPK's chair is chosen by the president from among nominations by parliament. The body has offices in at least seven major cities.[27]

  The BPK has been proactive, periodically announcing findings that reveal disturbingly high levels of financial irregularities in the running of state institutions. The more open political environment clearly has encouraged this proactive behavior. However, the body does not have power to demand that the government follow up on the results of its findings. For example, the BPK announced that only 870 of the 2,508 cases of irregularities revealed for the first semester of 2001 have been followed up by authorities (*Kompas*, September 26, 2001).

- *Badan Pengawasan Keuangan dan Pembangunan* (BPKP, Financial and Development Audit Body):[28] At first glance, many of its functions appear to overlap with those of the BPK. Like the BPK, it examines the books of all government institutions and examines suspected irregularities. But the BPKP is an instrument of the executive body of government, whereas the BPK stands outside of that branch. As an instrument of the central government the BPKP is potentially important in monitoring irregularities in the implementation of local autonomy and decentralization, especially because it has greater presence at the local level. The minister of finance, for example, can request that the BPKP investigate irregularities in provincial or local budgets but cannot do the same with the BPK for reasons relating to the structure of government. Essentially then, the BPK—which is on par with the executive body—acts as an external auditor of the finances of government institutions whereas the BPKP acts as an internal auditor (*Bisnis Indonesia*, July 19, 2000). Like the BPK, the BPKP regularly announces the uncovering of irregularities in government finances but it too has no authority to command other authorities—the police and the Attorney General's Office—to investigate the cases that it uncovers.
- *Komisi Pemeriksa Kekayaan Penyelenggara Negara* (KPKPN, Commission to Investigate the Wealth of State Officials):[29] This is a body formed by and responsible to the president. The KPKPN has the authority to investigate the wealth of a wide array of state officials, including the president, ministers, governors, regents, prosecutors, state enterprise commissioners, and national and local parliamentarians. The KPKPN, whose membership is nominated by parliament, consists of at least 25 people.[30] The membership mixes representatives from government and the general public. The body has embarked on a highly publicized program of tabulating the wealth of state officials by asking them to declare on detailed forms the extent of their wealth and how it was accumulated. It has publicly announced the results of these tabulations, over the protestations of some officials.

The KPKPN has had limited success in its efforts. It was reported in April 2002 that of the 48,000 forms it has distributed to officials, only 20,000 were returned. To remedy the situation, KPKPN announced its intention to solicit assistance from the police and prosecutors to prompt recalcitrant officials to cooperate (*Kompas*, April 24, 2002). But this tabulation effort has also been hampered by the limited capacity of the KPKPN to verify the truth of the declared wealth of officials.[31] The commission also has the authority to examine complaints filed by members of the public, NGOs, and state administrators relating to corruption in government institutions. The eventual establishment of the above-mentioned Anti-Corruption Commission may see the KPKPN merged into the new body when it is formally set up.

- *Komisi Ombudsman Nasional* (National Ombudsman Commission):[32] This is a body authorized to monitor and examine public complaints about the administration of the state and the provision of public services. It was established on the basis of a presidential decision in 2000. An aim of the commission is to increase the level of public participation in eradicating corruption. Theoretically it has the authority to investigate irregularities found in the administration of the state. The commission consists of 11 members, including prominent legal experts and a few activists.

  Like the BPK and BPKP, the National Ombudsman Commission has no authority to compel law enforcement agencies to follow up on its findings, and many government bodies may not bother to reply to its inquiries. The commission is also reported to be short on funding and other resources.

- *Tim Gabungan Pemberantasan Tindak Pidana Korupsi* (TGPTPK, Joint Investigation Team for the Eradication of Corruption):[33] The team was established in 2000 by the attorney general in response to calls for more proactive governmental efforts to eradicate corruption. A widely respected judge was appointed to chair the 25-member team, which comprises police officers, prosecutors, accountants, academics, and activists. The team was initially bolstered by what was then the attorney general's policy: anyone reporting or testifying against corruption would be granted immunity from prosecution. The TGPTPK was designed as an interim body, however, and its short life (until July 2001) was sometimes controversial. The team's work came to an end as a result of a Supreme Court decision that found the TGPTPK's existence contrary to the Criminal Procedures Law of 1981 and the Anti-Corruption Law of 1999. The Supreme Court decision created a public controversy because the team had been investigating alleged corruption by three members of the Supreme Court itself, and the justices who were under investigation had filed a defamation suit against the team.

- *Komisi Pengawas Persaingan Usaha* (KPPU, Business Competition Supervisory Commission):[34] Strictly speaking, this body is not an anti-corruption institution. However, its purview, which encompasses ensuring healthy business competition in Indonesia, is very much related to issues relevant to corruption, given the past abuse of public office directed toward the granting of monopolies, special licenses, and privileges to politically connected businesses. Its membership comprises academics, business analysts, and economists. The KPPU was set up in relation to a 1999 Anti-Monopoly Law. The commission reports to parliament and to the president.[35]

Anticorruption Laws

Until recently Law No. 3/1971 was the main reference point in dealing with cases of corruption.[36] Although it defines penalties for state officials who undertake corrupt activities, it was clearly an ineffective deterrent in light of the severity of corruption in Indonesia during the period of the New Order to the present day. After the fall of Suharto there was a new impulse to deal with the chronic problem of corruption. That impulse was reflected in MPR Decree No. 11/1998, although, ironically, the body that produced it was a product of the corrupt New Order itself. On the basis of that decree, at least two laws were enacted. One was Law No. 28/1999 dealing with the property of high ranking government officials, and the other was Law No. 31/1999, which superseded the 1971 legislation as the main legal reference against corruption.

In many ways the new legislation is harsher than the older law. For example, those found guilty of corruption during an economic crisis or natural disaster may be sentenced to death. Severe fines are also imposed as a minimum penalty for a corruption offense. Most important, the law now shifts the burden of proof in corruption cases from the prosecutor to the defendant.

There was at least one important limitation of Law No. 31/1999, however: it does not stipulate a transition from the use of the 1971 legislation to the new one. Hence it has been argued that the 1999 law cannot be applied to cases or offenses that predate its inception.[37] Moreover, no matter how severe penalties may be under the law, if the likelihood of suffering those penalties is low the law is essentially useless.

Anticorruption Coalitions

There has been a notable increase in civil society–based initiatives to monitor and help eradicate corruption. This has been made possible by the greater political freedoms enjoyed since the fall of the authoritarian New Order, and in many cases by the cooperation of foreign donor agencies. Civil society–based accountability organizations and their spokespeople regularly criticize the government for its slow handling of corruption cases and so raise public awareness of those cases. In the past, such open criticism would have met with a stern response from the authorities and possibly resulted in imprisonment. Below are profiles of some of the more important of these independent accountability institutions.

- *Indonesia Corruption Watch:*[38] This high-profile organization was established on June 21, 1998, just a month after the fall of Suharto, by a group of disparate individuals with reputations for being critical toward the Suharto regime. The organization was clearly a product of the *reformasi* movement that aspired toward a clean government, "free from corruption, collusion, and nepotism." The initial idea for ICW came from public figures and NGO activists.[39] ICW has been the most publicly vocal and aggressive of the society-based anticorruption institutions, regularly making press statements and conveying commentaries on the state of corruption in Indonesia. Its vision is to develop a strong civil society able to check the behaviors of corrupt powerholders and their collaborators in the private sector. ICW conducts research, produces publications, holds seminars and advocacy activities, and is headed by Teten Masduki, who is also a National Ombudsman.
- *Masyarakat Transparansi Indonesia* (MTI, Indonesian Transparency Society):[40] This civil society–based organization sees itself as part of a moral movement to cleanse the government and the private sector of corrupt practices. Among other tasks, it holds itself responsible for socializing the virtues of transparent practices in all aspects of life and for monitoring public policy to ensure that it meets with the public interest. MTI's activities include organizing meetings, conducting research on transparency-related issues, and disseminating research results to decisionmakers in business, government, and the public at large.

  The founders of MTI include academics, journalists, government ministers, a businessman, and a religious leader.[41] Its chief executive initially was Mar'ie Muhammad, minister of finance under Suharto, who in spite of that has a reputation for personal integrity. Although the MTI is a credible organization, the strong links of some of its members to the New Order may be a potential liability.
- *Partnership for Governance Reforms:*[42] The partnership is a collaboration between the international community and Indonesia to promote and support governance reform. It brings together the Indonesian government, legislature, judiciary, civil society, the corporate sector, and the international community. The partnership, in existence since 2001, fosters policy dialogue and analysis on governance issues and makes public information on key aspects of governance reforms in Indonesia. It also provides financial assistance to Indonesian agencies active in governance reform efforts. The partnership has carried out various activities in the areas of anticorruption measures, civil service reform, civil society and media strengthening, corporate governance, electoral

reform, legal and judicial reforms, and police/security reform. The coalition combines internal and external champions and is able to back its recommendations for reform with financial support.

- *Transparency International, Indonesia Chapter* (TI-Indonesia):[43] This organization is affiliated with Berlin-based Transparency International. It aims to create greater transparency and accountability in the administration of government and business. Like many other accountability institutions, it is involved in compiling and analyzing information related to transparency and in raising public awareness of corruption issues. It is also developing a media-based anticorruption campaign. TI-Indonesia conducts seminars, workshops, and training sessions. Its supervisory body includes a lawyer, a former judge, and a noted journalist, and its executive body consists of a mixture of business practitioners, academics, and well-known NGO activists.

- *Local anticorruption watchdogs*: There has been a proliferation of local anticorruption watchdogs in the relatively short period of time since the fall of Suharto. Some of these have roots in older NGO movements; others were responses to the holding of free elections in 1999; and still others were a direct reaction to the increasing importance of local governments in the context of decentralization policies.[44] In 2000 a loose coalition of such organizations formed an entity called GERAK, or the People's Anti-Corruption Movement, which coordinates such activities as training and advocacy.[45] Although they proliferate, local anticorruption organizations lack experience, skilled personnel, and resources, including funding.[46]

Leadership and Management

A key problem with the institutions and agencies harnessed to combat corruption is in finding the people who have the credibility to lead the fight. Past association with the corrupt New Order may become a liability for many of Indonesia's elites. There was some uproar about the composition of membership in the KPKPN, for example, because some of the individuals were thought to be less than "clean." A few former government officials, however, have been able to emerge from the New Order with relatively intact personal reputations. Some of these—like Mar'ie Muhammad—are involved in anticorruption institutions.

The specific circumstances in Indonesia call for greater nongovernmental, public participation in the fight against corruption. It is here that civil society–based organizations like ICW and MTI can have a greater impact, because it is likely that there will be more public trust in those organizations. As mentioned earlier, well-known and credible activists are in the forefront of these civil society–based efforts against corruption.

That having been said, anticorruption accountability institutions such as the BPK and the BPKP must be better equipped and endowed to improve their performance and civil society groups must monitor that performance. No matter how unconvincing their past performances have been, those are the institutions with the trained personnel and most of the powers necessary to carry out widespread auditing activities.

Nevertheless, the NGOs have a potentially larger role to play. At the very least they complement the governmental institutions. But, more crucially, if they are embraced by the government (rather than viewed as a threat) their presence will bestow a great deal more legitimacy on the effort of combating corruption. A related problem, however, is that some NGOs feel that they would lose their public credibility if they were perceived to be working too closely with the government. One possible way to develop a productive relationship between state and nonstate agencies is to provide greater public access to governmental auditing results, which would allow at least some of the better-established civil society–based groups to verify official audits. There has been some progress in this direction in the form of periodic BPK and BPKP announcements of their findings.

More public trust could be gained if civil society–based organizations played a more direct, if semiofficial, role in some of the auditing exercises. It is unfortunately a fact that the independent auditing of accounting firms does not necessarily receive the trust of the general public, given the perception that some of these have been paid off in the past to produce favorable reports. Although the involvement of nongovernmental bodies, like ICW or MTI, could be seen as encroaching on the authority of government institutions, such an arrangement would help gain the confidence of a very jaded public. ICW, for example, appears to rely greatly on whistleblowers rather than on official sources.[47] But the NGOs also have to be more professional and better equipped. They are all relatively new in the field and their personnel need to be trained in accounting and other skills necessary for effective monitoring.

Another chronic problem is ensuring that relevant authorities pursue allegations of irregularities, whether found by BPK and BPKP or by ICW and MTI. Given the large number of cases already disclosed, it is possible that the police and court system would be working full time just dealing with a fraction of those cases, if they chose to do so. Of course, not all cases should and can go to court because internal mechanisms of punishment should be at work in the different government agencies and bodies as well. However, the prosecution of the significant offenders remains necessary for the purposes of deterrence and underlining the seriousness of the anticorruption effort.[48]

Monitoring and Reporting Mechanisms

Improvements have been made in mechanisms of monitoring and reporting. Organizations like the BPK and the BPKP are more seriously active than they used to be, although they have not managed to erase from memory their less-than-impressive performance during the Suharto era. More civil society–based organizations are also carving out a role for themselves as advocates of clean government. The press is in a better position to demand accountability from public officials than during the authoritarian New Order, when publications were routinely closed down for printing critical opinions or controversial stories. Clearly this is a positive result of the fall of Suharto and of the economic crisis, both of which have encouraged greater public scrutiny of the behavior of officials.

Thus, such key bodies as the tax office, state banks, IBRA, the Bank of Indonesia, and others are subject to new auditing, disclosure, and monitoring requirements. The Bank of Indonesia, as the central bank, is taking more seriously its role of supervising state banks. Moreover, a governance and oversight unit for state and recapitalized banks has been established, and the audit of state banks has been carried out by international firms.[49] The central bank itself now has to report to parliament. Although there are clear limitations to what can be achieved in the current institutional context, these efforts represent some progress that should be sustained and strengthened.

There are still many areas where disclosure is inadequate. Virtually still off-limits in terms of monitoring are the many businesses that are officially and semiofficially run by the armed forces, including the lucrative field of forestry concessions.[50] Also overlooked are monitoring and reporting at the local level. The focus on Jakarta in the past is understandable, given the heavy concentration of wealth and power there. But trends toward decentralization have given greater levels of power and authority over some resources to local officials—notwithstanding the tug-of-war still taking place in regard to local autonomy laws. There is a real danger that the process might just transfer KKN from Jakarta to the regions. Indeed, numerous interviews I have conducted with local parliamentarians, officials, and businesspeople in North Sumatra and Yogyakarta, suggest that this transfer is already happening. It was recently reported that local officials "in a number of provinces and regencies already face audits for allegedly abusing as much as 40 per cent of the 60 trillion rupiah...transferred to regional governments to pay for civil servants' salaries" (*Straits Times*, May 31, 2002). For that reason National Ombudsman Anton Sujata suggested establishing regional ombudsmen (*Kompas,* February 23, 2002). But it is here that the role of civil society is even more important. Thus, civil society–based monitors in the regions also need to have upgraded skills and resources. As in every sector of Indonesian life, most of the skills and resources are concentrated in Jakarta.

Conclusion

Despite progress in enacting reforms to control corruption, corruption remains endemic in Indonesia. The problem is not some inherent, immutable feature of Indonesian culture, nor is it best described in terms of the simple lack of political will or of necessary institutions per se. The crux of the problem lies in the nature of the interests that have captured, appropriated, and ensconced themselves in the institutions of state power since the beginning of the New Order. From that standpoint, the lack of real inroads into eradicating corruption thus far is not entirely surprising. The new framework of governance in post-Suharto Indonesia continues to be shaped by many of the same interests that were active during Suharto's time. For them, an effective system of checks and balances constitutes no less than a fundamental threat, especially if the system involves more meaningful and wide-ranging public scrutiny and accountability,

In other words, the kind of interests that remain salient in today's Indonesia are those of the predatory type incubated during Suharto's rule that are now reinventing themselves in the current so-called era of *reformasi* and democratization (Robison and Hadiz 2002). These interests remain predominant in the judiciary, police, military, political parties, parliaments, and civilian bureaucracy as a whole, as well as in the business community. Furthermore, such interests can be expected to have a stake in keeping monitoring institutions weak and in safeguarding the conditions that make possible the plundering of state coffers and the forging of illicit alliances with business.

Although the kinds of social groups with a genuine vested interest in transparency, accountability, and the eradication of KKN remain relatively marginal and comparatively disorganized, through *reformasi* they have become more vocal. Although reforming existing institutions remains important, real progress in combating corruption ultimately depends on the ability of these reformist interests to organize coherently in order to capture the mainstream of political life and thereby drive the process to forge new, more effective, anticorruption institutions and practices.

Notes

1. The former president spells his name "Soeharto"; in the Western press, however, his name is commonly spelled "Suharto."

2. Although corruption by definition involves officials, Hamilton-Hart (2001) noted that it also can involve members of society as victims or cobeneficiaries. This is an important point, especially in a society like New Order Indonesia, where the dividing line between the public and private spheres was often blurred. The New Order was established in 1966 by a coalition of anticommunist forces led by General Suharto, who governed Indonesia until his downfall in 1998.

3. At present, the state financial audit body, the BPK, has raised the issue of the use of "Banpres" money (traditionally a nonbudgetary, nontransparent presidential discretionary fund) under Megawati Sukarnoputri's administration (*Tempo,* April 22–28, 2002). Among the concerns is that all nonbudgetary funds are supposed to have been transferred to the Department of Finance after 1999.

4. The term "bossism" probably emerged from the experience of local and city politics in the United States in the early to middle part of the 20th century. In Southeast Asia, it has been widely used in the context of the Philippines and Thailand (the *chao pho,* or godfather). In this region it essentially refers to local "strongmen" who control the electoral and bureaucratic machines of provinces, towns, or villages and who embody the alliance of local business, political interests, and frequently organized crime.

5. This understanding of good governance is taken from Camdessus 1997.

6. For many observers, Indonesian judges (and prosecutors and lawyers) would seem to enjoy a very low level of social esteem, with some Indonesians referring to the existence of a "judicial mafia."

7. There have been speculations that Suharto's ability to escape trial because of ill health was somehow the result of foul play, although no one has been able to furnish evidence. Similar suspicions were raised when a court released Akbar Tanjung—the Golkar chief on trial for corruption—from police detention, prompting the *Jakarta Post* to editorialize about the need to "probe the judges' involved in making this decision, in the belief that some wrongdoing had been committed" (*Jakarta Post,* April 9, 2002).

8. Defense lawyers too are not immune from criticism. Tommy Suharto's lawyer was detained for allegedly bribing witnesses in his case.

9. Previously, 80 percent of Supreme Court judges were reported to have taken bribes (*Straits Times,* August 26, 2000).

10. One police officer was quoted as having said "Gambling dens are cash cows for us. If we need money, we can just visit a certain den to get some cash. The operators, including the police officers protecting them, usually start shaking when they see a provost officer" (*Sunday Times,* April 21, 2002, p. 14). That account has been confirmed by one of Indonesia's more respected former police officers, Awaloeddin Djamin, who headed the force from 1978 to 1982. He suggested that the problem is simply one of supply and demand—gambling operators demand protection and police officers simply provide it. However, such a dismissive, almost nonchalant, attitude toward such a serious problem clearly may breed acceptance of police corruption within the force itself.

11. Personal interview with Herman Abdul Rahman, provincial parliamentarian, Yogyakarta, December 14, 2000.

12. Symptomatic of low public opinion and trust of the police force is some Indonesians' perception about police complicity in Tommy Suharto's long avoidance of justice, although no proof to that effect has ever been produced. It is significant that Tommy Suharto himself alluded to such police cooperation during his trial, but there has been no follow-up investigation.

13. ICW's Teten Masduki suggested that all major parties are beholden to conglomerates because of their need for campaign contributions (Masduki 2000, p. ix).

14. It has been alleged that a number of political parties, not only Golkar, received money from the same source, Bulog, in 1999 (*Straits Times*, November 29, 2001), reportedly as part of a scenario to get then–President Habibie reelected. *Tempo* devoted a major story to the practice (September 10–16, 2001).

15. For example, a provincial legislator in Yogyakarta has claimed that provincial parliamentary members received bribes to appoint certain individuals to the MPR as regional delegates (interview with Herman Abdul Rahman, December 14, 2000, Yogyakarta). MPR members set broad guidelines of national state policy and elect the president and vice-president of Indonesia.

16. The brother of the losing candidate, a major local businessman, complained that the municipal parliamentarians reneged on their promises to vote for his brother, even though he gave them money to return the initial bribe received from the winning candidate, and suggested that there were receipts to prove this (interview with Yopie Baturabara, businessman, September 8, 2001, Medan).

17. Some relatively petty cases may not qualify as corruption but would certainly qualify as abuse of power. For example, the Jakarta municipal parliament diverted funds earmarked for emergencies, including natural disasters, to buy 55 new cars for their official use (*Tempo*, October 1–7, 2001). Meanwhile, in early 2002 much of Jakarta was flooded by the combination of heavy rains and existing environmental degradation, and at least 65 people died. The official response to the human tragedy was typically slow, with bureaucrats citing the lack of funds.

18. Information is available at Transparency International's Web site, www.transparency.org.

19. I found this to be the case during fieldwork in North Sumatra. Officials at different levels of government would promote the role of their respective institutions in "facilitating" investment.

20. Even if accurate, however, such figures "do not capture forms of corruption that do not impose financial costs on the government." (Hamilton-Hart 2001, p. 74).

21. IBRA was criticized by some observers after it sold more than 72 percent of its stake in Indomobil to a consortium led by little-known PT Tri Megah Securities in late 2002. Reports alluded to suspicions that the Salim Group had secretly taken over the company again through intermediaries, something that it was legally barred from doing. IBRA had sold its shares at Rp 625 each, which was far

lower than the Rp 2,500 per share that the government paid when acquiring the company in 1998 (*Jakarta Post*, April 22, 2002). The new head of IBRA was alleged in a story published by *Tempo* to be partly responsible for the favorable debt restructuring terms enjoyed by two powerful conglomerates, Texmaco and Sinar Mas (*Tempo*, April 22–28, 2002).

22. Even the increases over the last two years in the salaries of civil servants have not improved the situation to a significant extent.

23. Anecdotal evidence of this practice abounds in offices as diverse as the foreign ministry and the local government of Bekasi.

24. An entrepreneur trying to start a business in information technology services in Batam Island told how it was difficult to calculate the amount of bribes and the level of project markups that were necessary to keep local officials cooperative (personal communication, April 28, 2002). Others have told how local authorities have gone overboard with charging new formal and informal taxes on business (*Medan Bisnis*, September 5, 2001; *Kompas*, September 19, 2001; also interviews with Yopie Batubara, head of the North Sumatra Chamber of Commerce and Industry, September 8, 2001, and with Surya Sampurna, businessman based in North Sumatra, July 6, 2001).

25. For example, the head of the Indonesian Chamber of Trade and Industry, Aburizal Bakrie, has been a vocal national spokesman against the policies of local officials who are eager to establish new forms of taxation that hinder business. However, some people point to his companies as having benefited from preferential treatment during the Suharto regime (*Kompas*, September 10, 2001).

26. See www.bpk.go.id.

27. The chair is currently Satrio Budhiardjo Judono, who was a minister during the Suharto era.

28. See www.bpkp.go.id.

29. Formed on the basis of Law No. 28/1999.

30. It currently consists of 35 individuals.

31. Many officials have gotten around ill-defined regulations by claiming that much of their wealth derived from inheritance or "gifts." Nevertheless, if officials' assets far exceed their official incomes, such claims need to be verified under the law.

32. See www.ombudsman.or.id.

33. The information below mainly relies on Awaluddin (n.d.).

34. This information comes largely from www.kppu.or.id.

35. It has been alleged that, contrary to regulations, some members of KPPU hold interests in commercial enterprises (*Tempo Interaktif*, April 17, 2002).

36. This section is based on Awaluddin (n.d., p. 11) and the pieces of legislation referred to here.

37. Some legal commentators argue that this omission was deliberately made in order to protect offenders during the New Order (*Kompas*, May 13, 2000).

38. The information here is taken from www.antikorupsi.org/about/index.htm.

39. They included Adi Andojo, the respected former judge who headed TGPTPK; Alexander Irwan, business analyst; Sonny Keraf, university lecturer; Bambang Widjajanto, then head of the Legal Aid Institute; Chusnul Mariyah, university lecturer; Christianto Wibisono, business analyst; Daniel Dhakidae, academic and journalist; Eros Djarot, filmmaker and journalist; Marsilam Simanjuntak, political activist; Masdar F. Mas'udi, NGO leader; Munir, human rights activist; Teten Masduki, labor activist; and T. Mulya Lubis, lawyer.

40. See www.transparansi.or.id.

41. Government officials include former Attorney General Marzuki Darusman, Juwono Sudarsono, Ma'rie Muhammad, Bambang Subianto, and Boediono—all of whom, incidentally, have strong Golkar and New Order connections. Teddy Rachmat of the giant Astra conglomerate is a member, as is Nurcholish Madjid, the highly respected religious leader.

42. The following account is based on information from www.kemitraan.or.id.

43. The information is from an undated brochure titled "Transparency International, Indonesian Chapter."

44. These include organizations based in such diverse localities as Palu, Sulawesi (Yayasan Merah Putih Palu); Malang, East Java (Malang Corruption Watch); Aceh (LSM Peka), Simalungun, North Sumatra (Simalungun Corruption Watch); West Nusa Tenggara (Somasi), and East Kalimantan (Kelompok Kerja 30). Cities such as Yogyakarta and Solo, in central Java, also have organizations labeled "corruption watch." The personnel in these organizations are diverse. They include people from a wide range of professions such as NGO activists, religious leaders, journalists, academics, and lawyers.

45. Many local organizations are not part of this coalition, however. The dynamics in different areas may also be distinctive. In Batam, for example, an NGO called Somasi initiated a dialogue with other local NGOs to establish an "independent commission to eradicate Corruption, Collusion and Nepotism"' (*Sijori Mandiri*, April 28, 2002) on the island. Batam is an important manufacturing center with close economic links to Singapore, but which has a history of corruption reportedly in part due to administration by the Batam Authority controlled by the Habibie family. In North Sumatra, FITRA, an NGO, filed a class-action suit against the *bupati* of Deli Serdang for alleged budgetary misappropriations. (On the formation of GERAK, see GERAK 2000).

46. GERAK has been working closely with ICW in Jakarta to gain greater access to sources of funding as well as to development training and advocacy programs and strategies (Luky Djani, ICW, personal communication).

47. Luky Djani, ICW, personal communication, May 6, 2002.

48. Hamilton-Hart even suggested that whether such offenders receive a fair trial is of secondary importance because although "there are probably long-term payoffs from the commitment to due legal process, in the short term it is massively overloading the attorney general's office, and makes the government itself subject to a corrupt court system" (2001, pp. 78–79). This is an ethically difficult

issue. The position amounts to suspending the rule of law, at least to an extent, for the sake of strengthening the anticorruption momentum and attaining badly needed immediate results. It is argued that deterrence is more urgent than are the niceties of the legal process. A step in the right direction has already taken place with the shifting of the burden of proof to the accused in new anticorruption legislation. However, the loophole in the 1999 anticorruption law discussed earlier, which makes those who committed corruption during the New Order beyond the law's reach, needs to be fixed sooner rather than later. That having been said, there is no substitute in the longer run for fundamental judicial reform, which would ultimately involve restructuring work processes for greater efficiency and transparency, increasing judges' pay, undertaking judicial audits, and possibly reassigning and replacing judicial personnel.

49. For example, the allegations of corruption against IBRA led to audits but no conclusive result was produced because of the poor nature of the financial data. IBRA itself has been placed under a ministerial-level Financial Sector Policy Committee and under the oversight of an independent review committee (Hamilton-Hart 2001, pp. 70–71).

50. Some people argue that these businesses are necessary to supplement Indonesia's comparatively meager defense budget, but the current situation has been said to be the existence of an almost untouchable quasi-official business kingdom (*Kompas*, September 11, 2001). Reports described the attempts of one crusading general, the late Agus Wirahadikusumah, to clean up the business practices of the elite unit, Kostrad: he apparently was thwarted when he was removed from his position as commander (*Tempo*, August 7–13, 2000).

References

The word "processed" describes informally produced works that may not be available commonly through libraries.

Anderson, Benedict. 1972. "The Idea of Power in Javanese Culture." In Claire Holt., ed, *Culture and Politics in Indonesia*. Ithaca, N.Y.: Cornell University Press.

Awaluddin. n.d. "Making National Anti-Corruption Policies and Programmes More Effective: A Case Study of Indonesia." Processed.

Camdessus, Michel. 1997. "Good Governance: The IMF's Role," Available at www.imf.org/external/pubs/ft/exrp/govern/govindex.htm.

GERAK. 2000. "Rakyat Memberantas Korupsi" ("People Get Rid of Corruption"). Proceedings of a national meeting of anticorruption organizations, August 27–31. Indonesia.

Hamilton-Hart, Natasha. 2001. "Anti-Corruption Strategies in Indonesia." *Bulletin of Indonesian Economic Studies* 37 (1): 65–82.

Hewison, Kevin. 2001. "Thailand's Capitalism: Development through Boom and Bust." In Garry Rodan, Kevin Hewison, and Richard Robison, eds., *The Political Economy of South-East Asia: Conflicts, Crises, and Change*. Oxford, U.K.: Oxford University Press.

Masduki, Teten. 2000. "Korupsi Politik" ("Political Corruption"). In *Peran Parlemen Dalam Membasmi Korupsi*. Jakarta: ICW and CIDA.

Partnership for Governance Reform in Indonesia. 2001. "A National Survey of Corruption in Indonesia." Final Report. Jakarta: Asia Foundation.

Robison, Richard. 1986. *Indonesia: The Rise of Capital*. Sydney: Allen and Unwin.

Robison, Richard, and Andrew Rosser. 2000. "Surviving the Meltdown: Liberal Reform and Political Oligarchy in Indonesia." In Richard Robison, Mark Beeson, Kanishka Jayasuriya, and Hyuk-Rae Kim, eds., *Politics and Markets in the Wake of the Asian Crisis*. London: Routledge.

Robison, Richard, and Vedi R. Hadiz. 2002. "Oligarchy and Capitalism: The Case of Indonesia." in Luigi Tomba., ed., *East Asian Capitalism: Conflicts, Growth and Crisis*. Milan: Fondazione Giangiacomo Feltrinelli.

World Bank. 2001. "Memorandum of the President of the International Bank for Reconstruction and Development, the International Development Association, and the International Finance Corporation to the Executive Directors on a Country Assistance Strategy of the World Bank Group for Indonesia." Washington, D.C. Processed.

Web Resources

Badan Pemeriksa Keuangan, www.bpk.go.id (not available in English language)

Badan Pengawasan Keuangan dan Pembangunan, www.bpkp.go.id (not available in English language)

Internet Centre for Corruption Research, www.gwdg.de/~uwvw/ icr.htm.

Komisi Ombudsman Nasional, www.ombudsman.or.id (not available in English language)

Komisi Pengawas Persaingan Usaha, www.kppu.or.id (not available in English language)

Masyarakat Transparansi Indonesia, www.transparansi.or.id (not available in English language)

Tempo Interaktif, www.tempointeraktif.com

Transparency International, www.transparency.org

7

Conclusion:
Lessons and Issues from
Challenging Corruption in Asia

Corruption is one of the greatest inhibiting forces to equitable development and to the combating of poverty....For many it constitutes the difference between life and death....We must reinforce our efforts...to deal with this scourge.

> – James D. Wolfensohn, Third Conference of International
> Investigators of United Nations Organizations and
> Multilateral Financial Institutions

Challenging Corruption: Addressing a Priority Public Policy Agenda in Asia

In the aftermath of the East Asian financial crisis that began in 1997, combating corruption has become a top priority for many countries in Asia. This change has been driven by the painful realization by a growing number of people that corruption imposes huge political, economic, and social costs. Public demands for controlling corruption have also been fueled by several corruption scandals involving high-level public officials in countries such as China, Indonesia, the Republic of Korea, the Philippines, and Thailand. In the international comparisons of perceptions and control of corruption, the low ratings of most countries in East Asia (see Table 7.1) are prominently reported in the local media and have helped raise awareness of the problem.

The shift in perceptions and attitudes about corruption is notable because it portrays, or at least portends, a shift in the political landscape and changes the structure of incentives and disincentives governing people's behavior. In a number of countries the corruption scandals exemplify the increasing risks that corrupt actors face. In those countries corruption has become a high-risk strategy for officials and vested interests. This is a significant departure from recent past when it was precisely those who chose to fight corruption who were choosing a high-risk strat-

Table 7.1. Control of Corruption in Selected Asian Countries, Selected Years, 1996–2002

| Economy | Estimates of the control of corruption | | | |
	1996	1998	2000	2002
Cambodia	18.7	2.7	35.3	20.1
China	58.7	57.9	46.7	42.3
Hong Kong, China	88.0	90.2	89.1	90.2
Indonesia	35.3	6.6	8.7	6.7
Japan	84.7	86.9	87.5	85.1
Korea, Rep. of	76.7	69.9	72.8	66.5
Laos	18.7	24.6	17.9	3.6
Malaysia	76.0	80.9	67.9	68.0
Mongolia	66.0	54.6	41.8	54.1
Myanmar	6.0	2.2	3.3	2.1
Philippines	38.0	45.9	37.5	37.6
Singapore	97.3	97.3	99.5	99.5
Thailand	42.7	61.2	46.2	53.6
Vietnam	30.7	28.4	23.4	33.0

Note: The Control of Corruption estimate shows the country's percentile rank. It refers to the percentage of countries worldwide that rate below the selected country. According to the authors, the ratings are based on subjective assessments from a variety of sources and are subject to substantial margins of error. In no way do they reflect the views of the World Bank, its executive directors, or the countries they represent.
Source: Kaufmann, Kraay, and Mastruzzi 2003.

egy. In some cases, the balance of forces is no longer preponderantly in favor of corruption.

That certainly is not to say that the there is an inexorable trend in controlling corruption. Rather, we simply note the fact that the growing knowledge, collective action capabilities, and enlightened leadership in some countries are making headway against corruption. The challenge remains formidable, of course. Corruption favors the status quo in many ways because the vested interests are powerful and organized, in part as a result of their pernicious practices. This is certainly the case in poor-governance countries with high levels of state capture and administrative corruption. In those countries, anticorruption groups have long found their efforts not merely ineffective, but downright dangerous.

In response to the recent shifts in public opinion demanding actions to combat corruption and the growing international concern about the problem, almost all governments in East Asia have included combating corruption among their strategies to promote growth, increase stability, and reduce poverty at the country, regional, and global levels. Recently, 20 governments endorsed an Anti-Corruption Action Plan for Asia and the Pacific as a framework for taking concrete steps to combat corruption in their respective countries (see chapter 2). Implementing the Action Plan is being supported by the Asian Development Bank (ADB), the Organisation for Economic Co-operation and Development (OECD), and other donor organizations and countries. This international action, among others, is important because it provides technical and financial support to overcome the expected resistance from corrupt interests who naturally prefer the status quo.

However, it is clear that apart from the obvious need for more political and economic resources to address the problem, what is needed fundamentally is a rethinking of strategies to make anticorruption policies and programs more effective. Since the problem first received international prominence in the mid-1990s there has been notably little significant change in most countries. Of course, it can be argued that we are in the early stages of the struggle against the problem and that there remain more questions than answers. A key challenge, in our view, is precisely the need to develop an analytical framework that can help officials in different countries ask sharper questions about their particular problems and, thus, develop more appropriate strategies to make their anticorruption agendas effective.

The Need for Improvement in Anticorruption Policies and Programs in Asia

Early indicators of progress in controlling corruption in Asia are not encouraging. By several measures, most countries have yet to show significant improvement. In some countries, the situation has even worsened. The poor record can be illustrated by looking at two sets of governance indicators over the 1996–2002 period. The first indicator is a "control of corruption" estimate prepared by Daniel Kaufmann, Aart Kraay, and Massimo Mastruzzi (2003) of the World Bank (see table 7.1).[1] The second is the Corruption Perceptions Index (CPI) published by Transparency International (see table 7.2).

In terms of the control of corruption, most of the countries showed consistently weak capacity to control corruption between 1996 and 2001. Some had significant drops—notably Indonesia and, to a lesser extent, China. Indonesia's drop was most precipitous in the aftermath of the Asian financial crisis. This regional assessment is echoed in the results of Transparency International's CPI. Most of the countries continued to demonstrate poor perceptions of corruption, with several countries showing declining ratings, while others are more or less stagnating. On

Table 7.2. Corruption Perceptions in Selected Asian Countries, Selected Years, 1996–2003

Economy	Corruption Perceptions Index				
	1996	1998	2000	2002	2003
China	2.43	3.5	3.1	3.5	3.4
Hong Kong, China	7.01	7.8	7.7	8.2	8.0
Indonesia	2.65	2.0	1.7	1.9	1.9
Japan	7.05	5.8	6.4	7.1	7.0
Korea, Rep. of	5.02	4.2	4.0	4.5	4.3
Malaysia	5.32	5.3	4.8	4.9	5.2
Philippines	2.69	3.3	2.8	2.6	2.5
Singapore	8.80	9.1	9.1	9.3	9.4
Thailand	3.30	3.0	3.2	3.2	3.3
Vietnam	n.a.	2.5	2.5	2.4	2.4

n.a. Not applicable.

Note: A score relates to the degree of corruption perceived by businesspeople, academics, and risk analysts, and ranges between 10 (highly clean) and 0 (highly corrupt).

Source: Transparency International, www.transparency.org.

average, the countries in the region rate below 5 on a scale of 0 to 10 in which the higher score represents the lower perception of corruption, which suggests that there is much room for improvement.

On the basis of that evidence it appears that although East Asian countries have long declared their intent to control corruption, their plans have not produced results. For most countries, corruption control has not improved. For some, it has clearly worsened. The lack of progress in controlling corruption is not for lack of government organizations or regulations focusing on anticorruption policies and programs. In most countries there are existing laws and statutes, but those have not been effective. In some instances the laws and the agencies created to fight corruption may already have become part of the problem.

The poor progress among Asian governments in combating corruption—despite various anticorruption policies and programs—testifies to the capabilities and cunning of corrupt interests. In many ways anticorruption actors have been no match for the resources and reach of corrupt officials. As the cases in this volume have shown, the beneficiaries of corruption are top-level officials who can prevent, obstruct, and overcome efforts to control their illicit activities. The playing field, thus, is generally graded in their favor, and the anticorruption actors are more often than not the underdogs.

In the lopsided situations facing reformist officials, their prospect for success is contingent on their ability to leverage fewer resources and overcome greater obstacles to collective action. Their odds are substantial. In this regard, a common challenge is to develop a strategy that is most appropriate and relevant to their particular situations. The conditions of corruption and the prospects for change vary across countries. There is no one-size-fits-all strategy. What is needed is an analytical tool that can assess what, where, when, and how anticorruption policies and programs can be applied to best effect, given the governance conditions.

An Analytical Framework for Improving Anticorruption Effectiveness

In chapter 2 we proposed a multidisciplinary analytical framework that may be used to make the design and implementation of anticorruption policies and programs more effective. This framework is analytically anchored on the premise that governance conditions and patterns of corruption differ across countries, and this variance helps to determine the impact of anticorruption instruments. Put differently, the framework emphasizes the importance of choosing and crafting anticorruption measures based on a country's quality of governance and nature of corruption. It does not prescribe "magic bullets" to pierce the armor of corruption. Rather, it suggests a way of thinking and doing that we hope is more strategic and potentially more effective.

As we outlined in Chapter 2, the framework follows a six-step approach:

1. Assess a country's governance and operating environment. This means determining a country's quality of governance and its patterns of corruption. Specifically, it calls for an evaluation of the robustness of the political, economic, and social institutions in the country. It emphasizes the need to examine its extent of state capture and administrative or petty corruption.
2. Review the range of anticorruption measures that are in use internationally and the conditions and prerequisites for the measures that have achieved success. This step suggests developing a global menu of anticorruption instruments that, in turn, can be buttressed by fact sheets for each instrument. The fact sheet would identify which aspects of the calculus of corruption are tackled by the measures, either on the rewards side or on the risks side. It would also describe the basic prerequisite conditions for the measure to be effective.
3. Link the analysis of country governance environment and patterns of corruption with the global menu of anticorruption measures. The linking is an analytical exercise to select and prioritize those measures that have the best chance of succeeding in a country's particular governance

and operating environment. Say, if a country is plagued by poor governance and high levels of state capture and petty corruption, the menu and fact sheets of anticorruption measures can suggest what may work best in such an environment. Of course, this analytical linking is much more than a cursory exercise; it needs to be conducted in depth.

4. Seek and build key anticorruption champions in the country. It is critical to forge strong partnerships and broad-based coalitions to support anticorruption agenda-setting and policy formulation and implementation. Without broad-based coalitions behind anticorruption efforts, the agenda can easily be blown away by the resistance to reforms. Nowhere is the challenge of collective action more difficult than in mobilizing the often disparate and disorganized sufferers of corruption. It is all the more difficult because the opposition to reforms coming from the beneficiaries of corruption is expectedly formidable, especially in poor governance contexts with high levels of grand and petty corruption.

5. Ensure authoritative and accountable leadership and management structures of anticorruption relevant to a country's governance and operating environment. They require clear authority, broad powers, and significant resources to be able to stand a chance when pursuing corrupt interests in the country. This is particularly plausible in poor governance environments with high levels of state capture, where the leadership and management structures would be subject to prey and capture by corrupt elements. Thus, it is critical that the leadership and management structures are both sufficiently shielded and equipped to tackle corruption.

6. Develop and strengthen processes and mechanisms for regularly monitoring and reporting feedback on anticorruption policies and programs. This is crucial because accurate feedback analysis allows anticorruption officials to assess the changes in the environment in which anticorruption instruments are being applied. It would provide them with information regarding the location, strength, and organization of those opposed to—and those who support—reforms. This information is crucial for mobilizing and deploying limited resources against corrupt interests.

In this book scholars from four countries (the Philippines, Republic of Korea, Thailand, and Indonesia) have presented case studies of the problem of corruption in their respective countries and how the problem is being challenged. Drawing on these case studies from the perspective of the analytical framework, we highlight some lessons and issues in combating corruption in Asia. We suggest avenues that may be explored to make national anticorruption policies and programs more effective.

In line with the components of the framework, each of the case study presented a discussion of common themes: the evolution of a country's governance environment; some of the recent measures to combat corruption; key institutions and champions involved in combating corruption; and leadership and management structures for the fight. Our discussion is solely for illustrative purposes and, thus, only broad conclusions will be drawn regarding what is working and where the effectiveness may be improved. More specific recommendations can only be made by subjecting each anticorruption program in a country to an in-depth analysis using the analytical framework.

Country Governance Environments: Shaping Successes and Failures of Anticorruption Efforts

The analytical framework discussed in chapter 2 highlights the importance of crafting anticorruption measures according to a country's governance and operating environment. Understanding the nature of a country's governance helps explain why some anticorruption measures are making headway while others are not showing results (or, worse, the wrong results!). More important, using analysis of country governance to shape anticorruption strategies is critical for making the programs more effective. In turn, success in anticorruption contributes to improving the governance environment. No success against corruption, no improvement in governance.

This analytical approach to anticorruption builds on growing research and experience in governance and strategies and with their relevance in different country environments. In chapter 2 we discussed the relationship between governance environment and anticorruption strategies, and how that can be applied to develop appropriate anticorruption strategies suited to a country's governance environment. Using the framework on the four case studies in this volume could help explain the successes and failures thus far in challenging corruption in Asia. It could also delineate areas where improvements can best be made.

In this volume, the four countries covered are characterized by different assessments of governance quality and patterns of corruption (see table 7.3). We arrived at this snapshot categorization based on findings of governance research to date, particularly the World Bank's Governance Research Indicators project, and the country case studies themselves. Table 7.4 shows the aggregate indicators of governance for the four countries during the period 1996–2002.

Among the four countries studied, Indonesia shows poor governance and high levels of state capture and administrative corruption. The Philippines and Thailand are categorized as fair governance, with medi-

Table 7.3. Country Governance Environment, Selected Countries

Country	Quality of governance	Corruption conditions	
		State capture	Administrative corruption
Indonesia	Poor	High	High
Korea, Rep. of	Good	Low to medium	Low
Philippines	Fair	Medium to high	Medium to high
Thailand	Fair	Medium to high	Medium to high

Source: Authors' assessments.

um to high levels of state capture and administrative corruption. South Korea is considered a good-governance country, with low to medium levels of state capture and low administrative corruption.

Indonesia's governance situation took a negative turn following the Asian financial crisis when its political and economic conditions unraveled rapidly. As seen in table 7.4, Indonesia's indicators for political stability, government effectiveness, regulatory quality, and control of corruption dropped dramatically after 1996. The Philippines and Thailand are broadly classified as fair governance, although there are important differences between the two countries. As shown in table 7.4, both countries have comparable levels in terms of voice and accountability, government effectiveness, and regulatory quality. But there are notable differences in recent years in terms of political stability, rule of law, and control of corruption, with the Philippine rates poorer than those of Thailand. A great deal of the divergence is explained by the corruption-wracked administration of former Philippine President Joseph Estrada and his ouster by popular protests in 2001. Korea's ranking as a good-governance country is reflected in its higher ratings of various indicators among the four countries. Its political stability indicator is not as strong as the others, in part because of its geopolitical situation and relatively recent democratic transition. The low to medium rating in state capture is partly a result of continuing issues related to business–government relationships as well as a result of the scandals linked to former president Kim Dae-jung.

From the logic of the analytical framework, our analysis of countries having poor governance environments and high state capture and administrative corruption suggests that anticorruption instruments need to pursue a set of policies and programs that go beyond relying on government leadership and regulation. This is because state institutions are

Table 7.4. Governance Indicators, Selected Years, 1996–2002
(Percentile Ranking of Selected Countries)

Governance indicator	Year	Indonesia	Korea, Rep. of	Philippines	Thailand
Voice and accountability	2002	34.8	67.7	54.0	57.1
	2000	32.5	68.6	60.2	58.1
	1998	12.0	68.6	63.4	55.5
	1996	16.2	68.1	58.6	52.9
Political stability	2002	12.4	60.5	29.7	62.7
	2000	3.0	64.8	40.0	57.0
	1998	9.1	56.4	49.7	59.4
	1996	30.5	54.3	43.3	55.5
Government effectiveness	2002	34.0	79.4	55.7	64.9
	2000	33.2	72.8	60.3	64.1
	1998	26.8	75.4	66.7	62.8
	1996	66.5	78.2	67.6	73.7
Regulatory quality	2002	26.3	76.3	57.7	65.5
	2000	28.1	67.6	62.2	77.3
	1998	47.3	58.7	72.8	56.5
	1996	65.7	78.5	68.5	70.2
Rule of law	2002	23.2	77.8	38.1	62.4
	2000	15.1	74.6	41.6	69.7
	1998	14.1	77.3	60.0	69.2
	1996	39.8	81.9	54.8	71.1
Control of corruption	2002	6.7	66.5	37.6	53.6
	2000	8.7	72.8	37.5	46.2
	1998	6.6	69.9	45.9	61.2
	1996	35.3	76.7	38.0	42.7

Note: These indicators have been constructed for 175 countries, based on 275 governance variables from 20 sources and 18 organizations, including Freedom House, Gallup International, Economist Intelligence Unit, DRI/McGraw-Hill, the World Bank, the Heritage Foundation, and the European Bank for Reconstruction and Development, among others. The methodology of aggregation is sensitive to measurement of errors; the authors placed greater weight on survey results with smaller measurement errors and lesser weight on those with higher margins of error. By drawing on multiple sources, the governance indicators reduce their margins of error which would not have been possible if they relied on one or few sources. For a fuller explanation, see chapter 2 in Radelet (2003).
Source: Kaufmann, Kraay, and Mastruzzi 2003.

generally weak and the agencies and officials are more likely to be part of the problem. At the extreme, to pursue anticorruption reforms through state agencies may almost be like putting a fox in the henhouse. In this context, the opportunities for reform are more likely to be found through external actors and processes. Thus, the following five policies are among those we recommend:

1. Forge broad-based anticorruption coalitions to put pressure for anticorruption actions. This is, in effect, about building and strengthening demand for reforms, without which there is little impetus for change.
2. Follow policy reforms that eliminate administrative opportunities for corruption. Because the state's investigative and prosecutorial capacity is weak, it is important to stop corruption before it can occur.
3. Reinforce media independence and citizen participation. This complements the strategy of supporting and shaping demand for reforms. Such external demand can help shift the balance of forces for change within and outside government.
4. Enhance the effectiveness and accountability of independent oversight institutions. This is assuredly a difficult task because the operating environment is powerfully hostile to effective oversight; in this area, leadership and management structures are critical.
5. Build the capacity and independence of prosecutorial agencies and the judiciary with appropriate checks and balances for holding them accountable to the public. This is critical, and perhaps it is the most challenging recommendation, because corrupt interests often penetrate, if not permeate, these institutions. A key challenge is the choice of leadership and management structures that can withstand inducements and can advance reforms.

When we compare Indonesia with, say, the Philippines, it is evident that there are notable differences across all dimensions of governance. To be sure, before the 1997 crisis Indonesia could show that it approximated the Philippines in some areas, such as government effectiveness and regulatory quality (see table 7.4). To date, in the estimates of the governance indicator for voice and accountability, the rating is significantly better for the Philippines than for Indonesia. This suggests that in the Philippines anticorruption instruments that build on civil society initiatives may have a greater chance of success than they do in Indonesia. The governance environment is poor in Indonesia and it shows a high degree of state capture as well as high administrative corruption, and the research findings on such conditions suggest that the near-term policy payoffs are going to come from actions in the broad categories listed in items 1–3 above. This is not to say that nothing should be done to improve laws or enhance institutions of accountability. Of course those are important areas for action and necessary for long-term governance improvement. However, it would not be realistic to rely on them to produce results in an anticorruption drive in the near term because the key institutions (including the police, the courts, and independent commissions) are themselves regarded as corrupt.

In contrast, in the case of the good governance environment of Korea, the international experience would suggest that, in addition to items 1–3 above, anticorruption measures initiated by the executive branch of the government as well as by regulatory authorities can have meaningful impact. That is true because the institutions of the state are fairly robust and there is a vigorous presence of civil society organizations. State agencies also have significant insulation against the predation of corrupt interests and are equipped with sufficient authority and sizable resources to overcome resistance to reforms.

In view of the foregoing, we believe the key point is to carefully choose and design anticorruption instruments according to the characteristics of a country's governance environment and its patterns of corruption. This approach is not a guarantee of success, of course, but more of an assurance that the anticorruption approach is appropriate to the situation at hand. The spectrum of anticorruption measures is wide and varied, as shown in the list compiled under the ADB-OECD Action Plan for Asia and the Pacific as well as in the menu that we compiled (table 2.2, chapter 2). This means that analyzing, selecting, and prioritizing the instruments that are likely to produce results for particular countries will require finding the best fit between policy and place.

The link between the governance environment and the effectiveness of anticorruption instruments is apparent in the four case studies presented in the book. The case studies analyzed the country governance environments and their respective patterns of corruption. They reviewed the country's political, legal, economic, and social dimensions and referred to some internationally available indicators of governance. They also discussed progress made and difficulties encountered in combating corruption. In the analyses of the case studies, the following points emerge:

- All four countries have a history of corrupt practices embedded in collusion between public officials and private interests. With the partial exception of Korea, they suffer from medium to high degrees of state capture and administrative corruption. As a result, anticorruption measures emanating from the executive branch of the government have generally not been successful in those four countries.
- In Indonesia, Korea, and Thailand the public's access to information was severely restricted until recently. This made active public and

media involvement difficult to accomplish and generally hampered efforts to expose corruption. In the Philippines the downfall of Ferdinand Marcos in 1987 led to reforms that substantially expanded the scope for public and media involvement. In Indonesia, Korea, and Thailand, political reforms, especially constitutional reforms after the East Asian financial crisis, have opened up the scope for public involvement. This opening up of space for public and media involvement has led to success in exposing and pursuing corruption cases. The freer press became instrumental in strengthening external demand for reforms while providing some protection against the attacks of corrupt elements.

- In Indonesia and the Philippines, the justice system has not been effective in successfully prosecuting cases of alleged corruption involving high-ranking political and government officials. This demonstrates weak rule of law. The Indonesian case study described a situation in which the police and the courts themselves are plagued by corruption. The situation in the Philippines is arguably not as problematic because major reforms are underway, particularly in the judiciary. As what international experience and research would have indicated, the weaknesses in the rule of law have resulted in a palpably poor track record of convictions in alleged corruption cases. In this regard, anticorruption should not rely on investigation and enforcement but on corruption prevention by reducing the scope of and opportunities for corruption.

- The Indonesia and Philippines case studies discussed the significant role that political fundraising plays and the ways in which it leads to state capture. Political corruption naturally weakens and subverts the will to combat corruption in general. In that environment in both countries, the politicians have been perceived as paying lip-service to the battle against corruption. Effective actions to challenge corruption have not materialized. As long as high state capture persists, the anticorruption measures initiated by the executive branch are not likely to be effective. Anticorruption champions would be well advised instead to invest resources in civil society initiatives to generate pressures for increasing transparency and accountability of public institutions. In this regard, it would be critical to build broad-based coalitions to shift the balance of forces that are often disproportionately in favor of corrupt elements as a result of their own networks and resources.

- The country cases studies cited instances when nongovernmental organizations (NGOs) and the media, individually or jointly, have played a role in exposing corruption and have mobilized public opinion for anticorruption action. These successes were made possible in part by constitutional and legal reforms that created enabling conditions for civil society initiatives. The reforms, in effect, served to provide added protection, if not ammunition, to anticorruption coalitions that are often outgunned, figuratively and sometimes literally. Further efforts in this area would be useful in improving effectiveness in challenging corruption in poor- to fair-governance countries.

- Parliamentary oversight has had varying functions and effects in the four countries studied. Even after the downfall of Suharto, parliamentary accountability has been weakest in Indonesia (and to a lesser extent in Thailand) because of perverse incentives embedded in campaign financing and pork-barrel politics. In the Philippines, prodded by civil society and media involvement, parliamentary oversight played a role, albeit limited, when it instigated impeachment proceedings against former president Estrada. It is in Korea, however, that parliamentary oversight appears to be making most inroads, in great part because of the country's relatively good governance environment. This suggests that reforms anchored on accountability by legislative assemblies are prone to be weak in poor to fair governance environments.

- The case studies show that availability and accessibility of information is a prerequisite for effective civil society actions. Experience in all the countries studied testifies that credible and detailed information on corruption has been effective in mobilizing public opinion and forcing accountability on high-level public officials. Information access is a powerful tool in all levels of governance, but especially so in poor to fair governance environments. The case studies also show the importance of the *quality* of information on corruption. In that regard, the importance of measures to strengthen access to quality information is underscored.

- The case studies discussed the role of different types of accountability institutions that are independent of the executive branch. In Korea and Thailand such institutions are showing some early successes, whereas in Indonesia and the Philippines such institutions have been around for many years but their effectiveness seems to have been blunted by vested interests. In some cases the institutions themselves have become instruments of corruption. That situation is seen in part by looking at the rule of law governance indicators, which shows a serious decline in Indonesia and, to a lesser extent, the Philippines. This means caution is needed when anchoring anticorruption approaches in independent accountability institutions that are within poor governance environments.

- All four countries have laws on the books to increase the public's right to know, the freedom of the press, and the disclosure of information. However, Korea and the Philippines seem to be farther along in that direction. The existence of enabling legislation has been a highly effective tool in promoting public access and thus in combating corruption.

- All four case studies addressed the proposition that cultural factors somehow make corruption acceptable. In all cases that proposition is being disproved by growing social movements against corrupt practices. To be sure, in poor to fair governance environments such as in Indonesia, the Philippines, and Thailand, the challenge of making corrupt practices unacceptable remains. In that regard, programs such as social marketing campaigns and investigative journalism have helped shift popular attitudes against corruption and those attitudes have been helpful in building broad-based anticorruption coalitions.
- In all four countries public awareness about the harmful consequences of corruption and the pervasiveness of corruption in the country is at high levels, fueled by media and civil society initiatives. In such a situation investing further resources in increasing the supply of quality information about incidences of corruption and increasing the capacity of media and civil society initiatives may not necessarily be as important as putting resources in other more relevant anticorruption measures.

Anticorruption Coalitions: Serious Challenges to Corruption in Asia

The analytical framework we propose is founded on the proposition that having technically sound anticorruption policies (that is, strategies that advance anticorruption policies and programs on the basis of a detailed understanding of a country's governance environment) is not sufficient to ensure effectiveness. The odds are particularly high when it comes to poor to fair governance environments where the forces of corruption are likely to have captured organs of the state and compromised bureaucratic duties. In such a context, shifting the balance of forces in society toward anticorruption policies and programs requires building a critical mass of state and nonstate actors assembled in a coalition. The coalition can be critically important in prioritizing anticorruption policies and programs at the top of the government's agenda. The stronger the coalition, the greater the probability that the policies and programs will be chosen and implemented despite expected resistance and opposition from vested interests from within and outside the government.

In relatively open societies, generally in good governance environments, usually there will be no visible opponents of reforms aimed at combating corruption. However, there will likely be more or fewer undercurrents of resistance. At one extreme, in some societies, when the general perception is that there is very little chance of success in bringing about change, nobody will be willing to stick his or her neck out on an anticorruption agenda. In those contexts it becomes very important to find and nurture those leaders in society who are supportive of an anti-corruption agenda. The participation of such leaders in the battle against corruption can have a ripple effect in terms of improving the effectiveness of anticorruption policies and programs. Leaders and champions of anti-corruption efforts can be found in various civil society groups, as well as in government. In certain poor-governance countries the domestic champions may not be able and willing to step out and play a public role, but in those situations international organizations and external support can play a major role.

The four case studies presented examples of emerging anticorruption champions, as well as formal and informal coalitions, that are making a difference despite the serious resistance to reforms from vested interests. Their stories suggest important lessons in developing and applying appropriate strategy to outmaneuver powerful forces. These anticorruption champions and coalitions are playing decisive roles in making sure that the problem of corruption and the issues related to fighting corruption stay current and remain a priority on the government and public agendas.

In the Philippines, civil society organizations (CSOs) and investigative journalism have played a major role in terms of exposing corruption in government procurement as well as other corrupt behaviors of high-level public officials. Taking advantage of the space created by the constitution and laws for public involvement in civic affairs, these CSOs have stepped in and are working independently or in partnership with champions in the public sector who are willing to take on the issue of corruption. For example, the chief justice of the Philippine Supreme Court initiated a partnership with the CSOs to monitor and report on the performance of judges. Similarly, the department of budget and management partnered with a CSO to create a procurement watch monitoring system to monitor public sector procurement. Various other citizens' organizations monitor the public works as well as performance of officials and they generate a volume of information that keeps the issue of combating corruption at center-stage in citizens' minds. Notably, the Philippine Center for Investigative Journalism plays a unique role in exposing corruption in the Philippines by taking full advantage of laws and regulations related to the public's right to know. Their work represents best practice in Asia. These groups of anticorruption champions are being helped in their work by international organizations, NGOs, donors who are providing support to generate information on the nature and extent of corruption and providing technical assistance in combating corruption. The Philippines case study also indicated that the public institutions of accountability have yet to show credible results. The failure of these institutions is largely explained by a country governance environment with a medium to high degree of state capture by vested interests.

In the case of Indonesia, since the downfall of the Suharto regime anti-corruption coalitions are just beginning to emerge following the establishment of legal and constitutional foundations for civil society and media freedoms. Even in the early stages, these two sectors (the press and NGOs) have managed to expose cases of corruption in an unprecedented manner. They played a critical role in the exposure and trial of several high-level public officials. However, the domestic coalitions in Indonesia are at a very young stage and are not yet reaching levels that can outweigh and outmaneuver corrupt forces. Recognizing this need, international organizations such as the World Bank, the United Nations Development Program, and the Asian Development Bank have entered into a partnership with domestic champions in combating corruption to form a Partnership for Governance Reform. This is a good example of building a coalition of domestic and external partners to combine resources and coordinate action. In addition to these groups, newly created independent accountability institutions in the public sector have the potential of becoming a potent force in challenging corruption, provided they are supported and held accountable by the media and civil society groups and, eventually, by the parliament.

In the case of Korea, the case study described the partnerships between major state institutions of accountability and anticorruption champions from civil society. The effectiveness of coordination among these champions can be improved, as noted in the case study, but the coalition members have already played important roles in bringing some recent high-profile cases to prosecution, and thereby raising credibility and public expectations. An interesting aspect of Korea's situation is that the exposure of alleged cases of corruption by media and civil society groups has been taken up by accountability institutions and has resulted in convictions. This situation underscores the importance of the fact that although civil society organizations and media can expose the alleged cases of corruption and fuel the public outrage, the success in bringing alleged culprits to justice will depend on the capability of the prosecutorial agencies and the effectiveness of the judiciary system. Korea, with its relatively good governance environment, is fortunate to have developed effective prosecutorial agencies and the relatively strong rule of law. In the cases of Indonesia and the Philippines, these institutions are not very effective and the probability that culprits will be brought to justice remains remarkably low. Thus, although most severe penalties against corruption are on the books in both countries, they have been rendered meaningless by weaknesses in detection, investigation, and prosecution.

In the case of Thailand, the case study discussed a recent procurement episode to illustrate how a coalition of NGOs, academics, and the media came together to expose corruption in procurement of medicines by health ministry officials. The coalition used the space created by the 1997 constitution to demand and get action against the alleged perpetrators. Regarded as among the strongest anticorruption constitutions in the region, the 1997 document has provided the bases for creating various institutions of public accountability as well as providing the foundation for the public's right to know. The constitution also supplied the basis for wide-ranging roles of civil society organizations. Thus, in Thailand anticorruption champions have grown and are working as part of a broad coalition surmounting differences to work together to control corruption. As a result, the balance of forces is no longer as disproportionately in favor of corrupt interests as before.

Experience from the four country case studies in this volume emphasizes the importance of anticorruption champions and coalitions in challenging corruption. Policies and programs to nurture and support such champions and coalitions certainly should be a key component of anticorruption efforts, but it is important to remember that the space and foundation for such groups to succeed were created by legislative and constitutional reforms. A key lesson from the Asian experience is that measures aimed at increasing active public involvement in challenging corruption have enormous impact and should be given a high priority.

Varied Anticorruption Leadership and Management Structures Produce Varied Outcomes

There are different leadership and management structures dedicated to fighting corruption. Among the common forms are an ombudsman, national anticorruption agencies, supreme audit institutions, investigative and prosecutorial agencies, parliamentary oversight bodies, multisector advisory groups, full-time ministers, and independent commissions. The global record suggests that the effectiveness of these existing management and leadership structures varies a great deal. Their differences depend greatly on the characteristics of a country's governance environment. These include factors such as political support, political and operational independence, access to documentation and the power to question, the ability of protect whistleblowers, the capability to introduce greater transparency and disclosure in public sector operations, reputational legacy, the credibility and integrity of public leadership, and the adequacy of funding arrangements. The experience in Asia is consistent with this international experience.

In the Philippines the leadership and management of anticorruption efforts can be classified into two groups. The first group includes institutions set up by the executive branch, such as presidential commissions, advisory bodies, a national anticorruption action plan, and so forth. The

second group consists of civil society organizations and the constitutionally mandated bodies such as the ombudsman, the Commission on
Elections, the Commission on Audit, and the judiciary. The case study
indicated that the performance of the leadership and management structures created by the executive branch has not been very effective. In some
instances those structures have become part of the problem. As one
would expect, that would not be surprising given the country's governance characteristics that have allowed for the persistence of state capture and administrative corruption. The case study also indicated that the
independent accountability organizations have a mixed record because
they depend on the executive branch and the politicians for their funding, and both have not been forthcoming in full measure. In a way this is
not surprising because corrupt officials and politicians are not about to
strengthen the bodies that can run after them.

The Korea case study pointed to the important role of political leadership that President Kim Dae-jung played in the early years of his presidency. This resulted in many significant reforms, some of which ultimately led to the exposure of corruption scandals within his own family.
The early success of the executive branch's effort in Korea compared with
the other three countries in this volume, particularly Indonesia and the
Philippines, is reflected in the differences among the countries' governance indicators. This is apparent, for example, in the rating of the degree
of government effectiveness, where Korea is significantly ahead of the
other countries (see table 7.4). The case study also points out that the public's outrage with corrupt behaviors created strong pressure on and support for the independent accountability institutions to take action. Once
again a relatively high degree of voice and accountability helps to explain
this success. In fact the public demands for clean government shaped the
recent election campaigns and the new leaders are all promising to take
further action to improve the effectiveness of anticorruption policies and
programs. Thus, in Korea corruption has increasingly become a high-risk
strategy for corrupt officials.

In the case of Thailand, the case study did not go into the details of
leadership and management structures, but the study of Indonesia
offered some discussion of the those structures for combating corruption.
The study suggested that the public institutions in the financial audit
area, which were set up to lead the fight against corruption, suffer from
degrees of state capture and therefore have not been very effective. At the
same time, the work of civil society organizations is at an early stage. It
has not yet reached the point where it can be a highly effective pressure
point in demanding accountability of public sector officials and a force
for improving the performance of the public sector accountability institutions. However, judging from the experience of other poor to fair gov-

ernance environments, external support for civil society and public involvement is important because it can provide the necessary political support for accountability institutions to do their jobs.

Anticorruption Monitoring and Reporting Systems: Good Ones Emerging in Asia

The sixth and final component of the analytical framework emphasizes the important role of monitoring and reporting systems on corruption and counter-corruption activities in a country. Fundamentally, what is measured is what is achieved. Monitoring and reporting systems serve not only to evaluate the pace and progress of anticorruption but to provide benchmarks or targets for what can be accomplished. They are also crucial barometers for where, when, and how opposition and resistance to anticorruption are likely to emerge. In environments where the struggle is intense because of poor governance conditions, such information is vital.

In this regard, it is necessary that the producers of this information be capable and credible—and be perceived as such—and that the methodology they use is sound and defensible. The data gathered will be ammunition for champions of anticorruption reforms, equipping them with timely and relevant information on corruption patterns and anticorruption performance. The modes of monitoring and reporting vary, and the constraints of choice are determined by resources and capabilities that are available. Among these choices are public opinion surveys, small group discussions, investigative journalism, and research studies.

Anticorruption efforts in Korea, Indonesia and Thailand have been helped by the results of diagnostic surveys involving households, public officials, and businesspeople that revealed the prevalence and consequences of corruption. The Philippines has also developed monitoring and reporting systems on patterns of corruption using a scorecard methodology. Several of these efforts have been supported by the World Bank and their findings have been used to develop appropriate anticorruption policies and programs.

The various methods for monitoring and reporting can and should also serve as important benchmarks or targets for performance. For example, take public opinion surveys. In the Philippine case study presented in this book, a 2001 survey showed about 49 percent of Filipinos perceived a "great deal" of corruption in the public sector. This is both an assessment statistic and a target for improvement. In that regard, the government's anticorruption agenda can adopt this figure as a benchmark. That is, it can decide that after the first year of its anticorruption work, the number will be reduced by half, to about 25 percent; in the second year, it could be reduced by half again, to about 12 percent.

With benchmarks, countries can adopt a hard rule to promote performance in anticorruption work. It is important to monitor and provide information on what is happening with regard to corruption and the battle against it. But it is equally important to use the information as a goal to improve performance. Reviewed regularly, the comparison between anticorruption results and performance targets ensures accountability and results among anticorruption advocates.

No less crucial in monitoring and evaluating is the use of information to determine the location, nature, and strength of resistance to and support for anticorruption. For example, survey results can indicate what segments of the bureaucracy and society are supportive or opposed to certain reforms, and they can define the intensity of their preferences. In poor governance environments where the balance of forces is often disadvantageous to reformers, such information can be critical to building coalitions and implementing programs. Monitoring and evaluation results can also reveal what means and messages are least or most effective, thus providing the officials implementing anticorruption policies and programs with information that can be used to calibrate or adjust measures to greater effect.

How Asia Can Improve the Effectiveness of National Anticorruption Programs

From the perspective of the analytical framework we have discussed it is possible to draw insights into what is and is not working in against corruption in Asia. At the same time it is possible to identify measures that are likely to improve and enhance the impact of policies and programs. Our analysis of what works and where the effectiveness of programs can be improved is certainly more for illustrative purposes than for offering exhaustive diagnostics and prescriptions. To do the latter would require a much more in-depth analysis and application of the analytical framework.

In our view the anticorruption policies and programs that have made significant impact among the Asian countries studied in this volume are the following:

- Recent reforms in transparency and openness—such as the widened space for mass media, increased flow of information and improved access to information on public and private sector affairs, and intensified involvement of citizens in anticorruption and public affairs—are helping to increase the probability of detection, investigation, and prosecution of corruption.
- Public pressure (through the media, NGOs, and in some cases international channels) has contributed to the ouster from public office of sev-

eral high-ranking officials. This outcome correlates well with and is a reflection of the growing freedom of media and civil society in Asia. Despite the poor governance conditions of Indonesia and the fair governance environments of the Philippines and Thailand, the expansion of freedoms has made an impact, particularly in detection and investigation. Where those countries remain weak is in the justice system that has constrained enforcement and punishment, unlike in the relatively good governance environment of Korea. Ultimately, detection and investigation, however effective, cannot credibly increase the risks of punishments for corruption if there is no effective prosecution, much less conviction.

- Accountability institutions seem to be performing better in Korea and to some extent in Thailand than they are in Indonesia and the Philippines. In the case of Korea, it is clearly a reflection of the low degree of state capture in the country. Korea's good quality of governance—as manifested in the county's relatively well-functioning institutions—enables accountability institutions to operate effectively. Combined with strong civil society and media freedoms, the risks of sanctions for corruption are becoming punitively high. In poor-governance countries such as Indonesia, the accountability institution—surrounded by dysfunctional institutions—finds it difficult to be accountable to itself. Instead of increasing the risks of being punished for corruption, the accountability institutions are faced with incentives to be corrupt themselves.

- Although the anticorruption legislative structure is being improved in all countries, enforcement is relatively better in Korea and in Thailand than in Indonesia and the Philippines. This is consistent with the former two countries' comparatively better regulatory capacity, government effectiveness, and rule of law. The existence of an anticorruption legislative structure is a prerequisite for successful results but it needs to combine with other strong dimensions of governance to make a difference.

- Korea and, to a lesser extent, the Philippines and Thailand, offer examples of successful use of information technology to reduce opportunities for administrative corruption. Examples of pioneering programs are Seoul's Online Procedures Enhancement for Civil Applications system and the Philippines's and Thailand's adoption of electronic processes to streamline certain government services, such as in customs, internal revenue, and vehicle and land registration and titling. The experiences of these countries suggest that technology tools can be useful corruption reduction and prevention mechanisms for countries with varying levels of governance. Of course, among the preconditions for relative success of information technology in anticorruption efforts is the spread of and support for technology infrastructure in the country.

- The growth of civil society–based anticorruption initiatives is relatively advanced in Korea and the Philippines, with Indonesia and Thailand catching up. In all cases civil society initiatives have brought some noteworthy successes and deserve to be fully supported by international and domestic sources. The social movements and nongovernmental groups have magnified the reach of anticorruption initiatives, and have helped tilt the balance toward reforms. In poor to fair governance environments civil society can make up for the inadequacies of the state to intensify the risks of being punished for corruption and to reduce corruption opportunities.
- Anticorruption coalitions are powerful proponents of change, as demonstrated in the experiences of the country case studies. Without the clout of the coalitions it would seem inconceivable that anticorruption agendas would have emerged, much less made an impact. To date, they continue to challenge corruption. In many ways these coalitions—more or less formal associations of NGOs, civic associations, business groups, academic institutes, and so forth—have been fairly successful because they have reduced the risks of fighting against corruption. They prove the adage that there is strength in numbers.
- The growing indigenous sources of information on and analyses of corruption in several countries play a vital role in mobilizing public opinion. As discussed in the country case studies, they are indispensable ingredients to building a critical mass for anticorruption endeavors. Without accurate information there is no informed awareness and, consequently, no active decisions against corruption. Thus, the efforts to promote and protect information institutions need to be supported and expanded to sustain the challenge to corruption in Asia.

In many ways, the above comparative experience resonates with several of the measures recommended in the ADB-OECD Anti-Corruption Action Plan for Asia and the Pacific. Decisionmakers can view the plan as a menu from which a country can select anticorruption policies and programs that are most likely to work in its governance environment. Building on the case studies and applying the analytical framework, the following broad measures in the plan present good prospects for improving the effectiveness of national anticorruption policies and programs:

- Systems to promote transparency and accountability through disclosure and monitoring of personal assets and liabilities of public officials
- Measures to ensure officials voluntarily report acts of corruption and to protect the safety and professional status of those who do
- Policies and programs to promote fiscal transparency

- Relevant auditing procedures applicable to public sector management that provide timely public reporting of official performance and decisionmaking
- Appropriate transparent procedures for public procurement that promote fair competition and simplify administration procedures
- Participatory institutions to promote public scrutiny and oversight of governmental activities
- Laws and regulations governing public licenses, government procurement contracts, or other public undertakings that deny private sector access to public sector contracts as a sanction for bribery of public officials
- Support of nongovernmental organizations that promote integrity and combat corruption by raising public awareness of corruption and its costs, mobilizing citizen support for clean government, and documenting and reporting cases of corruption
- Creation of various channels that provide a meaningful public right of access to appropriate information
- Cooperative relationships with civil society groups, such as chambers of commerce, professional associations, NGOs, labor unions, housing associations, the media, and other organizations
- Involvement of NGOs in monitoring and reporting public sector programs and activities.

In the final analysis, it is the governments and stakeholders in Asia who will have to make the evaluation and selection of their respective anticorruption policies and programs. It is they who will have to make the decisions of policy prioritization, resource allocation, and implementation strategies. It is they who will have to design and deliver the anticorruption agenda. What we have sought to provide is an analytical framework that can help decisionmakers discern and decide on what will work best in their own governance and operating environments. We offer a framework that allows decisionmakers to draw from the rich experiences of the global community and to act on that knowledge in a manner informed by the unique circumstances and possibilities of their own countries. The risks may be high, particularly in poor to fair governance environments, but then so are the rewards. We hope that in this effort we have helped to reduce the risks of reformers and have increased the prospects of making a difference in their good efforts.

Note

1. This work is an updated and expanded version of a continuing research project on governance indicators that began in 1998. See Kaufmann, Kraay, and Zoido-Lobatón (1999).

References

Kaufmann, Daniel, Aart Kraay, and Massimo Mastruzzi. 2003. "Governance Matters III: Governance Indicators for 1996–2002." World Bank Policy Research Working Paper 3106. Washington, D.C.

Kaufmann, Daniel, Aart Kraay, and Pablo Zoido-Lobatón. 1999. "Governance Matters." World Bank Policy Research Working Paper 2196. Washington, D.C.

———. 2002. "Governance Matters II: Updated Indicators for 2000/01." World Bank Policy Research Working Paper 2772. Washington, D.C.

Radelet, Steve. 2003. *Challenging Foreign Aid: A Policymaker's Guide to the Millennium Challenge Account.* Washington, D.C.: Center for Global Development.

Index

www.ingramcontent.com/pod-product-compliance
Lightning Source LLC
Chambersburg PA
CBHW020657270326
41928CB00005B/169